BUSINESS
FAIRY TALES

Cecil W. Jackson

Australia • Brazil • Canada • Mexico • Singapore • Spain • United Kingdom • United States

THOMSON
TM

Business Fairy Tales
Cecil W. Jackson

COPYRIGHT © 2006 by Texere, an imprint of Thomson/South-Western, a part of The Thomson Corporation. Thomson and the Star logo are trademarks used herein under license.

Composed by: Interactive Composition Corporation

Printed in the United States of America by R.R. Donnelley, Crawfordsville

1 2 3 4 5 09 08 07 06

This book is printed on acid-free paper.

ISBN: 0-324-30539-7

Library of Congress Cataloging in Publication Number is available. See page 282 for details.

For more information about our products, contact us at:

Thomson Learning
Academic Resource Center
1-800-423-0563

Thomson Higher Education
5191 Natorp Boulevard
Mason, Ohio 45040
USA

TABLE OF CONTENTS

ACKNOWLEDGMENTS

Without enormous support and assistance from others, this book would not have reached its "happy ending."

To Chris and Mike Bell, I sincerely appreciate your friendship, encouragement, and insightful comments from the book's inception to its publication.

To James Kellenberger, thank you for sharing your expert knowledge—and taking the time to discuss philosophy and ethics with me—as I wrote the chapter on making ethical decisions in the business world.

To Doug Schaeffer, thanks for stepping up to the plate with your research skills and your ability to locate hard-to-find information.

To the folks at Thomson—Steve Momper, Colleen Farmer, Elizabeth Lowry, and Maggie Sears—I appreciate the parts you played in getting the project going, keeping it going, and getting it done!

To the Leventhal School of Accounting and the Marshall School of Business at the University of Southern California, thank you for your unhesitating support of my proposal to develop and offer classes in Fraudulent Financial Accounting and Forensic Accounting.

To Jack Larsen, your enthusiastic response to the text was most heartening.

Thanks also to the graduate and undergraduate students in my Fraudulent Financial Accounting and Forensic Accounting classes who responded with such enthusiasm to the various chapters in progress. To past students Mohneet Singh and Jackson Li, I value your cheerful assistance.

To my children, Kate and David, thanks for the delightful diversions when I needed a break from balance sheets and bankruptcy reports, and your patience and good humor throughout this project.

Without a doubt, I owe my biggest debt of gratitude to my wife, Sandra, who—fortunately for me—is familiar with the writing and publication process. You helped in so many ways: from devising catchy metaphors to assisting with multiple revisions and maintaining enthusiasm for the project from start to finish. This book would not have been completed without you.

Cecil W. Jackson

CHAPTER 1

GOLD DUST: INTRODUCTION TO THE PROBLEM OF FICTITIOUS FINANCIAL REPORTING

Although gold dust is precious, when it
gets in your eyes it obstructs your vision.

Hsi-Tang Chih Tsang, Chinese Zen Master

ONCE UPON A TIME. . . . All good fairy tales begin with "Once upon a time," and business fairy tales are no exception. Once upon a time, public companies and large corporations were regarded as bastions of the U.S. economy, citadels where investments were safe, and employees could count on secure jobs and solid pensions. Almost all fairy tales have villains who prey on the unsuspecting and the innocent, who take advantage of the trusting and the unwary; business fairy tales are no exception. Villains abound in these stories of greed and betrayal, of blatant duplicity and moral bankruptcy. Blinded by gold dust, these corporate rogues were ruthless in their quest for riches. Central to almost every fairy tale of commerce and industry told in this book is the fact that these villains used fictitious financial reporting to hoodwink those who trusted them.

At the turn of the millennium, the nation's attention was riveted on the dangers of fictitious financial reports and the shortcomings of the current financial-reporting system as a result of the spectacular business and financial-reporting failures of Enron and WorldCom. In an Amended Complaint (May 1, 2003) charging Enron executives with fraud, Deputy Director of the Enforcement Division of the Securities and Exchange Commission (SEC) Linda Chatman Thomsen declared:

> At a point when Enron's touted groundbreaking broadband technology was little more than a concept—and its business model was not commercially viable— these defendants played important roles in perpetuating the fairy tale that Enron was capable of spinning straw—or more appropriately, fiber—into gold.

Within weeks of the beginning of Enron's meltdown in mid-October 2001, employees had lost billions of dollars worth of Enron stock in their 401(k) plans, stockholders had lost billions of dollars as the stock price fell from $60 per share to below $1, and debt holders were about to lose more than $3.9 billion that they were owed by Enron. On December 3, about

4,000 of Enron's employees were given notice to leave the company the very same day.

Unfortunately, Enron's accounting fraud was just one more case in an all too frequent litany of falsified financial reports that had grown in incidence over the 1990s and into the new millennium, where they reached pandemic proportions. WorldCom's bankruptcy was soon to follow, and, staggeringly, it topped Enron as it became the biggest bankruptcy case in the history of the United States. Furthermore, WorldCom's financial statements were misstated by the largest amount ever chronicled in this country, giving new meaning to the term "fairy tale." The combination of all these business and reporting failures finally led the nation to acknowledge that something was seriously wrong with the financial reporting system.

The U.S. Securities and Exchange Commission (SEC) embarked on a study of SEC enforcement actions over the period of July 31, 1997, through July 30, 2002. This *Report Pursuant to Section 704 of the Sarbanes-Oxley Act of 2002* (SOX Report) found 227 enforcement investigations in that five-year period, which led to the filing of "515 enforcement actions for financial reporting and disclosure violations" (1). What were the factors that led to such widespread alleged reporting fraud? What gatekeeping checks and balances were in place in the financial-reporting environment at that time? Who were the gatekeepers who neglected their duties? Why did these checks and balances fail?

In his *First Interim Report* (2002), Richard Thornburgh, WorldCom's Bankruptcy Examiner, presented a list of the gatekeepers who failed WorldCom, and this list of errant sentinels typified the failures that led to an analysis of the institutional and environmental problems in the financial reporting and auditing processes. Thornburgh found failure by WorldCom's management and senior accounting staff and the internal-control system, as well as failed checks and balances by the following gatekeepers:

- The board of directors, including general oversight failure as well as failures by the audit committee and the compensation and stock-option committee
- The internal audit department
- The external auditors
- The investment banking company
- The investment banker's stock analyst

Since management has ultimate responsibility for the preparation of the company's financial statements, it is not surprising that the huge rise in the incidence of fraudulent financial reporting enforcement actions at the turn of the millennium was associated with huge increases in incentives for management to present financial statements that overstated earnings. Time and again, the SEC's Accounting and Auditing Enforcement Releases alleged that management orchestrated frauds to meet Wall Street analysts' earnings expectations. In most cases, senior management compensation agreements included stock options that would provide significant additional remuneration if analysts' earnings expectations were met.

Former SEC chairman Arthur Levitt (2002) told of the losing battle that he fought when he tried to pass measures that he believed would cool the dramatic increase in the granting of stock options as a major form of executive compensation. As SEC chairman, Levitt had seen firsthand the temptations created by massive options grants. Levitt felt that if companies had to expense the value of stock options given to executives as compensation, the decrease in earnings reported in the income statement would dampen shareholders' willingness to agree to awarding stock options as an ever-increasing form of executive compensation.

By 2001, a troubling 80 percent of top management compensation "was in the form of stock options" (Levitt 2002, 111). In an article by Byrne and others, on May 6, 2002, *Business Week* reported: "In the past decade, as rank-and-file wages increased 36%, CEO pay climbed 340%, to $11 million." It was in this environment of the lure of tantalizing riches from stock options that many a top executive could not resist the temptation to present financial statements that satisfied Wall Street's earnings expectations.

At the same time that stock options were growing rapidly as a component of executive compensation, Levitt was also fighting a losing battle against another growing trend that concerned him. External auditors were collecting ever-escalating consulting fees from the same clients for whom they performed "independent" audits. At the beginning of 2002, an article in *Business Week* confirmed that consulting fees for external auditors were spiraling: "That accountants have become increasingly dependent on consulting is clear.... In 1993, 31% of the industry's fees came from consulting. By 1999, that had jumped to 51%." It may be a matter of debate whether keeping the audit client because of the audit fees alone was enough to make some auditors compromise their audits, or whether the double incentive of consulting fees was a deciding force. However, the high number of SEC enforcement actions revealed too many auditors who either accepted scope limitations on their audits—such as not demanding full access to the entire general ledger and not issuing a disclaimer or qualified report on the financial statements—or who knowingly yielded to incorrect financial statements. Clearly, many auditors could not take the increased pressure from management who stood to gain significantly from fraudulent financial reports. *Business Week* summed it up as follows: "Still, in many people's minds the rising importance of consulting has contributed to a decline in auditor skepticism. It simply looks bad to have Andersen earning more on consulting to Enron than on auditing." (Quotes from Byrnes et al. January 28, 2002)

Together with condemnation for accepting increasing consulting fees from audit clients, the auditing environment faced other tough criticism at the time of the colossal reporting failures. The self-policing practices of the auditing profession came under scrutiny. Since 1977, the Public Oversight Board (POB) had been responsible for monitoring audit independence and quality. However, this board did not have the power to subpoena, nor did it have any real power to punish wrongdoers, and with the onslaught of accounting frauds, the AICPA came to loggerheads with the oversight board. The board ceased to exist in May 2002.[1] The AICPA also had a peer-review system, but "no Big Five firm [had] ever failed a review" (Byrnes et al. January 28, 2002). Regrettably, the oversight division lacked the weapons to protect its domain.

Furthermore, as scrutiny of the Enron failure showed, independent auditors would frequently leave the auditing profession and join the staff of a company that they had audited. Clearly, there was often too much familiarity and camaraderie between a former employee of an audit firm and the external auditors, making it difficult for the external auditors to remain entirely independent.

Finally, audit firms usually audited the same companies year after year, developing friendships with management, growing complacent, and sometimes dropping their guard. Mandatory rotation of auditors could have prevented auditors from losing their independence in at least two ways: first, the forced rotation would have precluded the audit firms from building up too much familiarity, and second, knowing that a new firm would be arriving the following year and reviewing the work papers and the client's financial statements would have been an added incentive for external auditors to resist management's pressure to compromise their audits.

---

[1] The POB was replaced by the Public Company Accounting Oversight Board (PCAOB) which was created by the Sarbanes-Oxley Act of 2002.

In attempting to address yet another corporate governance concern, Levitt focused his attention on both chummy and absentee members of companies' boards of directors. In his book, *Take on the Street,* Levitt honed in on the many directors who lacked independence, as well as on those directors who were indifferent and had no interest in company activities. Levitt also observed that there were too many "inside" directors who were company employees, and there were too few "outside" directors. Further, he pointed out that too many "outside" directors apparently lacked independence in the sense that they were either friends or relatives of the company's CEO, were associated with competing businesses, or had been involved in business transactions with the corporation and had earned lucrative fees. All of these situations could, and often did, influence a director's autonomy in overseeing the direction of the company. Levitt (2002) described some of the responsibilities of a board of directors:

> One of its responsibilities is to advise the CEO and the top executive team with impartial common sense and various kinds of expertise. The board should meet regularly to discuss such issues as the ongoing health of the business, the current management team and its performance, the compensation of the top executives, and the future outlook of the company. (207–208)

Typical of many boards in the late 1990s and into the new millennium, WorldCom's board was criticized by the Bankruptcy Examiner for not monitoring the outrageous, unfocused growth of WorldCom. In addition, the board's compensation committee came under scrutiny for its "generosity" to the CEO, Bernard Ebbers. The audit committee of WorldCom's board of directors was scrutinized for its lax supervision of accounting issues.

Thornburgh, WorldCom's Bankruptcy Examiner, also criticized World-Com's investment banker, Salomon, Smith, Barney (SSB), and its star analyst, Jack Grubman. Thornburgh described SSB's distribution of coveted "Friends of the Company" IPO shares to Ebbers, WorldCom's CEO. Thornburgh then revealed the correlation between the allotments of these shares to Ebbers with WorldCom's allocation of investment banking work to SSB. Grubman is on record as complaining about pressure to provide favorable reports on certain companies in order for SSB to obtain more investment banking business from them. This was not an isolated problem. Arthur Levitt (2002) reported: "In April 2002, the Justice Department, Securities and Exchange Commission, and state regulators opened investigations of possible wrongdoing by research analysts at major Wall Street firms." These investigations were prompted by subpoenaed emails that seemed to confirm many rumors:

> Wall Street analysts often recommended to investors shares of companies that have an investment banking relationship with their firm; yet privately, analysts deride these same companies.... [A Merryl Lynch analyst] in one email referred to a company that he had bullishly recommended as "a piece of junk." (65)

In the rush to jump on the bandwagons of IPOs, hot dot.coms, and other get-rich-quick schemes, many investment bankers and analysts lost their independence, their impartiality, and their ability to provide their clients with sound and objective investment advise. Analysts' reports on the results of their research into companies became one more gatekeeping function that could not be relied upon. The promise of lucrative investment-banking work may have been the driving force behind an upgrade of a company's stock, and signals that the financial statements might be fraudulently prepared may have been ignored... for a fee. This was yet another case of gold dust obstructing the vision.

However, even if every one of the gatekeepers previously discussed failed in their duties, were there not other checks and balances in the form of internal control systems and internal audit departments to guard against the production and publication of fraudulent financial statements? Once again, Enron and WorldCom were symptomatic of the recurrent problems of inadequate and flawed systems of internal controls, as well as indicative of understaffed internal audit departments that came under the authority of the very managers they were meant to audit. The responsibility of management to institute controls ensuring the integrity of the accounting information captured was not clearly defined. The duties of the external auditors regarding the system of internal control were not well specified. Although members of WorldCom's internal audit department were finally instrumental in uncovering the financial reporting frauds and reporting them to the board of directors, WorldCom's Bankruptcy Examiner faulted both the company's system of internal controls and its understaffed internal audit department that ultimately reported to the CFO, Scott Sullivan, who was the major originator of the tall tales underlying WorldCom's accounting fraud.

Such was the financial reporting environment at the turn of the twenty-first century, as the management of so many companies, blinded by the lure of stock-option riches, recklessly pushed and pressurized everyone in the system to go along with the fabricated financial statements. Enron and WorldCom were not alone; they were just the largest of the fictions at the time. What happened to WorldCom and Enron was the result of a seriously flawed financial-reporting environment that permitted all of their gatekeepers to fail them in the same ways that hundreds of other companies' custodians failed their stakeholders as well. The frauds were not limited to any one particular industry or sector of the economy, nor were they limited to just a couple of varieties of sham reporting. The suspect companies ranged from medical corporations to theatrical companies, from manufacturers of kitchen electrics to conglomerates that sold electricity. In the five-year period ending July 30, 2002, the SEC filed 515 enforcement actions against "164 entities and 705 individuals" (SOX Report, 1).

In an attempt to deal with the morass of problems amid the huge public outcry, Congress passed the Sarbanes-Oxley Act of 2002. The Sarbanes-Oxley Act addressed most of the problems in the financial reporting environment discussed previously. The specific reforms instituted by this legislation—as well as further reforms needed—are discussed in a later chapter. Although many of the problems have been reduced, the litany of accounting frauds and misleading financial reporting still continues, as evidenced by new SEC investigations or findings announced almost every week—and this week is probably no exception.

Table 1.1, which follows, shows a list of the most prevalent and most serious methods of fictitious financial reporting usually leading to the SEC enforcement actions in the SEC five-year study period. This book tells the stories of a selection of the companies that spun these yarns. It helps the reader to understand the culture of greed, arrogance, and neglect that spawned these falsehoods. Each chapter also empowers the reader with the information necessary to recognize the danger signals that are frequently concealed in financial statements. These signals are vivid warning signs to the reader a company's financial statements may be an illusion, a figment of fictitious reporting.

Don't become one of the investors who buys stock in the next WorldCom—just before it takes a huge tumble.

Don't become a long-time employee who misses the warning signs and loses his or her job *and* 401(k) when the next Enron takes a dive.

Don't resign your regular job to join the newest high-flying company only to find yourself without a job in a couple of months when the next Sunbeam topples.

Equipped with the signals, readers will be forewarned.[2] With these indicators, readers will learn to recognize whether the financial statements they are examining are authentic, or whether they appear to be merely fairy tales.

---

[2] This book provides signals for each accounting scheme. For a summary of twenty-five of the most important signals, refer to Table 9.2 at the end of Chapter 9.

Table 1.1 The Top Twenty Methods of Fictitious Financial Reporting[1]

Fictitious Reporting Method	Illustrating Company[2]
The following schemes involve *improper revenue recognition:*	
1. Bill and Hold Sales, Consignment Sales, and other Contingency Sales for the purpose of improper timing of revenue recognition	SUNBEAM
2. Holding Books Open after the Close of a Reporting Period for the purpose of improper timing of revenue recognition.	SENSORMATIC
3. Multiple Element Contracts or Bundled Contracts when used for the purpose of improper timing of revenue recognition.	XEROX
4. Fictitious Revenue	CUC/CENDANT
5. Improper Valuation of Revenue	INSIGNIA
The following schemes involve *improper expense recognition:*	
6. Improper Capitalization of Expenses or Losses	WORLDCOM
7. Improper Deferral of Expenses or Losses	LIVENT
8. Failure to Record Expenses or Losses	LIVENT
9. Overstating Ending Inventory Values in order to understate the cost of goods sold	RITE AID
10. Understating Reserves for Bad Debts and Loan Losses	ALLEGHENY
11. Failure to Record Asset Impairments	LOCKHEED
12. Improper Use of Restructuring and Other Liability Reserves. The overstated reserves are released in future periods to fictitiously understate future periods' expenses.	SUNBEAM
The following schemes involve *improper accounting in connection with business combinations:*	
13. Improper Use of Merger Reserves. Overstated merger reserves are created in order to use their later release to overstate future periods' earnings.	WORLDCOM
14. Improper Asset Valuation	WORLDCOM
Miscellaneous schemes:	
15. Improper Use of Off-Balance Sheet Arrangements. Special Purpose Entities (SPEs) are used to overstate earnings and understate debt via contrived transactions.	ENRON
16. Inadequate Disclosures in Management Discussion & Analysis (MD&A) and Elsewhere in Issuer Filings	EDISON
17. Failure to Disclose Related-Party Transactions	ADELPHIA
18. Improper Use of Non-GAAP Financial Measures	ADELPHIA
19. Improper Accounting for Foreign Payments in Violation of the Foreign Corrupt Practices Act (FCPA)	BELLSOUTH
20. Inappropriate Accounting for Roundtrip Transactions	KRISPY KREME

[1] Revised and adapted by Cecil W. Jackson from SEC "Report Pursuant to Section 704 of the Sarbanes-Oxley Act of 2002" (SOX Report), based on a study from June 1997–July 2002.

[2] All of the illustrating companies, except for Lockheed and Krispy Kreme, were the subject of SEC enforcement actions. There was no SEC enforcement action for Lockheed. Krispy Kreme is still under investigation.

References

Amended Complaint Charging Five Enron Executives with Fraud and Insider Trading Relating to Enron's Broadband Subsidiary. U.S. Securities and Exchange Commission, May 1, 2003. www.sec.gov/news/press/2003-58.htm.

Byrne, John A., et al. 2002. "How to Fix Corporate Governance," *Business Week,* May 6. Available online via Academic Search Elite database.

Byrnes, Nanette, et al. 2002. "Accounting in Crisis," *Business Week,* January 28. www.businessweek.com.

First Interim Report of Dick Thornburgh, Bankruptcy Court Examiner. United States Bankruptcy Court Southern District of New York in re: WorldCom Inc. Case No.02-13533 (AJG), November 4, 2002.

Levitt, Arthur. 2002. *Take on the Street.* New York: Pantheon Books.

SOX Report. *Report Pursuant to Section 704 of the Sarbanes-Oxley Act of 2002.* www.sec.gov/news/studies/sox704report.pdf.

CHAPTER 2

THE SIZZLING SAGA OF SUNBEAM[1]

Sunbeam is presented mainly as an example of:
- Improper Timing of Revenue Recognition via bill and hold sales, consignment sales, and other contingency sales
- Improper Expense Recognition via the use of restructuring and other liability reserves

PART 1: THE HISTORY OF SUNBEAM

The Sunbeam story is ultimately the tale of a company that was gutted by management in a scorching turnaround attempt, while its executives falsely overstated profits in the vain effort to find a buyer for the charred company and cut themselves loose from the havoc they had wreaked. However, it is also the story of the collision and collusion of the forces that came together when fund managers hired a slash-and-burn chief executive officer who was convinced that he would not be harmed as he flew toward the sun. This is the saga of the analysts and journalists who watched and applauded the flight of the CEO, while the auditors overlooked the false profits reported by a company that had the guts ripped out of it after the appointment of Albert J. "Chainsaw Al" Dunlap as CEO in 1996.

Why did Sunbeam hire a CEO with a reputation for slashing and burning and "dumbsizing" companies? Why was Al Dunlap so enthusiastic about cutting plants and jobs quite so ruthlessly? Why did Wall Street not question how production and sales and profits could possibly increase as a result of having fewer plants, fewer product lines, and fewer workers? Why did virtually no one take heed of demoralized and scared employees looking for safer jobs, as key executives resigned in droves? What accounting mechanisms were used to overstate sales and earnings? Why did none of the executives inform the board of directors of the unfolding chaos? What went wrong, and why did it go wrong so rapidly and so relentlessly?

---

[1] Background information in this chapter is mainly from Byrne (2003), Byron (2004), Laing (1997; 1998; 1998), Scherer (1996), and Schifrin (1998).

To answer these questions, we have to look at how Sunbeam was performing in the 1990s as compared with the stock market in general, and the resulting irrational expectations. We have to examine the background and personality of "Chainsaw Al" Dunlap, and we must explore Wall Street's reactions to Dunlap's previous "turnaround" downsizings as well as Wall Street's reactions to "cost-cutting-at-any cost" in general.

The Dawn of the Company

Sunbeam began its life in 1897 as the Chicago Flexible Shaft Company, a manufacturer of agricultural implements. With the innovation of electricity, it began producing toasters and irons, and changed its name to Sunbeam Corp. In the 1960s it acquired Oster Co. and added blenders and electric blankets to the array of its then "high-tech" product range. However, competition for household electrical goods grew fast and furious, and in 1981, under increasing pressure, Sunbeam felt that its best option was to be acquired by Allegheny International, Inc. This turned out to be a poor choice, since Allegheny's CEO, Robert Buckley, was a man somewhat ahead of his time in that he was a forerunner of the high-living CEOs we are all too familiar with today. He regarded the company he ran as his own. Traveling the world in his corporate jets, and staying in lavish corporate apartments and condominiums, he felt entitled to large company loans at very low interest rates and to a salary of over $1 million a year. It was not surprising that his business focus became a little distracted, and between spectacular losses and extravagant expenditure, profits soon turned into losses; the unfortunate Buckley was fired in 1986.

The new management team began what would be a recurring theme for Sunbeam—team members instituted an aggressive downsizing program whereby they cut one-third of the company's jobs and sold off a number of the product lines. Not surprisingly, sales went down—not up—and in early 1988 the company filed for bankruptcy.

Sunbeam emerged from bankruptcy under the control of Michael Price of the Mutual Series Investment Fund and Michael Steinhardt of the Steinhardt Partners Fund. Each had contributed around $60 million, at the urging of two dealmakers named Paul Kazarian and Michael Lederman, who were then appointed to manage the company, with Kazarian as CEO. They renamed the business Sunbeam-Oster. Kazarian performed a true turnaround of the company, producing genuine profits and taking the company public very successfully.

However, although Kazarian cut out the extravagant waste of the Buckley era and also stopped the wild downsizing of his predecessor's turnaround attempt, he appeared to be a workaholic and was too intense for some. He was fired and replaced by Roger Schipke, who was as laid-back and gentlemanly as Kazarian had been intense. He may have overdone the gentility, however, for Sunbeam at this stage had many strong personalities pulling in opposite directions. Without a powerful leader, profits fell quickly and steadily.

As a result of basically buying Sunbeam out of bankruptcy, Price and Steinhardt, the fund managers, had an enormous amount of stock and an enormous amount of control of Sunbeam, even after it went public. It was now 1996, and these were giddy times for Wall Street. Price prided himself on being an exceptional stock selector. He knew how to find bargain stocks and he felt sure that Sunbeam could be made very profitable again and that its stock price could soar. He felt that he could make that happen; he just needed to appoint the right kind of CEO—a leader who could do another turnaround of Sunbeam. He needed a leader who had slashed costs in companies, who had cut production plants and products, and who had reported a profit so quickly after a period of losses that it was almost too good to be true. In fact, he knew of just such a man—Al Dunlap—who had done all this before for Scott Paper Co. What is more, Dunlap had then sold Scott Paper to Kimberly-Clark at a huge profit.

Perhaps Price had not followed what had happened to Scott Paper after its reported quick turnaround profits and its rapid sale to Kimberly-Clark. Perhaps he had followed but didn't care. The trouble was that after Kimberly-Clark acquired Scott Paper, they found it to be a mess. Scott Paper had had the guts ripped out of it. However, Michael Price needed a man who could slash costs and perform a company turnaround in no time at all, and he felt that Dunlap was just the man he needed to be the new CEO of Sunbeam.

PART 2: THE HISTORY OF AL DUNLAP

Al Dunlap's history—both his personal background and his business history of downsizing businesses that later suffered—was the first warning sign that alerted analysts like Andrew Shore of the PaineWebber, Inc., brokerage house to be on the lookout for unsustainable profits in Sunbeam.

Dunlap was 59 years old in 1996, when he was appointed CEO of Sunbeam. Although he claims that he was born poor and grew up even poorer, his sister said that his childhood was "very comfortable." Until he was

11 years old, he lived in a "three-story redbrick row house on Garden Street in Hoboken" in New Jersey and when he turned 11, "his family moved to Hasbrouck Heights, New Jersey, a middle-class community of peaceful, tree-lined streets and modest homes." Both Dunlap's sister and high-school coach reported that he always had a temper, "an aggressive one," according to his coach. His sister said that he "would just spin on you in a second." (Quotes from Byrne 2003, 97-98.)

Dunlap's childhood behavior sounds mild compared to his legendary temper tantrums at Sunbeam, where he would go into screaming rants that Christopher Byron, (2006) in *Testosterone Inc. Tales of CEOs Gone Wild*, described as "extreme fighting in the boardroom" (254). Clearly, the seeds for such anger had been sewn when he was much younger.

Dunlap worked hard at high school and got into West Point military academy. He completed his three-year military obligation, during which time he married Gwyn Donnelly when he was twenty-four and she was nineteen. Gwyn soon began to see another side of Al Dunlap—an unhappy side, an angry and controlling side. It has been reported that when Gwyn was four months pregnant, Dunlap angrily ordered her to find a job because she was "bringing in another mouth to feed." In Gwyn's divorce complaint, she alleged that Dunlap had once pointed a knife at her and had said, "I often wondered what human flesh tasted like." She also stated that he had a collection of guns and once, while cleaning them, he had remarked, "You better watch out and toe the line." He would go into ranting rages if she had not cleaned the apartment to his satisfaction upon his inspections. The complaint also stated that he had once threatened to bash her over the head with a telephone if she did not give it to him. He had become very angry when he had heard that she was pregnant and he later became angry if he saw his son's fingerprints on the furniture. Dunlap emphatically denied the divorce complaint. Ultimately, however, the judge found that Dunlap had engaged in "extreme cruelty" and awarded Gwyn sole custody of their son. Gwyn did not request any alimony upon her divorce in 1966 and got none. She received only a $4,000 lump sum and $15 a week child support until their son was twelve years old and $150 a month after that. Al never offered to increase the payments and never bothered to contact his son. When Dunlap's son turned twenty-one, he contacted the father who had not seen his child for nineteen years, but Dunlap's reaction was lukewarm and eventually the two lost contact again. (Quotes from Byrne 2003, 101-104)

Dunlap remarried in 1968, and his new wife, Judy, was always supportive of "Chainsaw Al." She appeared to admire his aggression and reportedly she once proudly told a party of people that Al did not get heart attacks himself, but he gave them to others! Al and Judy appeared to be very well matched. They did not have children, but both were dog enthusiasts, and their German Shepherds were their pride and joy. However, Dunlap's rage continued unabated toward the rest of the world. Al Dunlap "grew up angry at his parents, at his friends, at his classmates and teachers until, eventually, he was raging at the whole world. 'He was the most unpleasant, personally repulsive businessman I ever met in my life' said a New York image consultant who Dunlap had wanted to hire" (Byron 2004, 18-19).

Dunlap's business career echoed the same rocky pattern as his personal life. After graduating from West Point and completing his three-year military obligation, Dunlap got a job at Kimberly-Clark's New Milford plant in Connecticut. In 1965, he was transferred to Kimberly-Clark's plant in Wisconsin. The plant's superintendent was another cantankerous man who liked to chastise his employees. Not surprisingly, Al got on well with him, and perhaps even imitated him. Dunlap was recommended for the job as plant manager at Sterling Pulp and Paper, also in Wisconsin. Between his military training and his angry management style, he was soon giving unpopular orders for layoffs. In Dunlap's own autobiography, he relates that soon after assuming this new position, he began receiving death threats. Nevertheless, he kept that job for about six years, leaving only when the owner died.

Dunlap's next job was at Max Phillips and Sons, but he was allegedly fired after less than two months for his ill manners and insolence towards his boss. Not to be deterred, he got a job as chief operating officer at Nitec Paper Corp. in Niagara Falls, New York. Dunlap was meant to do a turnaround at Nitec, which was in a bit of a slump. However, Al's sojourn here lasted only about two years and also ended badly. Nitec's chairman, George Petty, fired him, declaring that "Dunlap had so completely alienated those around him that Nitec faced the mass resignation of all the company's vice presidents if he weren't let go." At that time, it appeared that profits had turned around positively, and so Dunlap negotiated a $1.2 million severance package. However, just after Dunlap left the company, "Nitec's auditors at the accounting firm of Arthur Young & Co. reported that the anticipated profits that Dunlap had been promising were apparently the result of massive falsifications and fraudulent accounting entries on the company's books." Even though there is no evidence that Dunlap had anything to do with the falsification, there had been no real turnaround. As a result, Nitec reneged on its promise of the severance pay, and Dunlap sued and settled for $50,000. (Quotes from Byron 2004, 77)

From Nitec, Al eventually found a middle-management job at American Can, where he rose to become head of the plastics division. From there, he moved on to Manville Corp, which filed for bankruptcy within a year after his arrival, as a result of asbestos lawsuits.

Serendipitously, Dunlap's next position truly seemed to be a perfect match with his genetic makeup—he was recruited by Lily-Tulip, Inc., to cut costs and turn around the company, which was making a loss and had too much debt. The specific mandate of slashing costs was almost too good to be true for angry Al, and he tackled the task with gusto. He even began to cultivate an image in the press of an executive who did not shy away from cutting jobs or offending colleagues. The press ran several articles on Dunlap in 1984, indicating that he was instilling fear into his workforce. This was the beginning of what would become the long saga of an angry man who cultivated and was even proud of a tough, ruthless public image—an image that was celebrated by the business press, and most unfortunate of all, an image that fed his already ruthless streak. He interpreted "mean" as "strong," and he titled his memoir *Mean Business: How I Save Bad Companies and Make Good Companies Great*. He was so desperate to be seen as the tough guy that eventually, as a 59 year-old man, he posed with bullets and machine guns to promote his "Rambo in Pinstripes" image. Dunlap took his cue from the media: nothing captured the business press's attention more than a slash-and-burn downsizing. And the more jobs he cut, the tougher and smarter the press made him look. By the end of his time at Lily-Tulip, Dunlap had cemented his public image as a ruthless, downsizing turnaround specialist, and he was proud of it; in fact, he was more than proud—it virtually became his new religion.

After Lily-Tulip, Dunlap went on to work in Britain, and then in Australia for Kerry Packer's Consolidated Press Holdings. He left Consolidated Press embroiled in conflict with a number of colleagues, as described in an article titled "Al Dunlap's Disgrace" (Williams 2001). However, the controversy in Australia did not seem to count against him at all when he went after the job of CEO of Scott Paper, which was also badly in need of a turnaround.

By the last quarter of 1993, Scott Paper was making large losses and its CEO, Philip Lippincott, wanted out. There were not many seasoned executives who wanted his job. Lippincott had already publicized a downsizing plan that would require laying off over 8,000 employees over a number of years. For "Chainsaw Al," it looked like a magnificent opportunity. Al Dunlap arrived to take the helm of Scott Paper in April 1994, and he slashed more than 11,000 jobs in less than one year. He sold off large publishing and printing businesses as well as the company's domestic timberlands and a number of overseas paper mills. It is difficult to second-guess which of these should have stayed and which should have gone, if any. However, when research and development expenditure is deeply cut, and maintenance on property, plant, and equipment is deferred, it is usually a pretty good guess that management is focused on short-term earnings instead of long-term growth and profit. It is easy to get profits up in the current year by cutting R&D, but that will kill future growth and profits.

In an interview with an executive from Scott Paper, John Byrne was told that "by the end of 1994, it just became a volume-driven plan to pretty up the place for sale. . . . We're talking about a whole new definition of short-term." In addition, "Dunlap slashed the company's research and development budget in half, to about $35 million, and eliminated 60% of the staffers in R&D." Dunlap also cut back on memberships in industry organizations and "eliminated all corporate gifts to charities." (Quotes from Byrne 2003, 27)

In a precursor to what would happen at Sunbeam, big sales discounts were given to accelerate sales, and "in the final months before the company was sold, the discounts were doubled." The stock price went up dramatically, based on reported profits. Dunlap managed to sell Scott Paper to Kimberly-Clark in July 1995, and he left Scott Paper $100 million the richer. Not surprisingly, Kimberly-Clark soon realized that Scott Paper, in fact, had had the guts ripped out of it. Predictably, with the highly discounted sales before Scott was sold, its sales were slow in the next period. Also, with plants closed, businesses cut, and workers retrenched, combined with little R&D and sparse maintenance, growth did not increase; inevitably, it fell. Kimberly-Clark took a $1.4 billion restructuring charge in respect of its integration of Scott Paper. Al Dunlap did not seem to care; he was out of Scott's as a very rich man, and a lucky one, since Kimberly-Clark was left with the mess. Furthermore, "Chainsaw Al" was not ready to retire. He was looking for a new company to "turn around." (Quotes from Byrne 2003, 28–32)

Wall Street Embraced Sunbeam's Downsizing Plans

When "Chainsaw Al" went looking for a new job after selling off Scott Paper, the general attitude toward downsizing at the time was that it was effective, and that Dunlap had the world's leading reputation for downsizing. In 1996, Sunbeam was making losses. The board was looking for a replacement for its CEO, Roger Schipke, who was considered too placid to provide the assertive leadership that the troubled company needed. Dunlap was the man for the job. On July 18, 1996, Albert J. Dunlap was appointed CEO of Sunbeam, Inc.

Although it was becoming obvious that Dunlap's cost-cutting turnarounds were not turning out to be such positive transformations after all, the business press generally ignored the short-lived nature of the profits that followed his ruthless downsizings. In the 1990s, Wall Street was happy to read optimistic news into almost any confidently announced plan. The more dramatically a plan predicted a spectacularly profitable vision of the future, the more the press and the analysts loved it. This was a time when companies were going public with no records of profits, sometimes not even of sales; a time when a simple click on a website was enough to be counted as a customer.

So when "Chainsaw Al" announced not only a vision of a profitable future for Sunbeam, but also a plan to achieve it, the press embraced his vision with gusto. After all, he was a brilliant businessman with a simple strategy— he was going to slash costs. And how was he going to slash costs? He was going to close productions plants, drop product lines, and slash workers' jobs. That was Dunlap's vision for Sunbeam. If the CEO of a company that was making losses suddenly and miraculously reported a profit in the financial statements without dramatically announcing a restructuring plan, that would be a little suspicious. One might wonder whether the financial statements had been fraudulently reported, or at least one might question whether they had been erroneously reported. Similarly, if management announced that it was going to increase sales by cutting products, and increase production by closing plants and firing employees, that would sound counterintuitive; the logic might be questioned and the predictions of increased earnings might not sound credible. However, if the CEO announced that he or she was going to perform a turnaround in a brief period by embarking on an aggressive "downsizing" cost-cutting plan, Wall Street would embrace the plan and celebrate the vision of a quick turnaround with high profits and even higher stock prices. Would that it were so simple.

The fact of the matter is that profits are maximized when total revenues exceed total costs by the greatest amount, which is not simply achieved by cutting production facilities and employees, or cutting R&D and marketing costs. Cutting is likely to reduce revenues more than it reduces costs, and that will lead to less profit. If the object is simply to cut costs, you can cut costs all the way to zero by liquidating the company. That will not maximize profits; it will produce a profit of zero. So cost-cutting is not an end in itself.

It has to be done very scientifically, being really careful to cut only costs that do not support greater revenues. Analysis, discernment, and precision are vital. The unintended consequences of cutting costs to increase short-term profits can easily cause long-term losses.

Downsizing or Dumbsizing?

An article in *BYU Magazine Online* titled "Downsizing or Dumbsizing?" succinctly captured the perils of these unintended consequences. It told the story of how, in 1994, professors Lee Tom Perry and Eric L. Denna presented a cost-cutting plan to the executive committee of Scott Paper Co. The plan was well received, but before any implementation, Perry and Denna's consultancy was ended when Al Dunlap took over as CEO of Scott Paper. Professor Perry later remarked, "Obviously, something needed to be done. But what bothers me about Al Dunlap is his lack of precision. He has a very simplistic view: smaller is better" (quoted in Jenkins 1997).

Sunbeam apparently did not realize that there is a crucial difference between a downsizing and a dumbsizing. Clearly, companies have to respond to changes and also have to initiate changes. The economist, Val Lambson, observed:

> The way capitalism works is that it sends signals through prices, telling people what they ought to be doing based on what's valued by consumers. The advantage of a free-market system is that it allocates the resources in a productive and efficient way. The results are beneficial for the whole. (Quoted in Jenkins 1997)

The organizational behavior specialist in downsizing, Kim S. Cameron, explained that downsizing has to be an improvement process, not a target: "If they merely cut positions and headcount, but do not address the fundamental problems causing inefficiency and lack of competitiveness, the problems are still going to be there even after downsizing." Cameron acknowledged that while downsizing is sometimes necessary, when it is done badly it is the most unproductive and futile method of trying to improve a company. He likened it to a "grenade strategy," explaining that when you fling "a grenade into a company. . . . it explodes, eliminating the positions of a certain number of people. The problem is you have no way of telling precisely who is going to be affected." (Quoted in Jenkins 1997)

Cameron pointed out:

> In the end, a corporation almost always loses company memory and company energy. The first is caused when informal networks are destroyed, information sharing is restricted, and experienced employees depart. The second is caused

by declining morale, loss of loyalty and commitment, and the departure of the most talented employees, who know that they are marketable. (Quoted in Jenkins 1997)

Of course, cutting R&D expenditure and maintenance expenditure is going to hurt you in the future. At the same time, as Lambson pointed out, "When there's a technological change, or a change in consumer tastes, the changes are reflected in the prices. That's a signal to industry producers—the black-and-white television industry, for example—to retrain, retool, and move into other areas, which may cause some downsizing." As Perry explained: "Increased resource utilization is good for both business and society. That doesn't mean downsizing is out of the picture, but the Al Dunlaps would be." (Quotes from Jenkins 1997)

Cost-accounting analysis shows that when a company closes down a segment, while it does lose that segment's revenues, it does not lose all of the costs that are allocated to it in typical income statements. Some of those costs—the common or allocated fixed costs—will remain and will simply have to be carried by the remaining divisions. Only the costs that are truly caused by the division continuing—the traceable costs—will be saved if the division is closed. Frequently, segments are closed without this analysis being done, and the result is often that the company is surprised to find that it has less profit, not more, after the segment is closed.

PART 3: DUNLAP'S CARROT-AND-STICK APPROACH

Dunlap structured his control over his management team at Sunbeam with one of the most severe *carrot-and-stick* combinations ever implemented in U.S. business. The *carrot* was that executives and managers were allocated large numbers of stock options that would make them multimillionaires if the Sunbeam stock price went up dramatically. This was a large carrot that caused many executives, even those who despised Dunlap from past experience, to join him again for the Sunbeam turnaround. It also encouraged a number of managers who were working for Dunlap for the first time at Sunbeam to stay put, since another key part of the carrot-and-stick deal was that the options Dunlap doled out vested only after three years. Many executives spent their entire tenure under Dunlap caught in a dilemma: they desperately wanted to leave, but they would be walking away from potentially millions of dollars of stock-option gains, as long as the price of Sunbeam shares stayed up or went higher. The final ingredient of the *stick* in Dunlap's carrot-and-stick approach was the raw fear he instilled in everybody who worked for him. All reports are that this really did apply to *everyone*.

The instillation of fear began on Al Dunlap's very first day on the job at Sunbeam. All the top executives assembled for a meeting in the boardroom of the Fort Lauderdale office in Florida. Dunlap walked into the meeting and began a "monologue on himself and the company." He then turned to the gathering of company officers and began ranting and raving, admonishing them for the "demise of Sunbeam!" He kept repeating that the "old Sunbeam is over today. It's over." In his description of the scene, Byrne wrote: "Glaring fiercely, Dunlap kept repeating the phrase, again and again, saliva spitting from his lips. His chest was puffed out and his face flushed bright red. The men stared in silence, incredulous at this outrageous performance." (Quotes from Byrne 2003, 2–3)

Dunlap then confronted the CFO, Paul O'Hara, and blamed him for delivering the financial performance estimates that Sunbeam had failed to meet for the last year. Next, Dunlap began asking the executives to present their summaries of the state of their units or departments. He started with the unfortunate James Clegg, the chief operating officer, who had expected to get Dunlap's job. Dunlap "cut him off and accused him of not knowing the details of his businesses." Dunlap snapped at anybody who hesitated. Richard Boynton, Sunbeam's national sales manager, later said, "He [Dunlap] just yelled, ranted and raved." Al kept this up for the whole of the first day and the meeting continued the next day. On the second day, Dunlap called Clegg out of the meeting and told him to leave the company, and to immediately sign the release form that honored his contract, including his salary for a year and his vested options. "Less than fifteen minutes after leaving the boardroom, [Clegg] returned to pick up his briefcase. 'I'm out,' he said to his shocked colleagues." (Quotes from Byrne 2003, 5-8)

Over the next few days, Dunlap fired five more executives. The fear factor was firmly in place. The big stick was looming over every senior executive and manager. The carrot in the form of extremely generous options beckoned to them with the promise of great riches, like the proverbial pot of gold at the end of the rainbow.

To grasp the unpleasant yet enticing position that the Sunbeam management team found itself in, one must remember that the year was 1996; the stock prices were rising boisterously; restructuring and downsizings were in vogue among Wall Street analysts and journalists; and the king of downsizing and restructuring, Al Dunlap himself, was promising to turn Sunbeam around in twelve months, maybe even less. On July 19, the day after the announcement of Dunlap's appointment as CEO, Wall Street analysts gave *buy* ratings to the stock and its market price jumped from $12.50 to $18.63.

By early November, the stock was trading around $25 per share. Considering how fast the stock market as a whole was climbing in 1996, Sunbeam's stock had moved upward relatively modestly after the initial jump on the announcement of Dunlap's appointment. To propel the stock price much higher, he wanted to produce a spectacular slash-and-burn downsizing plan for Wall Street. To get a truly dramatic, aggressive cost-cutting plan together, Dunlap turned to his long-trusted consultant, Don Burnett of Coopers & Lybrand, to head the project.

Dunlap announced his stunning cost-cutting plan on a conference call with analysts on November 12, 1996. The next day the *Wall Street Journal* ran an article dramatically titled, "Dunlap's Ax Falls—6,000 times—at Sunbeam." In the article, Frank and Lublin gave details of the plan announced by Dunlap:

- Immediately get rid of half of Sunbeam's 12,000 employees
- Shut down about 40 of its 61 warehouses
- Cut loose almost 90 percent of its product line
- Get rid of more than 50 percent of its twenty-six factories
- Eliminate the majority of its offices

The article went on to say that "Albert Dunlap all but gutted Sunbeam Corp. and demonstrated once again the genesis of his nickname: 'Chain-Saw Al.'" Dunlap's plan estimated "a one-time pretax charge of $300 million, of which $75 million will be paid as severance costs associated with plant closings." Furthermore, the reduction of 6,000 people "appears to represent one of the single biggest percentage cutbacks ever announced by a major US corporation." The downsizing expert and author, Alan Downs, commented, "You don't cut that dramatically without creating chaos inside the company" (quoted in Frank and Lublin 1996).

Surprisingly, for the first time Wall Street was not impressed with a Dunlap slash-and-burn announcement. The stock price did not rise. Perhaps the plan was so stunning that it gave cause for concern that Sunbeam was in worse shape than anyone had realized. Perhaps Kimberley-Clark's troubles with Scott Paper, after Dunlap's alleged turnaround, had left Wall Street a little weary of Dunlap's cost-cutting strategies. Maybe word had got out that some managers were in shock about what they considered to be economic-suicide: the closing of plants that they regarded as efficient and low-cost/high-profit facilities. Whatever the reason, Wall Street did not respond to this ruthless announcement. In fact, Sunbeam's stock price actually dropped 50 cents on the day of the announcement.

No wonder the stock market was a little skeptical. How could closing so many factories lead to increased production and sales? How could fewer people produce and sell more? However, whether by design or by coincidence, the dramatic announcements of cost-cutting had laid the foundation for lending credibility to the suddenly increasing false profits that would be reported in the near future. If Sunbeam had just begun falsely reporting overstated sales and profits in 1997, without any highly dramatic plan at all, the numbers in the financial statements probably would have been questioned a lot sooner. All Sunbeam had to do after this dramatic slash-and-burn action was report sales and profit growth and all would be believed. Accompanied by *reported* increases in profits, the plant and warehouse closings didn't have to be logical—they just had to be dramatic, and they were.

Two plant closings stood out as particularly ill conceived. Byrne reported conversations with employees and managers at the McMinnville, Tennessee, plant that indicate this was one of the most profitable plants at Sunbeam. It produced 15,000 hair clippers and trimmers a day, and its sales were growing. Further, the quality of its products was very high and its profit margins were much higher than Sunbeam's margins on its blenders or blankets. Sunbeam also had a very low lease cost at McMinnville, only "pennies per foot in rent, some $29,000 a year" (Byrne 2003, 131). However, there were plans to move the plant to Mexico to save labor costs, even though transport costs would be higher and moving the factory would cost millions of dollars. The plant manager and Donald Uzzi, senior vice president for sales, (who had replaced Newt White), as well as general manager William Kirkpatrick, fought to keep the McMinnville plant open and managed to save some of the jobs. Nevertheless, a line of clippers was moved out of McMinnville, and large amounts of sales were lost because of production shortages caused by the transition that the restructuring plan, typically, did not anticipate.

In the small town of Bay Springs, Mississippi, Dunlap's decision to close the plant that made the high quality wire for Sunbeam's electric blankets was possibly his most economically unfeasible. The city had given Sunbeam the rent-free use of the building for the plant. To keep jobs in the town, the mayor went on a public campaign to point out the economic stupidity of moving the plant. It was going to cost millions of dollars to relocate the plant in an absurd attempt to save a few hundred thousand dollars of transportation costs a year. As much as the mayor made sense, Dunlap resented the opposition and the plant was closed.

The numerous problems of trying to run Sunbeam after it was gutted by the restructuring plan were documented in a *Wall Street Journal* article by Lublin and Suris (April 9, 1997). There were bar-coding problems with shipping to their biggest customer, Wal-Mart, as well as a failed delivery of 150,000 irons among other items. There were also problems with the invoicing system and the computer system. In fact, Wal-Mart considered ending its relationship with Sunbeam due to these glitches. Other large customers claimed that shipments were late and that the staff turnover made continuity difficult.

Having pushed ahead with cutting jobs and closing plants, Dunlap began to apply his trademark brand of motivation—the fear and the dreams of stock option riches—to put the pressure onto his management. With gutted production facilities and a demoralized workforce, Dunlap began to pressure his management team to agree to incredibly high target estimates for sales and production.

The pressure to meet the sales figures fell first on the head of the sales department, who had to pass it down the line, and the same applied to the head of the production department. Managers simply couldn't make the unrealistic numbers, but they felt there would be repercussions if they didn't agree to them. And they didn't want to lose their stock options, which had increased in value but for the most part had not yet vested. They were in a bind. A number of employees left. Those who remained and accepted their unfeasible target numbers had to find ways to meet them.

One of the things that had swayed some of the managers in their decision to work for Dunlap in spite of their aversion to him, was that he had told them his plan for Sunbeam was to make a very quick turnaround and then to find an outright buyer for the company, as he had done with Scott Paper. If that could be done in a year, many of the managers felt it would be worthwhile to stick around and wait for their stock options to turn into huge financial windfalls. With such an incentive, they believed they could stomach anything for a year. However, the combination of what amounted to the gutting of the company in the restructuring plan, together with Wall Street's lukewarm reaction to it, caused some of the management to become skeptical. This was certainly the case with Newt White, executive vice president for consumer products. A few days after Sunbeam's downsizing announcement and Wall Street's cool response, White realized that this was not going to be a quick turnaround and there was not going to be a company gullible enough to acquire Sunbeam and cut them loose from their mess; so less than a week after Dunlap announced his plan, White left Sunbeam.

With White's departure, the first problem with cost-cutting became evident. Many believe that Sunbeam never recovered from the blow of losing him. When Sunbeam lost White, they lost an extremely talented and capable manager and a crucial amount of "company energy." His departure represented the loss of "informal networks" and "information sharing," of which Cameron spoke (quoted in Jenkins, 1997). White's leaving represented one of the unintentional consequences of indiscriminate downsizing: due to "declining morale," the most talented employees leave. According to White's friends, he "despised Dunlap" (Byrne 2003, 68). White could not tolerate the thought of a long stay in the environment that Dunlap was creating.

PART 4: AN OVERVIEW OF SUNBEAM'S FICTITIOUS FINANCIAL REPORTING SCHEMES

Scheme #1: Improper Timing of Revenue Recognition via Bill and Hold Sales, Consignment Sales, and other Contingent Sales

Under intense pressure to make the sales and profit targets, Sunbeam recorded future periods' sales in current periods. The U.S. Securities and Exchange Commission (SEC) findings explained how, for almost two years, Sunbeam's senior management deliberately embarked on a series of deceptive activities in order to increase the perceived value of the company (AAER 1393).[2]

The following is a summary of the alleged ploys that Sunbeam used, beginning with the first quarter of 1997 until the second quarter of 1998, to accelerate future quarters' sales in order to boost current periods' profits and give a misleading impression of sales growth:

1. Beginning in the first quarter of 1997, Sunbeam offered deep discounts and extended payment terms to get customers to place the next period's orders early. This acceleration of future quarters' sales into the present quarter "provided a misleading impression of the Company's results of operations for the present period." A worse consequence, of course, was that it "also resulted in the erosion of the company's profit margins and impoverished sales in later periods." In a nutshell, this began a death spiral because the ploy would have to be repeated in the future in order for the company to announce success in meeting target

---

[2] Sunbeam consented to the entry of the order without admitting or denying the findings or conclusions of law. As set out in AAER 1393, May 15, 2001.

sales. Further, the SEC Files reported that Sunbeam "failed to disclose this practice in its quarterly filing on Form 10-Q, as required under Regulation S-IC, Items 101 and 103." (Quotes from AAER 1393, 2001)

2. Beginning in the first quarter of 1997, Sunbeam recorded contingent sales or guaranteed sales as normal, current period sales. These were sales to customers where the sales agreements allowed the customers to return the goods to Sunbeam if they did not sell them. Some of these agreements even provided that, if returned, Sunbeam would pay for shipping and storage costs. Some of these customers did return the goods to Sunbeam in later quarters. Such non-GAAP sales increased Sunbeam's reported earnings; however, "GAAP does not permit the recognition of revenue in transactions lacking economic substance" (Cullinan and Wright 2003, 192).

3. Next, beginning the second quarter of 1997, Sunbeam became more aggressive and desperate and began using "bill and hold" sales to entice customers to place future periods' sales orders early. Sunbeam again offered discounts and extended payment terms and sometimes even the right to return the goods to Sunbeam if it turned out that they could not be sold. However, since the orders were so far in the future, the customers did not wish to hold the goods in their inventory ahead of time, so Sunbeam even agreed to hold the goods that they had "sold" in the current period until the customers really needed them in the next period. There are a number of criteria that have to be met before "bill and hold" sales are allowed to be recorded in a current period's sales and earnings:

   • The buyer, not the seller, must request that the transaction be on a bill and hold basis.
   • The buyer must have a substantial business purpose for ordering the goods on a bill and hold basis.
   • The risks of ownership must have passed to the buyer.
     Other relevant factors include: "whether [the seller] has modified its normal billing and credit terms for this buyer" and "the seller's past experiences with and pattern of bill and hold transactions" (AAER 1393, 2001).

   Sunbeam, nevertheless, recorded these sales as current period sales, even though they did not meet the criteria.

4. To coax more sales orders, Sunbeam increasingly gave customers the right to return goods, yet they did not increase the reserve for returns

in their accounting records. This overstated reported income. In addition, the SEC's findings alleged that in January 1998, the CFO, Russell Kersh, "ordered the deletion of all return authorizations from the company's computer system . . . [and] deleting the authorization file delayed acceptance of some quantity of pending returns long enough so that they did not count against net sales for the first quarter" (AAER 1393, 2001). Further, while sales with rights of return were growing, Sunbeam actually reduced its reserve for returns from $6.5 million at the end of 1991 to $1.5 million at the end of February 1998.

5. Sunbeam sold items in the first quarter of 1997 that were products that it was discontinuing as part of its restructuring plan. Sunbeam knew that sales of these items would not be continued since the product lines had been dropped. Also, they were sold at huge discounts to fully dispose of the products. These sales should have been reported separately from continuing sales, as an infrequent event, but they were recorded as regular ongoing sales. (This gave a misleading impression of Sunbeam's sales "growth" and its future profitability.) The SEC findings showed that such sales totaled $19.6 million in the first quarter of 1997 (AAER 1393, 2001).

6. Also pursuant to product lines that were to be closed as part of the restructuring, in 1996 Sunbeam overstated the amount by which the inventory had to be written down for all the segments that were going to be closed. This was part of their creation of "cookie-jar"[3] restructuring reserves. Then, beginning in the first quarter of 1997, profits were overstated as these inventories were sold at amounts above the amount recorded in 1996. In the first quarter of 1997, quarterly income was inflated "by approximately $2.1 million" (AAER 1393, 2001).

7. In the fourth quarter of 1997, Sunbeam entered into a thoroughly inconclusive "sales" agreement with a fulfillment house to sell an indeterminate amount of spare parts to the customer. The contract actually stated that it "would terminate in January 1998, absent agreement between the parties on the value of the inventory." Sunbeam even guaranteed a profit of 5 percent to the "customer" on any future resale of this inventory. Despite the conditional and indeterminate

---

[3] "Cookie-jar" reserves refer to reserves created by overstating a future liability in one period in order to release it in a future period, thereby fictitiously implying that the company has less expense in the future period.

nature of this agreement, Sunbeam recorded $11 million sales and $5 million profit on the "sale" in 1997, even though, as the SEC stated: "The sale price had no practical relationship to any payment Sunbeam might obtain." Upon the auditor's unwillingness to classify such an agreement as a sale, Sunbeam agreed to create a reserve of $3 million against the profit they had raised, but they left the balance of the income in the 1997 financial statements. (Quotes from AAER 1393, 2001)

8. Sunbeam recorded rebates on future purchases as deductions from the current period's cost of goods sold expense. In 1997 the company aggressively negotiated with suppliers to secure rebates that applied to purchase contracts covering future periods' purchases. One rebate contract included an up-front payment in respect of future purchases. Naturally, according to GAAP, rebates should decrease the cost of goods sold expense in the period that the goods are sold. Sunbeam applied these rebates to decrease cost of goods sold in the period that it signed the rebate contracts, instead of prorating them. The Commission found that "the suppliers' rebates obtained by Sunbeam beginning in the second quarter of 1997 were made in contemplation of future purchases, and therefore should have been recognized as the related sales were made" (AAER 1393, 2001).

9. Sunbeam captured extra revenue by extending its quarter-end date by two days. In the first quarter of 1998, in order to include the results of its newly acquired companies—Coleman, First Alert, and Signal Systems—Sunbeam changed its quarter end from March 29 to March 31. This is legal. However, in its press release on April 3, it made no mention of the fact that the shortfall in sales for the quarter was after *adding* two days' sales to the quarter. Sunbeam did, however, disclose the change in its 8-Q filing on April 3, 1998, and in the 10-K, which it filed on May 15, 1998.

10. Sunbeam was also accused of issuing misleading press releases, as well as conducting ambiguous and deceptive press conferences and conference calls with analysts. Sunbeam categorically denied its "channel stuffing,"[4] blatantly overstated its sales and earnings estimates, and deliberately failed to disclose any of the previously-mentioned nine manipulations that it had used to present a misleading impression

---

[4] "Channel stuffing" refers to persuading customers to place the next period's orders in the current period. The seller "stuffs" more inventory onto the customer than is currently needed.

of its sales and profit growth. In the press release announcing its results for the first quarter of 1997, Sunbeam's sales showed growth of 10 percent compared to the first quarter of 1996. However, in publicizing its results, Sunbeam did not disclose that most of that growth came from the sales of discontinued products and from the guaranteed sales, as explained earlier in point 2. Furthermore, the SEC declared, "As members of Sunbeam's management knew or were reckless in not knowing, these misstatements and omissions rendered Sunbeam's press release materially false and misleading." The SEC also found that although Sunbeam had ostensibly met its earnings targets for the third quarter of 1997 by relying on accelerating future periods' sales, "management publicly denied the contention of certain analysts that Sunbeam relied on channel stuffing to achieve its revenue targets" (AAER 1393, 2001).

When it came to the fourth quarter of 1997, all the tricks (as previously described—and more) were still not enough. Dunlap then blamed the warm weather for its effect on sales of electric blankets. However, "What investors didn't know would have caused Sunbeam stock to suffer a total collapse" (Byrne 2003, 169-170). Although just short of Sunbeam's own unrealistic targets, the *reported* results after all the ploys to accelerate future sales were supposedly *record* results. In its press release on January 28, 1998, Sunbeam maintained that the increase in its sales was a "clear indication that [Sunbeam's] strategy is working." The SEC subsequently concluded that "this press release and the associated conference call between Sunbeam and its analysts communicated substantially overstated results of operations" (AAER 1393, 2001).

With reluctance, Dunlap issued another (rather sudden) press release on March 19, 1998. The impetus for this was the "due diligence" examination that Morgan Stanley had done in respect of the $500 million bond offering that it was underwriting for Sunbeam. This "due diligence" study had picked up on the fact that major Sunbeam customers were overstocked with Sunbeam inventories and that Sunbeam's sales were going very slowly in the first quarter of 1998. Morgan Stanley's attorneys and Sunbeam's internal and external counsels insisted on a press release disclosing that the company's sales in the first quarter of 1998 might not meet analysts' expectations. Sunbeam issued a statement saying that net sales for the first quarter of 1998 "may be lower than the range of Wall Street analysts' estimates for $285 million to $295 million, but net sales are expected to exceed 1997 first quarter net sales of $253.4 million." It also stated that the shortfall "if any, would be due to changes in inventory management and order patterns at certain of the company's major retail customers." (Quotes from AAER 1393, 2001)

The SEC maintained that the "release inaccurately implied that Sunbeam's lower sales to retailers stemmed from a generalized effort among retailers to reduce inventory levels, rather than from Sunbeam's 1997 accelerated sales. In addition, information available to Sunbeam management did not provide any basis for projecting net sales in excess of those achieved in the first quarter of 1997" (AAER 1393, 2001).

Indeed, Sunbeam, in an April 3 press release just after its debt offering, announced that it expected to show a loss for the first quarter of 1998. The SEC release noted the following:

In the release and related conference call, Sunbeam management did not disclose:

- the inadequacy of Sunbeam's reserves for returns;
- bill and hold sales that pulled $35 million in net sales into the quarter; and
- the extension of the quarter by two days, which added $20 million in net sales to the quarter. (AAER 1393, 2001)

On May 11, 1998, Sunbeam issued its first quarter 1998 earnings release. It did not disclose how accelerated sales in 1997 had drained its current quarter's sales as it disclosed its loss of 52 cents per share. It also failed to disclose the "positive effect of the first quarter bill and hold sales and the failure to adequately reserve for returned product." Furthermore, Sunbeam made predictions for the year that were "contrary to internal analyses."

Scheme #2: Improper Use of Restructuring Reserves

According to SEC allegations, the other major category of misreporting by Sunbeam was that it created big reserves for the write-down of assets and for future losses or liabilities in order to boost future profits, as it later "discovered" that these reserves were not needed, and it then released those "cookie-jar reserves" back into earnings. Sunbeam created these overstated restructuring reserves upon the implementation of its downsizing and restructuring ploy, and on its acquisitions of Coleman, First Alert, and Signature Brands.

A legitimate reserve is usually created in recognition of a future liability or loss. The expense is recognized in the current period. When the future payment or loss occurs, the amount is offset against the reserve, and it is not reported as an expense in that later period. Sometimes companies abuse this procedure, and the SOX Report (*SEC Report Pursuant to the Sarbanes-Oxley Act*, 2002) described the abuse as follows:

> Reserves may be improperly used to manage earnings. These companies typically create reserves (by initially over-accruing a liability) in one accounting period and then reduce the excess reserves in later accounting periods. The reversal of the reserve creates net income that can be used to meet earnings shortfalls. (17)

What deceptive companies especially like to do is recognize the future expense in the current period as a special charge. The special charge is likely to be regarded as something that will not recur, and therefore it often does not impact the stock price negatively when recognized. It is best if the one-time charge has a positive-sounding name, like a "restructuring reserve." In the future, when the expense actually occurs and is offset against the reserve instead of being recognized as an expense, the earnings are inflated because the expense was moved to an earlier period. It then appears as though the "restructuring" worked and higher profits will recur, and the stock price often increases in response. Meanwhile, all that happened after the restructuring was that the company did not have to account for the expenses that were offset by the overstated "cookie jar" reserves that had been created earlier.

Sunbeam was not shy when it came to creating reserves on its spectacular downsizing restructuring plan. In the last quarter of 1996, it took a $337.9 million restructuring charge. The SEC found that at least $35 million of this was overstated (AAER 1393, 2001).

In addition, the SEC found that on its restructuring, Sunbeam had decreased the carrying value not only of inventory that it was dropping, but of inventory that it would continue to carry normally. As a result, inventory at the end of 1996 was understated by $2.1 million. Earnings in 1997 would be overstated by this amount when inventory was sold.

Sunbeam also created a $12 million litigation reserve in the last quarter of 1996 in respect of a possible environmental action. However, the Commission found that at least $6 million of this reserve was overstated. Also in the last quarter of 1996, Sunbeam created a cooperative advertising reserve of $21.8 million, which the commission found was created "without any test of the reasonableness" of the amount (AAER 1393, 2001).

Throughout 1997, Sunbeam overstated earnings by releasing parts of these overstated reserves in each quarter. For instance, in the second quarter of 1997, the company overstated its earnings by releasing $8.2 million of the non-GAAP overstated restructuring reserve, and another $5.8 million overstatement of earnings came from the release of the cooperative advertising reserve. By way of further example, Sunbeam's fourth quarter earnings were overstated by the release of $1.5 million of the restructuring reserves, and by $9 million when the company settled an environmental litigation case for $3 million and could release back into profit the remaining $9 million of the $12 million litigation reserve that it had created (AAER 1393, 2001).

However, it was in the area of accelerating the recording of future sales that Sunbeam presents itself as the ultimate case study in pulling every trick of the trade to boost sales and profits. Sunbeam created a whole new approach to playing fast and loose as it milked the widespread practice of channel stuffing for every last dollar.

PART 5: THE SUNBEAM INFERNO

On July 19, 1996, the day that Al Dunlap was appointed CEO of Sunbeam, the stock price jumped 57 percent, from $12.50 to $18.63. Wall Street was enthralled at the thought that this slash-and-burn downsizing specialist would quickly boost Sunbeam's stock price as he had boosted previous companies' share prices—never mind what had happened to those companies after the quick boost. The stock continued to rise after Dunlap said, in July, that he had begun a study for a downsizing plan that would produce a turnaround. By November 12, 1996, the stock price was up in the high $20s. That was the day that Sunbeam announced the actual details of the massive downsizing. This time, the stunning magnitude of the planned cuts in jobs, plant facilities, and products shocked Wall Street. The stock price actually dropped a little that day and remained in the high $20 range right into March 1997.

It was during this first quarter of 1997 that Sunbeam began producing financial reports that made it look as though the slashing of facilities, products, jobs, and research and development could, in fact, grow sales and earnings. Early in 1997, Sunbeam began to release back into earnings the false reserves that it had created upon its restructuring in 1996. It also began to accelerate future periods' sales into current periods via the wide array of tricks discussed earlier. Sunbeam did this every for every quarter in 1997, with its earnings management reaching its greatest level in the fourth quarter of that year (AAER 1393, 2001).

As previously mentioned, Sunbeam accompanied these misleading sales and earnings reports with unrealistic estimates of future growth and without any reference to the acceleration of future periods' sales. Based upon these illusory reports of earnings and sales growth as well as unrealistic estimates of future performance, the stock price broke out of the high $20s range in March 1997 and began a steady, steep rocket-like climb until it peaked at about $52 in March 1998, a few days after the announcement of Sunbeam's acquisition of three companies in one day: Coleman, First Alert, and Signature Brand. Sunbeam's stock price had risen 400 percent since Dunlap's appointment in July 1996; it looked as though his journey to the sun would succeed.

However, Sunbeam was on the verge of a blazing disintegration. By November 1998, the stock price would tumble to about $7 (AAER 1393, 2001). The more that Sunbeam accelerated future periods' sales into current periods, the harder it became to achieve the future periods' sales estimates. The company was caught in an ever-intensifying vicious circle. The customers weren't paying ahead of time for sales that were recorded ahead of time, and worse still, their inventories of Sunbeam products were building up steadily. Further, Sunbeam itself was storing massive amounts of these "sold" inventories.

While so many accepted the downsizing program as an explanation for that all-too-quick turnaround, for others, the downsizing made a quick growth in sales seem implausible. Some skeptics kept a careful eye out for signs of overstated sales and earnings. As early as mid-June of 1997, an article in *Barron's* questioned the validity of the sales growth in the light of the increase in both accounts receivable and inventories (Laing 1997). However, this went unheeded by the market which was blinded by the dazzling stock prices. Similarly, William H. Steele, an analyst for Buckingham Research Group in San Francisco, downgraded Sunbeam to a neutral rating in July 1997 based on the increase in inventories and on noticing that "changes in cash from working capital were negative" (Byrne 2003, 152). On March 2, 1998, when Dunlap's new employment contract was announced during a conference call, a Bear Stern's analyst, Constance Maneaty, questioned Dunlap on whether his generous new options package would be a drag on earnings in the future.

During this period, a real threat to the Sunbeam trajectory had been approaching in the form of Morgan Stanley's "due diligence" test for the debt offering that it was underwriting to raise the cash for the acquisitions of Coleman, First Alert, and Signature Brands. While Dunlap was talking up Sunbeam as part of the road show to drum up support for the debt offering,

Morgan Stanley's "due diligence" team had been speaking to Sunbeam managers as well as to Arthur Andersen, the external auditors, and to Sunbeam's biggest customers. Everything they heard indicated that Sunbeam's sales estimates for the first quarter of 1998 were not going to be met. Morgan Stanley then approached Sunbeam's internal counsel, David Fannin, and its external counsel, Blaine Fogg, who investigated further. On March 18, it was agreed that a press release had to be issued the next day, announcing that Sunbeam might not make its sales estimates. What was released, however, did not capture the severity of the problem. The company acknowledged that sales may be lower than the range of Wall Street analysts' estimates, but they "expected sales to exceed those of the first quarter of 1997." They also blamed the shortfall on "changes in inventory management and order patterns." Sunbeam's customers had so much inventory from 1997's accelerated sales that it was catching up with them in 1998.

Nevertheless, the announcement represented the first crack in the armor of Sunbeam's façade as a company whose sales and earnings were growing rapidly. The Sunbeam stock fell to $45.375 on the day of the announcement. In spite of this, the company still raised $750 million on the debt offering. Later this would be to the chagrin of those debt holders. However, the questions as to the validity of Sunbeam's real sales growth and its estimates were now exposed, and with inventory piled up in Sunbeam's warehouses and in its customers' warehouses, the answers to those questions would continue to impede management's efforts to maintain the Sunbeam illusion.

One day after the Sunbeam press release, on March 20, 1998, the *New York Post* carried an article entitled: "Sunbeam's Cloudy Outlook: Chairman Al Warns on Profits." The article questioned whether Dunlap would be able to deliver on Sunbeam's estimates of sales growth. More ominously, analyst Andrew Shore was reconsidering his earlier upgrade on Sunbeam's stock. Never a fan of Al Dunlap, he was again hot on the trail of stories of inventory piling up in the Sunbeam warehouses and in its customers' warehouses. He had also heard stories of turmoil within Sunbeam.

In early April, Shore received a tip-off that Sunbeam's head of domestic sales, Donald Uzzi, had been fired. The company was desperate to keep this quiet because Uzzi had been carrying an enormous load in trying to keep Sunbeam's sales from falling apart altogether. With the rumors of Uzzi's departure, as well as the resignation of Richard Coudis, head of corporate planning, Shore felt he had to take the risk of downgrading Sunbeam's stock on a "conference call that linked analysts in New York with more than 5,000 stockbrokers around the world. It had an electrifying effect.

Sunbeam's stock began to plunge, falling $4 within minutes" (Byrne 2003, 241, 242). If he was wrong, Shore's reputation would be in shreds. A few hours later, Shore was relieved to get confirmation that his call was correct when Sunbeam's internal counsel insisted on the release of a press statement explaining that:

- Sunbeam now expected to make a loss in the first quarter of 1998.
- Sales would not meet the amount predicted in their March release a few weeks earlier.
- Sales would be less than in the comparative first quarter of 1997.

That same day, Sunbeam's stock fell almost 25 percent, to $34.38. Andrew Shore was vindicated and congratulated. Sunbeam's internal auditor, Deidra DenDanto, who had been sidelined by management with her concerns about the bill and hold sales, resigned on the same day. Russell Kersh, the chief financial officer of Sunbeam, who had the ultimate responsibility for the accounting misstatements, could now just watch as the fireworks of falsely stated profits exploded before his eyes. As for Dunlap, he continued to "gloss over the first quarter repercussions of [Sunbeam's] 1997 earnings management as a surprising slowdown" (AAER 1393, 2001). By this stage, these nonsense charades were all to no avail.

Most of the Wall Street analysts began to downgrade Sunbeam's stock, and investigative journalists were hot on the trail of the telltale signs of fraud: growing accounts receivable and mounting inventory. The problem with a fictitiously recorded sale is that it remains as accounts receivable; it does not turn into cash like an honest sale does. Also, the inventory of a bill and hold sale has to build up somewhere—either at the seller's or the buyer's warehouses. Furthermore, cash flow from operations (CFFO) lags the falsely reported profits, and it gets really difficult to make sales in the following periods. Wall Street was finally catching on to Dunlap's "turnarounds," and so was the media. An article in *Forbes* magazine commented, "Seven months ago Al Dunlap declared victory in turning around . . . Sunbeam. . . . But since the middle of March its stock has fallen nearly 50% from $52 to a recent $28. . . . This turnaround hasn't turned and it isn't likely to." The article went on to point out how "in December 1997 Sunbeam had sold $60 million in accounts receivable to raise cash." Unfortunately, however, analysts had not questioned Sunbeam's numbers, "If they had, they might have seen that Sunbeam was coming apart." (Quotes from Schifrin 1998)

During a meeting with financial analysts on May 11, Sunbeam announced another downsizing plan. In respect of its acquisition of Coleman,

Signature Brands, and First Alert, Sunbeam planned to eliminate 6,400 jobs and close 8 of 24 plants. The *New York Times,* on May 12, noted that in the analysts' meeting, "Mr. Dunlap attributed the 'early buy' debacle to everything from a marketing executive who approved 'stupid deals' with retailers to El Nino. . . . Whatever the reason, the dismal performance was worse than investors had anticipated" (Canedy 1998c, D2). Worse was coming.

The final blast of the explosion for Dunlap and CFO Russell Kersh came a few weeks later in the form of an article by Jonathon Laing in *Barron's* investor periodical that made the accusation that "the earnings from Sunbeam's supposed breakthrough year appear to be largely manufactured." The article speculated that a lot of the supposed earnings had come from releasing back into earnings the overstated reserves that had been created upon Sunbeam's restructuring charge in 1996. Furthermore, the exposé assumed that, at the time, Sunbeam had also written down property, plant, and equipment values to reduce future depreciation expenses, and observed that earnings were boosted by a drop in Sunbeam's allowance for doubtful debts and discounts. It was also suspicious that "Sunbeam's inventories exploded by some 40% or $93 million, during 1997." In addition, there were "indications that Sunbeam jammed as many sales as it could into 1997 to pump both the top and bottom lines." The article in *Barron's* provided the final spark that exploded the Sunbeam façade. (Quotes from Laing 1998b, 18-19)

The following Monday, Sunbeam put out a press release saying that there was no factual support to the *Barron's* article's accusation that Sunbeam had largely invented its profits. The release was rather problematic, however, because it was very general and did not answer the specific questions raised. The next day, Sunbeam held a directors' meeting to consider the accusations against the company. The gathering included internal and external counsel, as well as Russell Kersh, the CFO, Robert Gluck, the controller, and Philip Harlow, the external auditor from Arthur Anderson. At the meeting, the directors found no comfort from the answers they received about the accounting numbers, or about the strength of the current quarter. Further, Dunlap and Kersh indicated that if they didn't get more support from the board of directors, they might tender their resignations. After the meeting broke up, the external directors discussed the situation and concluded that it looked like the end of the line for Dunlap, and possibly for Sunbeam as well. In the next few days, Fannin, the general counsel, met with the external counsel and they carried out some further internal investigations. On Saturday, June 13, Fannin and the outside directors met secretly. They decided that they should get rid of Dunlap and Kersh by accepting their offers to resign as tendered at the previous board meeting. Another board meeting was convened, and telephone calls were made to Dunlap and Kersh. With the two men on the line, Peter Langerman, one of the directors, read to them from a prepared statement:

> Here is what we propose:
>
> 1. You be removed from all positions with the company and its subsidiaries immediately. You may continue to serve as a director of Sunbeam unless you choose to resign from that position.
> 2. The board names a new Chairman of the Board and we expand our ongoing search to encompass a search for your successor. . . .
> (Byrne 2003, 324)

After firing Dunlap and Kersh, Langerman continued to investigate the depth of Sunbeam's problems. He learned that Sunbeam might contravene its debt covenants by the end of the month and that the $1.7 billion of loans could become repayable. The board of directors realized that bankruptcy was a possibility, and they decided to ask Ron Perelman (of Revlon Cosmetics) if he would get his man, Jerry Levin (who had been the CEO of Coleman) to run Sunbeam for a while. (Perelman had acquired a significant amount of Sunbeam stock on the sale of his company, Coleman, to Sunbeam.) Levin agreed to the request and began by rehiring executives who had quit under Dunlap, and then he initiated a thorough analysis of the financial statements. The SEC also began an investigation of Sunbeam in June. Arthur Andersen, the external auditors, began a review of Sunbeam's previous financial statements. It was immediately apparent to Levin, Arthur Andersen, and the SEC that Sunbeam's financial statements would have to be restated. An ongoing investigation would have to determine the amount of the restatements.

In November 1998, as a result of the investigations, Sunbeam "issued substantially restated financial statements for the six quarters from the fourth quarter of 1996 through the first quarter of 1998. As a result of the restatement for 1997, Sunbeam reported $93 million in income, approximately one half of the amount it had previously reported" (AAER 1393, 2001). Sunbeam had inflated its 1997 income alone by close to 100 percent. Sunbeam's amazing resurrection had been nothing more than a "manufactured illusion" (Byrne 2003, 345).

Within weeks of the firing of Dunlap, the stock price had fallen to below $10 per share. After the October announcements of the required restatements, Sunbeam was trading in the $7 range, a spectacular plunge from its peak of about $52 per share a mere eight months earlier (AAER 1393, 2001).

Although Jerry Levin did a valiant job in attempting to reverse the destruction of Sunbeam, the company filed for Chapter 11 bankruptcy protection in 2001, after making heavy losses in the previous year. Under the reorganization plan, banks would recover about 33 cents for each dollar they loaned Sunbeam. Shareholders received nothing.

PART 6: SIGNALS OF SUNBEAM'S SCHEMES

Signals of Sunbeam's Fictitious Reporting Scheme #1:

- Improper Timing of Revenue Recognition via bill and hold sales, consignment sales, and other contingency sales.

Signal #1: The quality of a company's leadership is the primary signal as to whether its financial statements are likely to be fraudulently reported. The ethics, ability, management style, and track record of the leadership of the company should be the first evidence an analyst or investor looks at in examining financial reports for credibility. The track record of the companies that Dunlap had managed before joining Sunbeam, most notably Scott Paper, made Andrew Shore a skeptic of Sunbeam's reported "turnaround" right from the start. Because of his long-term doubts about Dunlap, Shore was the first analyst to put in a downgrade on Sunbeam stock on the morning of April 3, 1998, just before Sunbeam's press release that it was not going to make its estimates for the first quarter of 1998.

This general signal of the quality and track record of company leaders should be combined with an analysis of whether the business plan outlined by management is likely to produce the reported results as published in the financial statements. Sunbeam's vicious cost-cutting plan of closing production plants and cutting products, jobs, and R&D expenditure was not likely to lead to fast sales growth as reported in record numbers in 1997. The implausibility of the reported financial results in relation to Sunbeam's major downsizing plan was a major signal of fictitious financial reporting.

Signal #2: The leading sign of an overstatement of sales is when accounts receivable increase as a percentage of sales, which is often measured as days' sales outstanding (DSO). If the next period's sales have been accelerated into the current period, or if the sales are completely fictitious, the company will debit accounts receivable and credit sales, as for legitimate sales. However, while legitimate sales will be paid relatively soon by the customers and will turn into cash, the next period's sales will probably only be paid next period, and will remain on the balance sheet in the current period as accounts receivable instead of turning into cash.

This signal of an overstatement of sales, and the accompanying profit, is easy to spot. One simply has to look at the income statement and extract the sales figures, and then look at the balance sheet and extract the accounts receivable amounts. Then, calculate accounts receivable as a percentage of sales. To illustrate the validity of this technique, let us examine an extract from Sunbeam's income statements in Table 2.1, and an extract from its balance sheet in Table 2.2. If we divide accounts receivable at the end of any

SUNBEAM Table 2.1[5]
Extracts from Quarterly Income Statement (in Millions)

	1996			1997				1998	
Gross Profit Margin:	Q2	Q3	Q4	Q1	Q2	Q3	Q4	Q1	Q2
Net Sales	253,896	231,770	268,863	253,450	287,609	289,033	338,090	244,296	578,488
(Cost of Goods Sold)	206,685	202,998	309,282	185,669	213,080	200,242	238,692	211,459	630,965
Gross Profit	47,211	28,772	(40,419)	67,781	74,529	88,792	99,398	32,837	(52,477)

SUNBEAM Table 2.2
Extracts from Quarterly Balance Sheets (in Millions)
PRIOR TO RESTATEMENT

	1996			1997				1998	
	Q2	Q3	Q4	Q1	Q2	Q3	Q4	Q1	Q2
Balance Sheet Accounts									
Cash & cash equivalents	35,794	24,638	11,526	30,415	57,970	22,811	52,378	193,543	43,151
Receivables, net	228,749	194,559	213,438	296,716	252,045	309,095	295,550	562,294	523,065
Inventories	327,093	330,213	161,252	14,811	208,374	290,875	256,180	575,109	646,626
Total current assets	621,411	586,012	624,163	609,654	634,848	692,552	658,005	1,438,638	1,278,465
Total assets	1,230,310	1,196,333	1,072,709	1,053,155	1,089,345	1,145,071	1,120,284	3,443,422	3,519,121
Total current liabilities	187,535	253,331	271,583	260,154	258,149	245,997	198,099	443,719	1,861,243
Retained earnings			35,118				141,134		(310,233)

---

[5] Tables 2.1 and 2.2 are derived from Sunbeam's SEC filings.

SUNBEAM Table 2.3

Receivables-to-Sales Ratio

	1997				1998	
	Q1	Q2	Q3	Q4	Q1	Q2
Receivables-to-Sales Ratio	29.43%	24.20%	28.13%	25.30%	48.51%	36.08%

quarter by the addition of the sales for the four quarters ending on that date, we see the trend of accounts receivable growing as a percentage of sales, as shown in Table 2.3, from 29 percent of sales in the first quarter of 1997, to 49 percent of sales in the first quarter of 1998.

Signal #3: The third sign to look for as an indicator of illegitimately reported sales is a sudden change in the gross margin percentage. It is difficult for a manufacturer to suddenly increase the company's gross margin percentage, and it is also suspicious if the gross margin fluctuates downward suddenly. Again, it is easy to find this signal. A simple perusal of the income statements over a number of quarters will alert the investor to suspicious changes in the gross margin percentage. Look at extracts from Sunbeam's quarterly income statements in Table 2.1. Calculating gross margin as a percentage of sales, as shown in Table 2.4, reveals sudden changes in the gross margin over the quarters, from 19 percent in the second quarter of 1996, to negative 15 percent in the fourth quarter of 1996. This was followed by a suspicious improvement in 1997 (after the so-called "turnaround") to 27 percent in the first quarter of 1997, to 31 percent in the third quarter of 1997, and then falling to 13 percent in the first quarter of 1998.

These sudden changes in gross margins were probably due partly to things like selling inventory, in 1997, at better prices than the restructuring purported to anticipate because some inventory had been valued at incorrectly low amounts. Also, Sunbeam's ploys—like understating the reserve for

SUNBEAM Table 2.4

Quarterly Gross Margin

	1996			1997				1998	
	Q2	Q3	Q4	Q1	Q2	Q3	Q4	Q1	Q2
Gross Profit Margin %	19%	12%	–15%	27%	27%	31%	29%	13%	–9%

returns and taking the benefits of rebates for future purchases into the current period—would also have falsely boosted the gross margins in 1997 and in the first quarter of 1998.

Signal #4: The fourth signal of inappropriately recorded sales is when cash flow from operations (CFFO) falls, or when it lags behind operating income or net income. For this information, once again, we simply have to look at the financial statements filed with the SEC. For the first three quarters of 1997, we see that Sunbeam reported operating income of $132 million in its income statement. However, looking at the statement of cash flows, we see that Sunbeam's cash flow from operations for the same period was *negative*. This signal is a huge red flag. If Sunbeam was operating at such a great profit, why would it be burning through operating cash?

The statement of cash flows is separated into three segments: the cash flow from operations; the cash flow from investing activities; and the cash flow from financing the business. So the section called "the cash flow from operations" should *not* show an amount of cash generated that is significantly less than the profit from operations—listed as "operating income" or "operating earnings" in the income statement—without a very specific explanation.

Certainly, from these first four signals alone, anybody reading the financial statements of Sunbeam at the end of 1997 should have been fully alert to the fact that its reported sales and operating profits were unreliable. The sales were simply not turning into cash received at the rate that they should have been if they were legitimate sales, and the gross margin percentages were fluctuating wildly without a clear explanation for the volatility.

Signal #5: The fifth signal that a company is overstating its sales is when it begins a policy of more aggressively recognizing revenue. The leading example of such an aggressive policy is the practice of recognizing sales revenue before the goods are shipped to the customer. The two major accounting strategies for doing this are "bill and hold" sales and "percentage of completion" accounting for contracts in progress. For Sunbeam, the relevant method in this category of overstatement of sales and profit was its "bill and hold" sales to get customers to place later periods' orders long before they would pay for the goods and long before Sunbeam delivered the goods to the customers. Of $35 million of "bill and hold" sales that Sunbeam recognized in the fourth quarter of 1997, $29 million was later reversed and restated as future periods' sales.

In the case of Sunbeam, this signal was easy to spot. One of the notes to the financial statements in the company's 1997 Annual Report mentioned this policy.

The lesson here is always to read the notes and footnotes to quarterly and annual financial statements in a search for a new, aggressive policy indicating that the company records sales before the goods are delivered.

Signal #6: When a company offers large discounts and extended payment terms to entice its customers to order early, it is a signal that the reported sales for the current period are overstated and that future sales will be impoverished by the early placement of the orders. The notes in the financial statements in Sunbeam's quarterly reports (Form 10-Q) should have disclosed this, under Regulation S-K, items 101 and 103. However, Sunbeam failed to divulge this information (AAER 1393, 2001). In order to get information on this kind of channel stuffing, analysts and investors should scan the 10-Q and 10-K reports, and also conduct article searches via search engines such as Google and databases such as LexisNexis or ProQuest. Search for data indicating that the company is offering unusually generous payment terms or discounts. If necessary, one could even interview the company's staff and customers, as was done in the due diligence tests by the underwriters of Sunbeam's debt offering in 1998.

In addition, any news reports of large warehouses being built to house the company's inventory (as was the case with Sunbeam), or of a company's major customers building warehouses or "reclamation centers" to store unsold or returnable inventory, should be taken as huge red flags that companies have accelerated current sales at the expense of future sales.

Signal #7: The recording of sales when the customer has a right to return the product is a signal of the overstatement of sales. Such sales are often known as "guaranteed sales," where the customers can return goods if they are unable to resell them, or they can get a reimbursement if they cannot achieve a certain resale selling price or "guaranteed markup." In Sunbeam's case, the SEC found that "in total, $24.7 million in fourth quarter [1997] sales to distributors were subject to rights of return" (AAER 1393, 2001). A reserve for such returns should be accounted for in the financial statements, according to the Financial Accounting Standards Board's SFAS 48. However, the SEC reported that since such sales were a significant change in approach for Sunbeam, and the likely return amounts were not known, it should not have reported these sales.

The investor should search the financial statements for any disclosure of recording such sales (although in some cases, like that of Sunbeam, a change in approach may not be properly disclosed). Also, one should conduct an article search for significant changes in company policy, or for "guaranteed sales," or sales with right of return, or for information about customers or the company building reclamation centers or warehouses—all telltale signs of returns waiting to happen.

Signal #8: Press releases indicating that previous sales growth estimates will not be met are clear warning signals. It is a strong indication of a desperate overstatement of sales and sales estimates when a company issues a second press release, downwardly revising the numbers of an earlier press release that was itself a downward revision of sales estimates. This was indeed the case with Sunbeam's March and April press releases discussed earlier. Perform Internet or database searches for press releases or for articles referring to press releases that revise earlier public statements in quick succession.

Signals of Sunbeam's Fictitious Reporting Scheme #2:

- Overstating Earnings via improper use of restructuring reserves

Signal #1: Large one-time charges in the income statement, such as restructuring charges and the creation of reserves on the balance sheet, should alert the reader to the possibility that future periods' earnings may be inflated as the reserves are released back into profits, or as the written-down assets are sold at normal prices. Sunbeam's income statement showed a massive restructuring charge of $154.9 million in the last quarter of 1996 that included the over-accruals for items such as the advertising reserve and the litigation reserve.

Signal #2: If restructuring reserves or reserves resulting from other one-time charges appear in the financial statements upon the arrival of a new CEO, it is an even stronger alert that future expenses are possibly being recognized early with the creation of improper reserves. Al Dunlap was appointed CEO of Sunbeam on July 18, 1996, and the massive restructuring reserves were created in the last quarter of 1996.

Signal #3: When reserves decrease fast, it is an indication that earnings in the period may have been inflated by avoiding expenses through the reversal of the reserves. One has to consider how the company will be able to continue showing profits in the future when it can no longer release reserves to bolster profits. Sunbeam's restructuring accrual decreased from $63.8 million in the last quarter of 1996 to $45.3 million in the last quarter of 1997, and then it was released steadily until it reached zero at the end of the first quarter of 1998.

Signal #4: The release of "cookie jar" reserves boosts operating income but does not produce cash flow. Therefore, once again, cash flow from operations (CFFO) lagging operating income is a signal of this method of fictitious reporting. In Sunbeam's financial statements, the effect of releasing "cookie jar" reserves together with accelerating sales (as discussed in Scheme I), combined to provide a very strong signal of its extremely aggressive earnings management.

For this manipulation one should, of course, search the financial statements for large one-time charges in the income statement, or for reserves decreasing in later periods on the balance sheet. When Sunbeam simultaneously reported large operating profits in 1997 but negative CFFO, it was time to bail out of the company and its stock as quickly as possible.

Are They Living Happily Ever After?[6]

≈ **Al Dunlap,** Sunbeam's former CEO and chairman, settled a $15 million class-action lawsuit with Sunbeam shareholders in 2002. In a civil settlement with the SEC that same year, and without admitting or denying the allegations, Dunlap agreed to a civil penalty of $500,000 and was prevented from ever again acting as an officer or director of a public company (LR 17710, 2002).

Dunlap and his wife Judy are reportedly living in Ocala, Florida, with a summer home in Wisconsin. In July 2005, the Dunlaps made a $5 million donation to fund the Albert J. and Judith A. Dunlap Children's Hospital at Munroe Regional Medical Center in Ocala ("Munroe Foundation Receives Largest Single Gift" 2005).

≈ **Russell Kersh,** Sunbeam's former chief financial officer, agreed to a civil penalty of $200,000 without admitting or denying the allegations. He was barred from ever again acting as an officer or director of a public company (LR 17710).

≈ **Morgan Stanley** was found liable for fraud by a jury in May 2005. Before the case was tried, U.S. District Judge Elizabeth Maass ruled that "Morgan

---

[6] The "Are They Living Happily Ever After?" sections in this book present selected information about certain people or companies and are not meant to be definitive or exhaustive lists.

Stanley helped Sunbeam ... to defraud investors." The investment firm was ordered to pay a total of over $1.4 billion in "compensatory and punitive damages" in respect of the sale of Ron Perelman's Coleman company to Sunbeam in 1998. Perelman had "accepted 14.1 million shares of Sunbeam stock in the buyout." Perelman lost close to $1 billion when Sunbeam collapsed.

Morgan Stanley has appealed the verdict, claiming that it too was "a victim of the Sunbeam fraud" ("Morgan Stanley ..." 2005).

≈ **Sunbeam** emerged from bankruptcy in 2002 as American Household, Inc. which was then acquired by Jarden Corporation in January 2005 ("Jarden ..." 2005).

References

AAER 1393. *U.S. Securities and Exchange Commission* Accounting and Auditing Enforcement Release. May 15, 2001.
www.sec.gov/litigation/admin/33-7976.

AAER 1394. *U.S. Securities and Exchange Commission* Accounting and Auditing Enforcement Release. May 15, 2001.
www.sec.gov/litigation/admin/33-7977.

Byrne, John A. 2003. *Chainsaw: The Notorious Career of Al Dunlap in the Era of Profit-at-Any-Price.* New York: HarperBusiness.

Byron, Christopher. 2004. *Testosterone Inc. Tales of CEOs Gone Wild.* New Jersey: Wiley.

Canedy, Dana. 1998a. "A Warning by Sunbeam Stuns Wall St." *New York Times*, March 18. Available online via ProQuest database.

_____. 1998b. "A Big Sales Gain for Sunbeam Proves Costly to Investors," *New York Times*, May 7, D1. Available online via ProQuest database.

_____. 1998c. "Amid Big Losses, Sunbeam Plans to Cut 6,400 Jobs and 8 Plants," *New York Times*, May 12, D2. Available online via ProQuest database.

Cullinan, Charles P., and Gail B. Wright. 2003. *Cases from the SEC Files: Topics in Auditing.* New Jersey: Pearson Education.

Dunlap, Albert J., with Bob Andelman. 1997. *Mean Business: How I Save Bad Companies and Make Good Companies Great.* New York: Fireside.

Frank, Robert, and Joann S. Lublin. 1996. "Dunlap's Ax Falls—6,000 Times—At Sunbeam," *Wall Street Journal,* November 13. Available online via ProQuest database.

"Jardin Complete Acquisition of American Household, Inc." News Release, January 24, 2005. www.jarden.com

Jenkins, Carri P. 1997. "Downsizing or Dumbsizing?" *BYU Magazine Online.* Brigham Young University, Spring.
www.magazine.byu.edu/article.tpl?num=26-Spr97.

Laing, Jonathon. 1997. "High Noon at Sunbeam," *Barron's*, June 16. Available online via ProQuest database.

_____. 1998a. "Into the Maw," *Barron's*, March 9. Available online via ProQuest database.

_____. 1998b. "Dangerous Games," *Barron's*, June 8. Available online via ProQuest database.

LR 17001. *U.S. Securities and Exchange Commission* Litigation Release. May 15, 2001. www.sec.gov/litigation/litrealeases/lr17001.

LR 17710. *U.S. Securities and Exchange Commission* Litigation Release. September 4, 2002. www.sec.gov/litigation/litrealeases/lr17710.

Lublin, Joann S., and Oscar Suris. 1997. "'Chainsaw Al' Now Aspires to be 'Al the Builder,'" *Wall Street Journal*, April 9. Available online via ProQuest database.

"Morgan Stanley Told to Pay $850 Million," *MSNBC.com*, May 18, 2005. www.msnbc.com.

"Munroe Foundation Receives Largest Single Gift: Al and Judy Dunlap Give $5 Million to Munroe Pediatrics," *Munroe Foundation: Munroe Regional Medical Center.* July 26, 2005. www.munroefoundation.com/dunlap.htm.

Scherer, Ron. 1996. "Towns Dread Job Cuts But Investors Applaud the Role of 'Chainsaw,'" *Christian Science Monitor*, November 8.

Schifrin, Matthew. 1998. "The Unkindest Cut," *Forbes*, May 4. Available online via ProQuest database.

SOX Report: *SEC Report Pursuant to Section 704 of the Sarbanes-Oxley Act of 2002.* www.sec.gov/news/studies/sox704report.pdf.

"Sunbeam's Cloudy Outlook: Chairman Al Warns on Profits," *New York Post*, March 20, 1998.

Williams, Pamela. 2001. "Al Dunlap's Disgrace," *Australian Financial Review*, July 21. www.newsstore.fairfax.com.au.

CHAPTER 3

HOCUS POCUS

This chapter presents the creative company chronicles of:
- **Sensormatic**
- **Xerox**
- **CUC/Cendant**
- **Insignia**

Overview

In a speech given several years ago, past SEC chairman Arthur Levitt (1998) spoke about the numerous companies that "operate in the gray area between legitimacy and outright fraud." He observed: "Integrity may be losing out to illusion." In order to achieve these illusory earnings and fabricated balance sheets, many companies resort to what Levitt described as "hocus pocus."

This chapter presents a brief overview of, at worst, some of the lesser known, intentional revenue-recognition accounting frauds and, at best, misguided attempts to "improve" a company's financial statements with "aggressive" accounting. In all cases, however, the main objective was either to boost the appearance of corporate profits or to enhance the seeming strength of the balance sheets, and in most cases, company personnel achieved this using their own versions of hocus pocus.

Why are so many company executives prepared to resort to such desperate measures to misrepresent or falsify accounting records? Some of the reasons are quite obvious: better balance sheets or greater earnings mean more investors, increased stock prices, more valuable stock options, bigger bonuses, improved financing terms, and so on. Essentially, all these reasons boil down to one basic and obvious motivating force: greed. However, there are other reasons that are not quite so apparent. As with Enron and WorldCom, many of the companies discussed in this chapter were managed predominately by men who at times seemed charismatic and plausible, men with strong personalities and even stronger egos. Some were desperate to avoid the embarrassment of failure at any cost. Others started to believe in their own mythology, and in the power of their own artifice. These were people who really bought the notion that they could live in their own fantastic world of fairy tales.

SENSORMATIC: MADNESS AT MIDNIGHT

Sensormatic is presented mainly as an example of Improper Timing of Revenue Recognition via holding books open after the close of a reporting period.

Introduction

Sensormatic Electronics Corporation was a publicly traded Delaware company with its head office located in Boca Raton, Florida. The company is still in existence but is no longer a public company. Sensormatic manufactures electronic security systems, and is probably best known for its anti-shoplifting security devices. It was known on Wall Street for meeting its budgeted figures for revenues and earnings. Moreover, these estimates were quite aggressive. For example, Sensormatic budgeted for revenue growth of over 20 percent per year over the period of 1988 to 1995. The company began facing enormous difficulty in meeting these phenomenal growth projections from at least the first quarter of its 1994 fiscal year. Surprisingly, despite this difficulty, Sensormatic's quarterly financial reports continued to meet analysts' earnings forecasts almost to the cent. Sensormatic's management was fully committed to meeting these forecasts, and apparently became quite creative in this regard.

In its proceedings against Sensormatic, the SEC examined the roles of a number of former senior executives of the company, including Ronald Assaf (former CEO), Michael Pardue (former COO and CFO), and Lawrence Simmons (former vice president of finance).

Sensormatic stock was used to finance acquisitions, and the stock price was sensitive to the company's revenue growth and to analysts' revenue and earnings estimates. Therefore, senior management was highly motivated in communicating positive information on Sensormatic's financial position and prospects to stock analysts, and management was aware of Sensormatic's high price-to-earnings ratio as well as the effect that faltering growth would have on the stock price. Senior executives became too eager in their quest to deliver earnings and revenue figures that met analysts' high growth expectations in every single quarter. Sales were seasonally lower in the third quarter of each year, and this quarter generally provided the biggest challenge. By the 1994 fiscal year, all quarters received significant assistance via nifty accounting that recognized the next quarter's sales a little early.

An Overview of Sensormatic's Fictitious Financial Reporting Schemes

The SEC found that Sensormatic misstated its quarterly revenue and earnings from at least the first quarter of fiscal year 1994 until the third quarter of fiscal year 1995.[1] Further, they claimed that Sensormatic's senior management, including Pardue and Simmons, were "aware of the methods used to effectuate the scheme, [and] also condoned and directed them. Others at various levels and in various departments also participated in these practices" (AAER 1017, 1998).

According to the SEC, memoranda were prepared close to the end of each quarter specifying sales goals that needed to be met before the close of the quarter, in order to comply with the aggressive sales budgets that had been published and distributed to senior management and to the various departments. When it became clear that the company could not reach the budget targets, "Sensormatic engaged in a variety of improper revenue recognition practices . . . that were not in conformity with Generally Accepted Accounting Principles ('GAAP') . . ." (AAER 1017, 1998).

Scheme #1: Holding Books Open after the Close of a Reporting Period

The SOX Report, which examined all the SEC Enforcement Actions for July 31, 1997, through July 30, 2002, found twenty-five enforcement actions in this period "involving the failure of issuers to close their books properly at the close of a reporting period" (8). Simply put, this fraud enables a company to report the next quarter's sales in the current period by simply holding the current period's books open for a few extra days after the close of a reporting period, for the recording of additional sales. This strategy was one of a "variety of improper revenue recognition practices" that Sensormatic allegedly used. The Commission contended that Sensormatic devised a

---

[1] Sensormatic consented to the issuance of the order without admitting or denying the findings contained in the order. As set out in AAER 1017, March 25, 1998.

complicated and expensive procedure whereby the computer records of goods or equipment shipped were actually backdated:

> Shortly before midnight on the last day of the quarter, the computer system that recorded and dated shipments was 'brought down' so that the computer clock date would reflect the last day of the prior quarter. The computer system then falsely recorded shipments as having occurred on the last day of the prior quarter. (AAER 1017, 1998)

Scheme #2: False Recognition of Early Shipments

The next improper revenue recognition practice Sensormatic used to meet its quarterly sales budgets was the ploy of shipping goods that customers had ordered for the next period to Sensormatic's own warehouses at the end of the current period. Then, in the financial records, the company would recognize this revenue *at the time of* the shipment to its own warehouse. This scheme was so elaborate that the company needed to create a set of what were known as "off-books" records in order to keep track of the prematurely shipped goods, to ensure that they were later shipped from the warehouses to the customers at the appropriate time, as originally requested by the customer. Sometimes the goods remained in the warehouses for several months before they were actually shipped to the customers.

Scheme #3: Slow-Shipping Requests

Another tactic Sensormatic allegedly used to accelerate its revenue recognition was what is called "slow shipping." When a customer had ordered items for the next quarter, Sensormatic sometimes shipped the goods early in order to record the sale in the current quarter. However, according to the SEC, to avoid having the goods arrive at the customer before the requested date, Sensormatic would instruct the carrier to delay the delivery for anything from a few days to a few weeks. Using this "slow shipping" strategy, the company could record a few extra days' sales in a particular quarter.

Scheme #4: Recognizing "FOB Destination" Sales at the Time of Shipment

When a sales order stipulates "FOB Destination," GAAP stipulates that the sale can only be recognized when the goods reach the destination, at which time ownership of the goods passes to the customer. However, the SEC alleged that, in the last week of some quarters, Sensormatic recognized some of its "FOB Destination" sales at the time of shipping, instead of the time the goods reached their destination. This was yet another of the "variety of improper revenue recognition practices" that the Commission alleged was used by Sensormatic in its attempt to meet analysts' quarterly revenue and earnings expectations.

The following table summarizes Sensormatic's misstatements over a two-year period:

Table 3.1 Summary of Sensormatic's Quarterly Misstatements[2]
1994—1995

	Amount of Improperly Recognized Revenue	Net Income As Reported By Sensormatic	Over/[Under] Statement Of Net Income	%Over/[Under] Statement Of Net Income
1994 Q1	$8.5 M*	$14.8 M	[$0.8 M]	[5.3%]
1994 Q2	$4.6 M	$18.8 M	[$1.9 M]	[9.1%]
1994 Q3	$15.8 M	$16.4 M	$3.6 M	28.1%
1994 Q4	$15.5 M	$22.0 M	[$0.9 M]	[3.8%]
1995 Q1	$12.8 M	$20.1 M	[$0.5 M]	[2.2%]
1995 Q2	$13.8 M	$25.3 M	$0.3 M	1.2%
1995 Q3	$30.2 M	$24.1 M	$6.7 M	38.3%
1995 Q4	$29.3 M	$18–$21 M**	$5.2 M	40.5%

*M = Millions
**Sensormatic's reported estimate in press release.

Scheme #5: Misleading the Auditors

The SEC also stated that Sensormatic carefully concealed its deceptive practices. Not only was the computer clock stopped to backdate sales after the end of a period, but documents were also provided indicating that shipments to the company's own warehouses were sales to customers. According to the Commission, Sensormatic directed that certain bills of lading be

---

[2] From AAER 1017, 1998.

withheld from the auditors because they would have indicated that the revenue was recognized prematurely. Through a concerted and deliberate effort to conceal information from the auditors, company executives "caused accounting records to be falsified, made false statements to the independent auditors, and intentionally circumvented the company's internal accounting controls" (AAER 1020, 1998). The SEC findings also alleged that during the 1994 audit, an employee was instructed to withhold documents from the auditors that would have "disclosed the improper recognition of revenue on out-of-period shipments." Furthermore, the employee was apparently told to "follow orders or quit" (AAER 1027, 1998).

Signals of Sensormatic's Fictitious Reporting Schemes #1–#4:

- Holding Books Open after the Close of a Reporting Period
- False Recognition of Early Shipments
- "Slow Shipping" Requests
- Recognizing "FOB Destination" Sales at the Time of Shipment

Essentially, all of Sensormatic's reporting frauds accelerated and overstated sales, which is ultimately the same effect that Sunbeam's accelerated sales achieved. Hence, the signals of the frauds are the same as the signals listed for Scheme #1 in the Sunbeam case in Chapter 2.

Are They Living Happily Ever After?

≈ **Assaf, Pardue, and Simmons** consented to the SEC's final judgment "without admitting or denying the allegations." Assaf, Pardue, and Simmons were ordered to pay "civil money penalties of $50,000, $40,000 and $50,000 respectively" (AAER 1020, 1998).

≈ **Sensormatic** was acquired by Tyco Inc. in November, 2001, and was removed from the New York Stock Exchange because "fewer than 600,000 shares remain[ed] publicly held" (NYSE 2001).

≈ **Ronald Assaf** resigned after Sensormatic was acquired by Tyco. Mr. and Mrs. Assaf are reportedly living in Boca Raton, Florida where they are very active in the community. In January 2003, they were honored for their philanthropy by the Community Foundation for Palm Beach and Martin Counties ("Community Foundation Honors . . ." 2003). In February 2005 they were "Honorary Chairmen" of an American Red Cross fundraiser ("Together We Prepare" 2005).

XEROX: NOT TO BE COPIED

> Xerox is presented mainly as an example of Improper Timing of Revenue Recognition via the misuse of multiple element contracts or bundled contracts.

Introduction

The Xerox Corporation is a multibillion dollar, Connecticut-based company that specializes in the production, selling, and leasing of duplicating machines and services. The company is known worldwide, and its name has become synonymous with "photocopying." In the period from 1997 to 2000, Xerox paid its auditors (KPMG) the sum of "$55.8 million for non-audit services." During the same period, Xerox paid KPMG "$26 million for auditing [its] financial statements." (Quotes from AAER 2234, 2005)

The SEC found that Xerox accelerated recognition of its equipment revenue by more than $3 billion, over the period 1997 through 2000, and "increased pre-tax earnings by $1.5 billion."[3] The SEC findings also alleged: "KPMG's failure to comply with generally accepted auditing standards ('GAAS') caused and willfully aided and abetted Xerox's violations."[4] (Quotes from AAER 2234, 2005)

Xerox provides a spectacular illustration of fictitious reporting by improper timing of revenue recognition through the misuse of multiple-element contracts or bundled contracts.

Xerox's Fictitious Financial Reporting Schemes

Scheme #1: Improper Use of Multiple-Element Contracts or Bundled Contracts

The major offending accounting actions in the SEC complaint were concerned with Xerox's treatment of its lease contracts. Typically, Xerox customer leases generate revenue from three streams:

1. The equipment revenue known at Xerox as the "box" revenue. This revenue is earned for making the physical asset (i.e. the copy

---

[3] "Pursuant to a consent to settlement by Xerox, the company also was assessed a civil penalty of $10 million. In consenting to settlement, Xerox neither admitted nor denied the allegations of the Commission's Complaint." As set out in AAER 2234, April 19, 2005.

[4] KPMG consented to the entry of this order without admitting or denying the finding therein, except as to the Commission's jurisdiction over it and the subject matter of these proceedings. As set out in AAER 2234, April 19, 2005.

machine itself) available to the customer, and it is legitimately recognized at the beginning of the lease in sales-type leases.

2. Revenue for servicing the equipment. GAAP requires this revenue to be recognized over the life of the lease.

3. Financing revenue on the effective loans to the lessees. GAAP also requires this revenue to be recognized over the life of the lease.

The SEC found that Xerox shifted revenue from the servicing revenue stream to the "box" revenue stream (i.e., to revenue received for physically transferring the equipment to the customer). This was done in order to recognize all the service revenue at the beginning of the lease. Xerox's internal name for the accounting method whereby it shifted this revenue was its "return on equity" method. The SEC found that Xerox also shifted certain portions of its financing revenue to the "box" or equipment revenue stream so as to recognize that revenue at the beginning of the lease. Xerox's name for the accounting method under which it made this shift was its "margin normalization" system. According to the SEC: "These two methodologies, which did not comply with GAAP, increased Xerox's equipment revenues by $2.8 billion and its pre-tax earnings by $660 million from 1997 to 2000." The SEC complaint alleged that Xerox failed to disclose its use of these methods "which were changes in accounting methods and changes in accounting estimates." (Quotes from AAER 1542, 2002)

Scheme #2: Estimates of Discount Rates and Residual Values

Further, an article in *The Accountant* described an SEC complaint against the Xerox auditors, KPMG, as follows: "Between 1995 and 2000, Xerox always assumed a 15 percent return...despite significant volatility in the returns actually earned by leasing companies" ("SEC Complaint" 2003). Leasing companies discount future cash flows when recognizing the amounts in current income. By choosing a particular discount rate, a leasing company can manipulate its reported income. The SEC also alleged that Xerox increased its reported earnings by changing estimates of the residual values of its leased assets. (Note, however, that KPMG strongly defended its audit work at Xerox.)

Scheme #3: Improper Disclosure of Sales of Leases

Xerox also sold approximately $400 million of its existing leases. This occurred after Xerox Brazil changed its emphasis from sales-type leases to operating leases. This revenue from the operating leases would have been received over a number of years, over the durations of the leases. However, the sale of the receivables to a lender caused the revenue to be recognized immediately and for the cash to be received immediately. The nondisclosure of these sales had the dual effects of making the operating income in the period of the sale look better than it was, as well as making the cash-flow situation look stronger: "This added $182 million in pre-tax profits to Xerox's 1999 results" (AAER 1542, 2002).

Other Misstatements

The SEC also alleged that Xerox boosted its earnings via creating cookie-jar reserves and then reversing those unneeded reserves back into profits in later periods. Additionally, the company improperly disclosed the gain on a one-time event with the result of boosting the appearance of extra profits from ordinary, recurring operations.

Signals of Xerox's Fictitious Reporting Schemes #1–#3:

- Improper Use of Multiple-Element Contracts or Bundled Contracts
- Estimates of Discount Rates and Residual Values
- Improper Disclosure of Sales of Leases

Signal #1: Examine the accounts receivable-to-sales ratio as measured, for example, by days' sales outstanding (DSO), or by days' revenues outstanding (DRO). When a company shifts revenue from a stream that should be recognized in a later period in order to have it recognized in a current period, its revenues, operating income, and net income increase, but its cash received does not increase. Instead, the company's accounts receivable will increase.

Signal #2: If the revenue streams are reported separately, and the stream in which revenue is immediately recognized increases in proportion to the stream/s where revenue recognition is delayed (over the life of the contract), it is a signal that the company could be shifting revenue to accelerate its recognition. If this is accompanied by Signal #1 (an increase in the accounts receivable-to-sales ratio), the alert becomes stronger.

Signal #3: Any disclosure in the financial statements, or in the press, that a company has "factored" or sold its accounts receivable—or any future revenue stream—should alert the reader to test for all signals of accelerating revenue recognition. Xerox sold accounts receivable without disclosing it immediately. In such a case, as soon as information is released that a company has factored its accounts receivable, realize that this in itself could be a signal that the company has accelerated its sales. In addition, be aware that this factoring of accounts receivable would have concealed Signal #1 above, because the factoring would have reduced the build up in accounts receivable.

Signal #4: When notes to the financial statements indicate a change in the method used to recognize revenue regarding either of the following, it should be seen as an alert, especially if other companies in the same industry do not make these changes:

1. Reclassification of a revenue stream in contract revenue
2. Change in estimates of

   • discount rates
   • residual values

Signal #5: When cash flow from operations (CFFO) decreases relative to operating income and net income, this is always the prime signal of a company recognizing any form of profit ahead of time. At Xerox, CFFO went from being 25 percent of operating income for 1995 to 18 percent for 1997. Then, for 1998, the company actually generated a negative CFFO of $1,165,000, compared to positive operating income of $1,333,000. This dramatic lagging of CFFO behind operating income should have been a major red flag, signaling that there was something seriously amiss regarding Xerox's reported profit. Suddenly, in 1999, CFFO suspiciously turned around dramatically—too dramatically—to positive $1,224,000, compared to operating income of $2,583,000—a ratio of 47 percent. Remember the old adage: Whenever something is too good to be true, it's usually not true. It was later revealed that Xerox had sold $1,495,000 of its receivables in 1999. It had also received pretax restructuring cash payments of $437,000. When the company's 1999 reported CFFO of positive $1,224,000 is adjusted for these non-recurring items, the CFFO for that year is actually negative, while the reported operating income in the income statement was a purportedly healthy $2,583,000. After making these adjustments, anyone looking at the signal of CFFO lagging reported operating income should have had no doubt that Xerox was dramatically accelerating its reported earnings. (For this signal and Signal #1, securitized amounts should be added back to accounts receivable and deducted from CFFO.)

Are They Living Happily Ever After?

≈ **Six former Xerox company officials** agreed to pay over $22 million in penalties, without admitting or denying the SEC's allegations (SEC Press Release 2003).

≈ A criminal investigation into Xerox's accounting practices was concluded in October 2004, and U.S. prosecutors did not file charges ("Xerox Cleared ... " 2004).

≈ **KPMG** "agreed to settle the SEC's charges against it in connection with the audits of Xerox Corp. from 1997 through 2000" (LR 19191, 2005). As a result of this civil litigation, KPMG agreed to pay a total of $22.475 million in penalties. KPMG was also ordered to develop reform plans to ensure that SEC violations do not recur (LR 19191, 2005).

CUC/CENDANT: PHONY FUNDS[5]

CUC/Cendant is presented mainly as an example of Improper Revenue Recognition via reporting fictitious revenue.

Introduction

CUC International, Inc., was a Delaware company that sold club memberships to its customers for automobile, dining, shopping, and travel services. Another Delaware company, HFS Incorporated, controlled franchise brand names in the hotel, real-estate brokerage, and car-rental industries. These two companies merged in December 1997, taking the name of Cendant Corporation, which carried on the combined activities of the two formerly separate companies.

The SEC maintained that the fraud began with the original CUC as far back as 1985, and was allegedly directed by CUC's chairman and CEO, Walter Forbes, from the very beginning. The SEC's complaint also alleged that CUC's president and COO, E. Kirk Shelton, joined Forbes in directing the scheme from at least 1991 onwards (LR 16919, 2001; AAER, 1372, 2001). The Commission also contended that Cosmo Corigliano, who served as controller of CUC from 1983 to 1995 and as CFO from 1995 to 1997, "assisted senior CUC officers who initiated the long-running financial

---

[5] The fraud occurred at CUC before the company merged with Cendant.

reporting fraud and later, as CUC's Chief Financial Officer, proceeded to orchestrate and refine the fraud" (LR 18711, 2004; AAER 2014, 2004).[6] Referring to the CUC case, Richard Walker, SEC director of enforcement, noted that "large, complex, and long-running financial frauds often originate at the highest levels of a company" (LR 16919, 2001; AAER 1372, 2001).

According to the SEC records, another pivotal individual involved in the execution of the schemes was Mary Sattler Polverari, a CPA who was hired by CUC in December 1995 and became manager of financial reporting in 1997. The SEC maintained Polverari carried out instructions that "included adjustments increasing revenue . . . and decreasing particular expense line items" (AAER 1275, 2000).[7]

An Overview of CUC's Fictitious Financial Reporting Schemes

According to the Commission, beginning in at least 1985, "certain members of CUC's senior management implemented a scheme designed to ensure that CUC always met the financial results anticipated by Wall Street analysts. The CUC managers utilized a variety of means to achieve their goals" (AAER 1275, 2000).

The SOX Report found eighty enforcement matters in which companies reported fictitious revenue, and the report described several ways in which improper revenue recognition involving fictitious revenue occurred: "The manipulation of revenue was accomplished through, among other means, the falsification of sales documents, side agreements with customers that were not recorded, and top-side adjustments by senior management (11)."

One of CUC's primary methods of fictitious revenue reporting was through the use of top-side adjustments. In addition to the top-side entries, CUC also transferred some amounts for deferred club membership revenues to current periods' revenues. Further, the company created huge, overstated merger reserves, which it used as "cookie jar" reserves to release into profits in later periods. After the merger of CUC with HFS, Inc., the newly established Cendant discovered the CUC fraud and, in 1998, this represented the biggest accounting fraud revealed in the United States. However, Enron and then WorldCom subsequently dwarfed this fraud, and now WorldCom holds the notorious record once held by CUC. (Note that in the WorldCom chapter of this text, WorldCom is analyzed as an illustration of the fraudulent

---

[6] Cosmo Corigliano and others "consented to the entry of the Final Judgment without admitting or denying the allegations of the complaint." (As set out in LR 18711, 2004)

[7] Mary Sattler Polverari consented to the entry of the order without admitting or denying the findings. As set out in AAER 1275, 2000.

use of merger acquisition reserves.) CUC is presented here as an example of overstating revenue by the use of *fictitious revenue*.

The CUC Scheme of Reporting Fictitious Revenue via Top-Side Adjustments

For the hands-on part of the scheme that required actually making the top-side adjustment, the alleged role of Mary Sattler Polverari was important. She received the financial reports from all the business units and compiled a monthly report showing the results of each unit. Each quarter she submitted the quarterly consolidating report to her supervisors. This was when the sorcery started. Polverari's supervisors would devise instructions of adjustments for her to make: "Typically the instructions included adjustments increasing revenue by a certain amount and decreasing particular expense line items by certain amounts" (AAER 1275, 2000). Most of the alterations were concentrated on the Comp-U-Card division. The adjustments always increased earnings, and they never had supporting documentation. Particularly illustrative of overstating revenue via reporting *fictitious revenue* by means of top-side entries was the following finding of the SEC:

> The adjustments were entirely top-side adjustments. That is, the adjustments were simply entered into Polverari's spreadsheet at Stamford—no journal entries were created, no entries were made to CUC's general ledger, and the adjustments were not carried down to the books and records of Comp-U-Card or any or the company's other divisions. (AAER 1275, 2000)

Clearly, the revenue recognized in this manner was entirely fictitious, with no accounting explanation provided for the entries. However, the explanation given to Polverari for the entries was amazingly frank—brutally frank, in fact. She was apparently informed that "CUC's chief financial officer had generated the adjustments to inflate CUC's quarterly results so that the results would meet earnings expectations of Wall Street analysts." Polverari was even told that some of the adjustments were made to achieve percentage targets for some expenses and that some of the adjustments were "to ensure that items such as receivables and cash were at levels he [the CFO] thought desirable." (Quotes from AAER 1275, 2000)

The Commission found that for the fiscal years ended 31 January 1996, 31 January 1997, and 31 December 1997, the top-side alterations aggregated $31 million, $87 million, and $176 million respectively. Since the top-side entries were not entered in the company's general ledger, something had to be done to align retained earnings with the annual financial statements. The

SEC maintained that, in April 1998, after the filing of Cendant's annual financial statements: "Polverari directed the subsidiaries to give the entries March 1998 effective dates and stated that the entries that 'would normally be charged to the P&L can be charged directly to Retained Earnings to avoid opening last year's books'" (AAER 1275, 2000). The Commission also found that in January 1998, managers directed approximately $115 million in unsupported post-closing journal entries reversing the company's merger reserves. (Refer to the WorldCom chapter of this text, Chapter 4, for a detailed analysis of improper use of merger reserves.)

Signals of CUC's Fictitious Reporting Scheme of:

• Reporting Fictitious Revenue

The major signals are the same as for other overstatements of revenues as discussed in the analysis of Sunbeam's accelerated revenue reporting.

Signal #1: Once again, accounts receivable as a percentage of sales as captured in such measures as days sales outstanding (DSO) is a leading signal of this fraud. (Refer to Sunbeam's signals in Chapter 2.)

Signal #2: Also, CFFO lagging reported operating income is a strong signal of a possible overstatement of revenue in the income statement. (Refer to Sunbeam's signals in Chapter 2.)

Signal #3: In a company that sells membership subscriptions, deferred revenue decreasing as a percentage of total revenue is an indication that the company may be aggressively recognizing subscription revenues that will really only be earned in future periods.

Signal #4: Yet again, when a company precisely meets analysts' earnings and revenue expectations quarter after quarter, it is often an alert that things may be too good to be true.

Signal #5: When major expense items remain identical quarter after quarter as a percentage of revenues, it is frequently a signal that the reported expenses and revenues are being manipulated. This is an especially strong alert when an expense contains a significant fixed-cost element. One would expect a fixed-expense component to increase as a percentage of revenues when revenues decrease. Likewise, it would be expected that the fixed-cost component of an expense would decrease as a percentage of revenues when revenues increase.

Are They Living Happily Ever After?

≈ **E. Kirk Shelton,** former CUC/Cendant president and CEO was convicted, in January 2005, by a federal jury "of all 12 counts of an indictment: including conspiring to fraudulently inflate reported earnings at Cendant and at a predecessor company, CUC International" ("E. Kirk Shelton is Guilty" 2005). On August 3, 2005, he was sentenced to ten years in prison and ordered to pay $3.27 billion to Cendant (Haigh 2005). He is appealing the sentence. As of January 2006, he was still out on bail (Burns 2006).

≈ **Cosmo Corigliano, Anne Pember, and Casper Sabatino,** three of Shelton's co-conspirators, each pleaded guilty in federal courts under plea agreements in which "the three defendants admitted participating in the conspiracy and acting under the instruction of their superiors" ("E. Kirk Shelton is Guilty" 2005). They could each be sentenced to up to five years in prison and fined.

≈ **Walter Forbes,** former Cendant chairman, stood trial with Shelton. Forbes's case ended in a mistrial. A retrial began in October 2005, in Hartford, Connecticut (Mills and Voreacos 2005). The retrial ended in February 2006, with the jury unable to reach a verdict and the judge declaring another mistrial. In 1998, when Forbes left Cendant, he received $47.5 million ("Another Cendant Hung Jury" 2006).

INSIGNIA: RETURN TO SENDER

Insignia is presented here mainly as an example of Improper Valuation of Revenue.

Introduction

Insignia Solutions is a British publicly traded company that does business in the United States through its subsidiary company, Insignia Solutions, Inc. It trades on the NASDAQ and develops and supports cross-platform compatibility software. Insignia generally sells its software to resellers, to whom it grants certain rights of return.

The Insignia Scheme of Failing to Value Revenue Correctly

The SOX Report listed Insignia Solutions PLC as an example of the failure to value revenue properly via *providing inadequate allowances for returns.*

The SEC found that Insignia Solutions allegedly "overstated its Revenue and Net Income . . . [and] . . . understated its allowance for returns" for the first and second quarters of 1996.[8] Insignia had a standard practice of recording an allowance for returns—in respect of inventory at resellers—that exceeded an estimated forty-five days of sales: "In effect, Insignia subtracted this allowance from its gross revenue to arrive at revenue." Therefore, if Insignia understated the amount of inventory held by its resellers, this would lead to it understating its allowance for returns and overstating its revenue. This was the method the company used for the improper valuation of its revenue. The Commission's findings quoted Insignia's own revenue recognition policy as stating that revenue is "recognized upon shipment if no significant vendor obligations remain and if collection of the resulting receivables is deemed probable." (Quotes from AAER 1133, 1999)

In December 1995, the sales manager effected a shipment of $1.2 million to a reseller. A side letter was signed, giving the reseller generous rights of return. According to the SEC release of May 1999: "After the shipment, the supervisors instructed a subordinate to 'drop the zero' or report only 10% of the inventory held by the reseller. . . . This had the effect of decreasing Insignia's allowance for product returns, thereby increasing reported revenue" (AAER 1133, 1999).

No restatement was needed for this in 1995 because there was a large enough allowance for returns at that point. However, at the end of the first quarter of 1996, when most of the goods were still unsold, the Commission found this resulted in the revenue being overstated by $1.1 million. Also, because the later return of the goods due to obsolescence was concealed from the finance department, a replacement order was recorded as a new sale. Further, in June 1996, a sale of $750,000 with a sixty-day right of return was recognized without an allowance for returns.

Insignia restated its financial statements for the first and second quarters of 1996. It reported restated revenue of $13.1 million in the first quarter, compared to $14.7 million previously reported. For the second quarter, the company reported restated revenue of $14.9 million, compared to $15.7 million previously reported.

On February 27, 1997, Insignia announced that it was restating its financial statements for the first two quarters of 1996. Following this announcement, the company's shares fell 35 percent, from $3.88 to $2.53 in one day.

---

[8] Insignia consented to the order without admitting or denying the findings. As set out in AAER 1133, 1999.

Signals of Insignia's Fictitious Reporting Scheme of:

- Failing to Value Revenue Properly via providing inadequate allowances for returns

Since overstatement of revenue in this manner leads to accounts receivable that do not get realized in the form of cash, the signals of the misstatements in the financial reports are the same as the signals for the overstatements of revenue discussed in the Sunbeam case in Chapter 2.

Signal #1: In addition, if the company separately reports the amount of its allowance for returns, a significant decrease in allowances for returns as a percentage of sales is a signal that the allowance for returns may be understated.

Signal #2: Also, any reference in the financial statements' notes to a change in policy regarding the method of recognizing the allowance for returns, or any changes in estimates for returns that lead to decreasing the allowance, should be taken as signals that the company may be understating its returns.

(Note that while Sunbeam is the leading case of improperly timed revenue, it also represents an example of overstating revenue by improper valuation of revenue. It overvalued revenue via its failure to fully recognize an allowance for the right of return of inventory. The Sunbeam case in Chapter 2 provides a discussion of how side agreements and special terms, given to accelerate sales, can lead to an increased likelihood of returns. However, Sunbeam also failed to set up adequate reserves for these returns.)

Are They Living Happily Ever After?

≈ **Insignia** was briefly in danger of losing its listing on the Nasdaq due to falling out of compliance with Nasdaq capitalization requirements. However, the company obtained additional funding and in January 2006 Nasdaq agreed that Insignia could "continue to be listed on the exchange" (Graebner 2006).

≈ **Insignia** now specializes in software that allows "operators of mobile devices [to] update and repair them remotely . . ." (Graebner 2006).

References

AAER 1017. *Securities and Exchange Commission* Accounting and Auditing Enforcement Release, March 25, 1998.
www.sec.gov/litigation/admin/337518.txt

AAER 1020. *Securities and Exchange Commission* Accounting and Auditing Enforcement Release, March 25, 1998.
www.sec.gov/litigation/litrealeases/lr15680.txt

AAER 1027. *Securities and Exchange Commission* Accounting and Auditing Enforcement Release, April 27, 1998.
www.sec.gov/litigation/admin/337528.txt

AAER 1542. *Securities and Exchange Commission* Accounting and Auditing Enforcement Release, April 11, 2002. www.sec.gov.

AAER 1133. *Securities and Exchange Commission* Accounting and Auditing Enforcement Release, May 17, 1999.
www.sec.gov/litigation/admin/34-41409.txt

AAER 1275. *Securities and Exchange Commission* Accounting and Auditing Enforcement Release, June 14, 2000.
www.sec.gov/litigation/admin/34-42936.htm

AAER 2234. *Securities and Exchange Commission* Accounting and Auditing Enforcement Release, April 19, 2005. www.sec.gov.

"Another Cendant Hung Jury," *The Los Angeles Times,* February 10, 2006.

Burns, Greg. 2006. "Enron Case Big Test of the "Idiot Defense": Ex-Chief Vows to Say He Was Blind to Crimes," *Chicago Tribune*, January 2. Available online via InfoTrac OneFile (Gale).

"Community Foundation Honors Two Local Residents at Annual 'Celebration of Philanthropy' Event," *Community Foundation for Palm Beach and Martin Counties.* January 24, 2003.
www.yourcommunityfoundation.org

"E. Kirk Shelton is Guilty on All Counts of Accounting Fraud," *RisMedia,* January 5, 2005. www.rismedia.com

Graebner, Lynn. 2006. "Insignia Solutions Keeps Nasdaq Listing," *San Francisco Business Times*, January 17. www.sanfrancisco.bizjournals.com

Graubert et al. vs. Insignia Solutions. 1998. Defendant's Memorandum in Support of Settlement, *United States District Court Northern District of California, San Jose Division,* April 20.
www.securities.stanford.edu/1009/INSGY97/006.html

Haigh, Susan. 2005. "Cendant Official Must Pay Back $3.27 Billion," *Washingtonpost.com,* August 4. www.washington.post.com

Levitt, Arthur. 1998. "The Numbers Game: Remarks at NYU Center for Law and Business," September 28.
www.sec.gov/news/speech/speecharchive/1998

LR 16919; AAER 1372. *Securities and Exchange Commission* Litigation Release, February 28, 2001.
www.sec.gov/litigation/litreleases/lr16910.htm

LR 17465. *Securities and Exchange Commission v. Xerox Corporation* Litigation Release, April 11, 2002.
www.sec.gov/litigation/litreleases/lr17465.htm

LR 18711; AAER 2014. *Securities and Exchange Commission* Litigation Release, May 14, 2004.
www.sec.gov/litigation/litreleases/lr18711.htm

LR 19191. *Securities and Exchange Commission v. KPMG LLP, et al.*
   Litigation Release, April 19, 2005.
   www.sec.gov/litigation/litreleases/lr19191.htm
Mills, Jane, and David Voreacos. 2005. "Ex-Cendant Chief at Retrial Denies
   Inflating Income; Forbes Testifies Subordinates Handled Books," *The
   Record* (Bergen County, NJ), November 17. Available online via
   LexisNexis database.
NYSE. 2001. *New York Stock Exchange Press Release*, November 9.
   www.nyse.com/press
SEC Press Release. 2003. *Securities and Exchange Commission News Release.*
   "Six Former Senior Executives of Xerox Settle SEC Enforcement
   Action Charging Them With Fraud," June 5.
   www.sec.gov/news/press/2003-70.htm
"SEC Complaint Reveals What Caused it to Sue KMPG," *The Accountant*,
   February 23, 2003. Available online via *LexisNexis* database.
SOX Report. *Report Pursuant to Section 704 of the Sarbanes-Oxley Act of
   2002.* www.sec.gov/news/studies/sox704report.pdf
"Status of High-Profile Corporate Scandals," *Washingtonpost.com,*
   Associated Press, November 23, 2005. www.washington.post.com
"Together We Prepare," American Red Cross website, February 4, 2005.
   www.redcross-pbc.org
Whiteman, Lou. 2003. "No Cause for Alarm," *The Daily Deal*, July 14.
   Available online via InfoTrac OneFile (Gale).
"Xerox Cleared in Criminal Investigation," *United Press International*,
   October 20, 2004. Available online via *LexisNexis* database

CHAPTER 4

WORLDCOM WIZARDRY:
FROM WORLDCOM TO WORLD-CON[1]

> WorldCom is presented mainly as an example of:
> - Improper Accounting in Connection with Business Combinations via improper use of merger reserves and improper asset valuation.
> - Improper Capitalization of Expenses.

PART 1: THE WIZARDS OF WORLDCOM

Introduction

During a *CNBC* television interview hosted by David Faber in September 2003, Robert Hudspeth, a former WorldCom vice president, described how "there seemed to be a disconnect" between WorldCom's internal numbers and the numbers touted on Wall Street. Hudspeth added that it was hard to explain to members of his 4,000 sales force why investors were being told that WorldCom's revenue was increasing, while the sales force knew that revenue was declining. Hudspeth then commented: "All we did is submit numbers to [head office in] Clinton and the magic happened" (Faber 2003).

Faber's response to this comment struck at the heart of the matter: "The Justice Department has charged Scott Sullivan, WorldCom's former chief financial officer, with being the mastermind behind that magic." Since that television interview, several WorldCom officers have been found guilty of fraud for making that magic happen.

The Chief Wizard: Bernard Ebbers

The WorldCom fairytale started not so long ago, in a land not that far away, with a young man who wanted to be a prince, but turned into a wizard instead. At six foot four, Bernard J. Ebbers was a starter on the

---

[1] Background information in this chapter is mainly from *First Interim Report of Dick Thornburgh* (2002), Jeter (2002), Krim (2002), Malik (2003), *Second Interim Report of Dick Thornburgh* (2003), and *Third and Final Report of Dick Thornburgh* (2004).

varsity basketball team at Victoria Composite High School in downtown Edmonton, Canada. He already had the ambiguous traits of coming across either as painfully shy or as powerfully driven and charismatic. His basketball team won the city championship in his senior year; for Bernie Ebbers and Brent Foster, best friends on the team, it looked as though that championship was going to be the peak of their careers. For a few years after high school, both spun their wheels doing odd jobs, like delivering milk. Then their old high-school coach took Brent Foster with him on a trip to Seattle. While Foster waited for the coach in a bank, he picked up a brochure lying on a desk in the lobby—a seemingly trivial, distracted act that changed the course of so many lives. The brochure was, oddly, an advertisement for Mississippi College in the town of Clinton. The charming pictures of the campus and town looked enticing, and Foster decided that this was the fresh start that he needed.

The very traditional Mississippi College is the oldest Baptist college in America, and the town of Clinton is lined with tall, old oak trees, interspersed with striking magnolias. On a subsequent visit to Mississippi College, the deeply religious and conservative young Foster had a good feeling about the college and the town, with its many grand Victorian-era homes. The fact that Clinton's city hall had been the site of General Sherman's headquarters during the siege of Jackson struck a chord with the competitive young Foster, who enrolled in the school. When Foster returned home to Edmonton for the summer, it was clear to his old high-school pal, Bernard Ebbers, that Foster was back to his peak.

Bernie Ebbers knew what he had to do: he too had to go to Mississippi College with his friend. So at the end of that summer, Bernie joined Foster and his new wife on their honeymoon road trip back to Mississippi College. Even more devoutly Baptist than Foster, Ebbers liked the school and the town of Clinton immensely and really took to southern small-town life, finding the green openness a refreshing change from downtown Edmonton. Bernie joined the college basketball team and soon was awarded a basketball scholarship. Before long, he too was back to his peak and growing in confidence every day, his earlier shyness now counteracted by a kind of arrogant swagger.

Bernie's basketball scholarship, however, ended after one year, when his Achilles tendon was torn by a broken bottle during a fight with some local thugs. To get by financially, he helped coach the junior varsity team, and this led to a high-school coaching job at nearby Hazelhurst, after he graduated with a degree in physical education.

A year later, Ebbers went to work for a clothing manufacturer, where he remained for five years, before buying a cheap, run-down hotel and restaurant in Columbia, Mississippi. By this time, he was married to Linda Pigott, and they had three children, Treasure, Joy, and Faith. In 1977, he combined with a few friends and began an expansion that led to nine hotels by 1983. This was the year that a court order instigated the break up of AT&T into AT&T and seven local phone companies, so as to allow more competition in the long-distance telephone industry: "The divestiture forced AT&T to lease long-distance phone lines at deeply discounted rates to small, regional companies who could then resell the lines' data-carrying capacity, or bandwidth, to small businesses" (Jeter 2003, 17, 18). That was the impetus for WorldCom. The actual inception of WorldCom occurred when Murray Waldron, a businessman from Tennessee, decided to get into the business of reselling long-distance phone service in country towns.

Ebbers—now living in Brookhaven and running nine hotels—was introduced to this business venture by David Singleton, a friend from Ebbers's prayer group at the First Baptist Church in Brookhaven. Singleton invited Bernie to a meeting about starting a company to resell long-distance phone service. Ebbers was aware of the court-ordered breakup of AT&T and had heard of small companies that were taking advantage of the leases that AT&T was forced to option out. He was ready to listen when he got the call from Singleton.

Waldron, Singleton, Ebbers, and Waldron's friend Bill Fields met the next day in a coffee shop in Hattiesburg, Mississippi. It was September 1983. They had chosen Hattiesburg because it looked like a rural area's hub town on the map, and it didn't have a long-distance phone company. Legend has two competing stories about how the company's initial name was concocted. Either way, what both stories have in common is that the first meeting about starting a company to resell long-distance phone service was in a coffee shop in Hattiesburg and that Waldron was present. One story goes that the men at the meeting asked their coffee-shop waitress to suggest a name for their new company. On a napkin, the waitress wrote the letters "LDDC," for "Long Distance Discount Company." The men at the meeting made one small change to "Long Distance Discount Services." At this point, LDDS, the company that was destined to evolve—via over seventy acquisitions—into the infamous World-Com, was born. As the story goes, Waldron still has that napkin in his office.

Cynics of corporate folklore say that the story of the napkin and the waitress is not completely accurate, and that the meeting occurred without all four founders. However, it sounded better for company mythology if the arrogant, self-conscious, yet charismatic Bernie Ebbers and the other three founders were present at the site of this slice of Americana being lived out on a cold night in a unpretentious but warm Hattiesburg coffee shop. These men were about to embark on a wild roller-coaster ride with their new company. Almost twenty years later, on July 21, 2002, that same company would declare one of the most spectacular bankruptcies in corporate history.

WorldCom, in the end, was betrayed by virtually every single entity or division entrusted with any fiduciary duty intended to guarantee the honest reporting of its financial affairs—from the preparation of the financial reports to the gatekeeping intended to provide the checks and balances to ensure the proper accounting behind the preparation of those reports. Even the board of directors abrogated its responsibility and ignored the outrageously unfocused growth of WorldCom via more than seventy uncoordinated acquisitions of other companies. The failed checks and balances listed by Richard Thornburgh, WorldCom's Bankruptcy Examiner, in his *First Interim Report* (2002) included:

- The internal control system
- The audit committee
- The compensation and stock-option committee
- Arthur Andersen, WorldCom's external auditors
- WorldCom's internal audit department
- The board of directors
- The management
- The investment banking company of Salomon Smith Barney
- The chief investment banker and analyst, Jack Grubman
- Members of WorldCom's senior accounting staff

For many years, thousands of employees, customers, corporate investors, and private individuals were hoodwinked by accounting manipulations of massive proportions. How did WorldCom spin so out of control? Why did all the checks and balances fail? How did Arthur Andersen neglect to detect the massive and poorly hidden frauds? Why did Salomon Smith Barney's analyst recommend the deteriorating company so highly? Why did the directors allow the chaotic list of acquisitions and the colossal loans to Bernie Ebbers? How did the fairytale turn into a nightmare?

WorldCom's Early Years

After the September meeting in the Hattiesburg coffee shop, Ebbers, Singleton, Fields, and Waldron contacted friends and acquaintances. Together with an additional five investors, the nine of them incorporated LDDS with about $600,000 capital, and they divided its one thousand shares between themselves. On January 14, 1984, the first long-distance telephone call was made on LDDS's system. At this stage, LDDS basically leased bandwidth and resold it for long-distance telephone calls. The company's switching equipment, which they had purchased for $450,000, was located in their small building opposite the University of Southern Mississippi. The first customer was a realty company, Floyd Franks & Associates, which was owned by Ole Miss's former wide receiver, Floyd Franks. With a recommendation like Floyd Franks's, soon after their opening in January 1984, they had 200 customers. Still, they had capacity for many more customers and with fixed costs high, they needed to expand their customer base. Also, without a technical expert to optimize the configuration of the circuits, their line costs were very high. After the AT&T breakup, LDDS wasn't the only company to get the idea of long-distance discounting. There were a number of start-ups, most of them running at a loss just like LDDS, which was losing about $20,000 a month in 1984. By the end of that year, LDDS had gone into debt to the tune of over $1.5 million.

Ebbers took over the running of the company in 1985, and besides a ferocious focus on cutting costs, he immediately set his sights on acquiring some of the small, long-distance resellers. Between the market competition and the requirements of the Public Utility Commission, the charges to customers were pretty well set. However, the cost of bandwidth depended on the volume, as larger volume led to lower costs per minute. Ebbers decided that he had to get more customers and more bandwidth and sell the bandwidth cheaper than the other small-town competitors, and he had to do this while the big boys like MCI were focused elsewhere. Ebbers craftily decided that the best way to increase customers and bandwidth— without getting the attention of the big players—was to buy the smaller companies. His first acquisition was The Phone Company in Jackson, Tennessee, where Waldron had once worked briefly to get experience in the telephone business. After this, Ebbers and his cronies bought ReTel Communications, also in Tennessee. Next, in order to acquire a small telephone reseller in Arkansas, Bernie convinced his colleagues to do something that they would do over and over and over again, until WorldCom's final bankruptcy—they issued shares in their company (LDDS) to get the cash to pay for the acquisitions.

Many folks around Brookhaven, Mississippi, became multimillionaires from the stocks they bought in LDDS in those early years. (Around that time, LDDS's first two CPAs quit the company—ostensibly because of "personality clashes." Looking back, one has to wonder if they really were just that.) With these acquisitions, the company's sales grew and the volume of reswitching equipment grew as well. With each acquisition, the new company's revenue, assets, and profits were included with those of the original LDDS.

By now, Ebbers was a keen acquirer of companies and was growing into a fanatical one. He became convinced that it was time for LDDS to go public. He realized that if LDDS was listed on the stock exchange, it would be able to raise cash readily by issuing stock. Furthermore, instead of paying cash for additional acquisitions, LDDS could pay for new companies simply by issuing LDDS shares to the shareholders of those companies. As long as the publicly traded stock price of LDDS increased, there would be no end to the number of acquisitions it could make. As long as LDDS publicly *reported* increasing profits and increasing sales in its financial statements, it could carry on acquiring companies, and there would be no limit to the growth of its stock price. To Ebbers, there was no doubt—LDDS had to go public.

There were two ways that LDDS could become a public company. It could make a public offering, or it could acquire a publicly traded company and in the process, it would then become publicly listed and traded. It chose the latter approach, and in 1989 LDDS purchased the publicly listed Advantage Companies, Inc., of Atlanta. LDDS was now a public company.

The Assistant Wizard: Jack Grubman

Ebbers now had to interface with investors as well as public institutions, and as a result, he had his first fateful meeting with Jack Grubman, the Salomon Smith Barney stock analyst. (Ebbers and Grubman would later go on to overestimate the demand for internet traffic capacity at that time. Neither of them had much of a clue about the technicalities of either the Internet or Internet traffic or the workings of the telecom industry as a whole.) Ebbers and Grubman had an instant rapport. Both had colossal ambition-to-knowledge ratios—always a dangerous set of attributes—and both were newly rich, from working-class roots. Both understood about leaving out pertinent facts to build half-truths. Both possessed the need to impress. Grubman, for example, had lied about having "attended the Massachusetts Institute of Technology" (Jeter 2003, 62). Interestingly, both men also shared the need to be generous with money gained dubiously. Both were driven and troubled, yet charismatic. They formed a bond and some-times drank beer and shot pool together.

The Accounting Wizard: Scott Sullivan

Shortly after going public, LDDS swapped some of its new publicly traded stock for stock in Advanced Telecommunications Corp (ATC). With this transaction, Ebbers and Grubman acquired another cohort who seemed very different from them. Scott Sullivan was a brilliant, quiet, reserved, and conservative young CPA who had previously audited for one of the Big Eight audit firms, and had then moved to south Florida to become CFO of a telecommunications company. When Ebbers acquired ATC, he also got Sullivan, who became "vice president and assistant treasurer of LDDS" (Jeter 2003, 50).

Sullivan commuted from his home in Florida to a condo in Mississippi, where he seemed to be almost obsessive about his job and often worked into the early hours of the morning. He was just what Ebbers needed: a serious and seriously smart sidekick, the brains to Bernie's brawn. In spite of their differences (or perhaps because of them), Sullivan and Ebbers got along ex-tremely well, and he became "the real force" behind Bernie's deals (Malik 2003, 7).

Sullivan apparently liked the idea of acquisitions as much as Grubman and Ebbers did—but for a different reason. Sullivan understood the poten-tial of acquisitions to provide opportunities to manipulate the profits, or earnings, that a company reports in its financial statements. Of course, re-ported earnings drives share price, and a high share price can, in turn, be used to finance more acquisitions and turn the whole cycle again . . . and again, and again. Thornburgh, the WorldCom Bankruptcy Examiner would eventually explain: "WorldCom grew in large part because the value of its stock rose dramatically. Its stock was the fuel that kept WorldCom's acquisi-tion engine running at a very high speed. WorldCom needed to keep its stock price at high levels to continue its phenomenal growth" (*First Interim Report* 2002, 6).

Sullivan seemed to believe that a company didn't need actual earnings to *report* profits of a given amount. The Bankruptcy Examiner went on to observe: "WorldCom put extraordinary pressure on itself to meet the ex-pectations of securities analysts. This pressure created an environment in which reporting numbers that met these expectations, no matter how these numbers were derived, apparently became more important than accurate financial reporting" (*First Interim Report* 2002, 7).

PART 2: THE ACQUISITIONS SPREE

The three men who influenced WorldCom used the company for their own convoluted reasons. Ebbers wanted the company to grow as big as possible and as fast as possible; Grubman sought to be a leader in the telecom-analyst sector; and Sullivan worked on producing high reported earnings and high stock prices.

The acquisition of ATC in 1992 seemed like a good move. The lease cost of lines was high and with ATC Ebbers got a good bunch of his own fiber-optic lines. With these lines, LDDS could use the Internet to transmit not only data, but also voice and video.

At the end of 1994, on the quest for more acquisitions, LDDS acquired IDB Communications Inc., a global-satellite business that included IDB WorldCom—a company with a large international division. Possession of IDB WorldCom gave the company an international platform in Eastern Europe and eventually gave LDDS its new name, WorldCom.

Still high from that deal, Ebbers and Sullivan went on to acquire a company that had undergone a very interesting change to its core business. WilTel, previously Williams Oil and Gas, had experienced a severe drop in demand for its gas and had wondered what to do about the idle capacity in its gas pipelines. When the demand for fiber-optic lines grew, it figured that it could save a lot of money by simply threading fiber-optic lines through its existing but idle natural-gas pipelines. LDDS acquired WilTel in 1995 for $2.5 billion cash, getting a cable network with over 11,000 miles of fiber-optic cable. After that gratifying deal, Sullivan was promoted to CFO; the name of LDDS was formally changed to WorldCom; and the three cohorts were gearing up to rock the financial world.

By now, with all the acquisitions, there were just too many companies that had been added to the collection without being properly integrated into a synergetic whole. There was little liaison between the companies, and much of the work was duplicated. Employees had already started to cynically mock WorldCom. They ridiculed the famous Michael Jordan/WorldCom "teamwork" commercial because the various WorldCom companies actually eschewed teamwork and despised each other.

In 1996, the Telecommunications Act was passed, allowing for competition in the local telephone market. This gave WorldCom another boost, and the company grew exponentially that year.

Ebbers's ego also continued to grow. The folksy part of his personality became more pronounced; he dressed and swaggered more and more like John

Wayne. People who saw him only from afar—and he was very visible all around Mississippi—couldn't get over what a down-to-earth billionaire he was, always in blue jeans and boots. He was also a big donor to a variety of civic causes and colleges all over Mississippi. In addition, WorldCom was a godsend as an employer in the state, providing employment to so many Mississippi College graduates that the college even structured courses specifically for WorldCom's needs. While folks from a distance saw Ebbers as a hero, or a pious saint still teaching Sunday school, some of those closer up were beginning to see him get meaner as he got bigger. Although he was down-to-earth around town, with his down-home clothes and his unpretentious truck, he was always on the prowl for companies, and he was also buying up huge ranches and other properties, as well as a sixty-foot yacht that he appropriately called "ACQUASITION" [sic].

The misspelled "Acquasition" fittingly described his ego as well as his only real business strategy of collecting an increasingly out-of-focus conglomeration of companies. Bernie was a walking mass of contradictions: self-conscious, yet "in your face" and insatiably egotistical; devoutly religious and a generous donor, yet bad tempered and penny pinching. He was controlling on minute details, yet without any macro plan or focus for all the acquisitions that he was pushing through management and the board of directors at an unprecedented, frenzied pace. It was as if Bernie and WorldCom were both on the long manic swing of a bipolar cycle.

The Bankruptcy Examiner would eventually assert: "WorldCom did not achieve its growth by following a predefined strategic plan, but rather by opportunistic and rapid acquisitions of other companies. The unrelenting pace of these acquisitions caused the company to constantly redefine itself and its focus" (First Interim Report 2002, 6).

WorldCom continued to grow too fast and in too many directions. In 1996 the company set its sights on becoming a major Internet provider and turned its attention to UUNet, which was the leading Internet provider in the world at that time. UUNet had been one of the first companies to offer email and Internet access to individual users. As the company began to attract a vast amount of investment money, John Sidgemore, from General Electric, was appointed CEO. UUNet then began providing large businesses the means to transmit data via the Internet. Next, they provided hardware for Microsoft's online service, MSN. UUNet had gone public in 1995 and its stock price had soared until competition from AT&T and MCI began to knock the price down in 1996. As a result, Sidgemore led UUNet to accept a buyout offer from MFS Communications on August 12, 1996. About two weeks later, on August 26, 1996, WorldCom acquired MFS Communications, swapping WorldCom stock for MFS stock. This was a $12 billion deal whereby WorldCom acquired UUNet at the same time. By this time, UUNet had over four million dial-up ports for users to log onto the Internet.

With this acquisition, WorldCom had broadband and networks all over the world and had become a major provider of Internet access and data transmission. WorldCom's stock price soared on the grounds of its reported profits combined with its vast Internet capacity and the world's belief in the projected astronomical growth in Internet traffic.

The Myth of Internet Growth

Everyone accepted the enthusiastic claim that internet traffic was "doubling every 100 days." The only problem was that this expectation of Internet growth was not accurate. Om Malik (2003) clarified the misconception in his book *Broadbandits:* "Think of 'internet traffic doubles every 100 days' as an urban legend" (13). Compared to demand at that time, there had been a massive overinvestment in fiber-optic lines and Internet backbone hardware; in fact, the investment anticipated at least ten times the actual demand. Not only was the demand grossly overestimated, but all the large companies, including WorldCom, Global Crossing, Quest, AT&T, Enron, Sprint, and others, were building and acquiring capacity to meet that fictitious demand. Each company was seemingly unconcerned about the fact that what each of them was doing was being done ten times over by their competitors.

Broadbandits points out that Andrew Odlyzko and Kerry Coffman, two AT&T scientists, couldn't believe that Internet traffic was doubling every 100 days, so they undertook a research study to analyze its growth. In their paper, "The Size and Growth of the Internet," Odlyzko and Coffman "proved that the whole notion of Internet traffic was doubling every 100 days was hogwash." The actual growth rate of the Internet at that time was about 70 to 150 percent per year. The researchers found that every reference to Internet traffic doubling every 100 days led back to Sidgemore and Ebbers at WorldCom. In August 1997, Sidgemore had stated in an interview with *Telecommunications Magazine:* "We're seeing growth at an unprecedented level. Our backbone doubles every 3.7 months. . . . So three years from now, we expect our network to be 1,000 times the size it is today. There's never been a technology model with such an extraordinary rate of growth like this before." (Quotes from Malik 2003, 13–15)

Not only was the demand for the Internet growing much more slowly, but in addition, at least 30 percent of Internet access was still ordinary, old-fashioned dial-up access, and the broadband capacity for demand at that time was being vastly overbuilt. However, to justify the acquisitions in Internet capacity, WorldCom had to insist that the demand for it was growing at an incredible speed. Grubman joined in spreading the hysteria about Internet traffic and broadband growth. With Sidgemore, Grubman, and Ebbers screaming about capacity being the only limitation, nobody in the industry wanted to believe Odlyzko and Coffman's study about the truth of Internet traffic growth. The rest of the industry ignored the proverbial iceberg and chanted their mantra, "Internet traffic is doubling every 100 days," as they swarmed across the nation and under the oceans, installing ten times more fiber-optic lines than necessary.

Ebbers and Sullivan continued their acquisition frenzy. They were perhaps driven by a quest for power, as well as an intense greed—they did not want to lose the value of all the shares they held in WorldCom, and the pursuit of acquisitions was their method of hiding the fact that the motley group of companies that WorldCom had put together was not nearly as profitable as they were reporting in their financial statements. Sullivan and Ebbers had to have more acquisitions in order to maintain the mirage of soaring earnings and stock value. They did it with smoke and mirrors, and accounting magic.

Making Accounting Magic with Acquisitions

Acquisitions provide an easy vehicle for accounting tricks to make a company or corporate group report more profit than it is really earning after the acquisition period. (Acquisitions can also make the group's revenue appear to be growing when, in fact, the parent company and the acquired company may be stagnating.) The falsely overstated earnings, in turn, drive the group's stock price higher, and then the company can use its stock as currency for the next acquisition, which can again be used to overstate profits after the acquisition period. The entire cycle can then be repeated again and again. In the *First Interim Report* (2002) the Bankruptcy Examiner described WorldCom's efforts to overstate its profits:

> We have found that as early as at least 1999, responding to the pressures on WorldCom's earnings, management undertook a succession of measures designed to shore up the Company's income statement. These measures deteriorated into a concerted program of manipulation that gave rise to a smorgasbord of fraudulent journal entries and adjustments. (105)

When a company acquires another company, there are a number of periods in time that the parent company can use to manipulate profits. For example, sometimes the parent company recognizes a big one-time expense or "restructuring charge" with respect to the acquired company *in the period immediately after the acquisition.* This expense is ostensibly to anticipate some event in the future and to provide for it in the current period—that is, to set aside current-period profit and create a reserve now for when the expense, or liability, materializes in the future. Examples of situations for which reserves could be set up are:

- The parent or acquiring company anticipates that the realizable value of the acquired company's assets is less than the assets' value as stated on the balance sheet—in other words, the asset will have to be sold at a loss in the future. For example, the company's inventory may have to be sold below its currently stated cost. Hence, a reserve is created for this probable, expected future loss.
- It is "probable" that the company will have liabilities in the future for a situation for which the liability has not yet been recorded in the acquired company's books—for example, a liability for taxes or litigation or employee severance payments.

Of course, all the previously mentioned reserves should only be created if it is probable that the unfavorable future condition actually will come to pass. Creating such reserves for the future falsely—when the unfavorable condition is not really probable—has two advantages for the acquiring company. First, since the charge is described as a "one-time charge" in the period immediately after the acquisition, analysts may not see the expense as "recurring," meaning that they do not see it as indicative of the future—and the value of any financial instrument, such as a share certificate, is the present value of its future income stream. So the current charge (expense) in the income statement is often "discounted" by analysts and investors. In other words, it may be largely ignored by the market because it was related to the previous management, and the current thinking tends to be: "The new owners are going to turn things around."

The second advantage of false reserves is the big payoff. As the future periods approach, when the earnings fail to meet the hyped expectations, the company has a "cookie jar" in the form of the reserves that it does not really need. It can then conveniently discover that the reserve wasn't required and release this surplus reserve back into the earnings in the income statement for the new period. So, when a reserve that was created is reversed because it isn't needed, it erroneously appears to be an increase in the earnings in the period into which it is released. Conversely, at the origin of the reserve, it overstates expenses and understates profits in an apparently nonrecurring manner in the period in which it was first created. As the Bankruptcy Report pointed out, "It is the inappropriate release of these reserves that results in one form of earnings management" (*First Interim Report* 2002, 107). WorldCom got to the point that it needed acquisition after acquisition in order to release false reserve after false reserve to prop up its earnings, period after period.

There is another similar accounting trick that a company can employ to use acquisitions to present false earnings and a false balance sheet. In this ploy, the parent company, *at the time of the acquisition,* creates a "purchase acquisition accounting reserve," and an unscrupulous company can overstate this reserve and manipulate future profits by releasing the reserve in the future. To the extent that a company overstates the reserves, it overstates goodwill by a corresponding amount. This would be done at the exact time of recording the purchase of the acquired company (as opposed to the period immediately following the acquisition). No expense has to be recorded.

Also at the time of the acquisition, the company can understate the fair value of the assets it is acquiring by making it look as though it has paid a greater part of the purchase price for goodwill, and less for the acquired assets. Economists define *goodwill* as an ability to earn future supernormal profits. (Accountants, on the other hand, have never managed an intelligible, consistently applied, systematic treatment of goodwill, just some cursory rules on how it is calculated. Consequently, we have the ludicrous situation that a company making huge losses can have *goodwill* on its balance sheet, when it actually has *badwill,* or the tendency to earn *less* than normal profits.) At the time of the acquisition, the parent company ascribes a fair value to the net value of the acquired company's assets, less its liabilities. If the parent pays more for the company than the net value, the excess of the purchase price over the fair value of the net assets is all allocated to goodwill. The advantage of ascribing part of the purchase price to goodwill instead of, say, to plant and machinery, is that plant and machinery would have to be amortized reasonably quickly over the estimated useful life of the asset. However, until 2001, goodwill had to be amortized only over forty years, resulting in much smaller amortization expenses during each period in the company's income statement, and therefore higher reported earnings. Since 2001, the incentive to overstate the allocation of the purchase price to goodwill instead of to tangible assets is even greater because, nowadays, goodwill arising on acquisition need not be amortized at all unless it becomes impaired. Also, overstating the amount of the purchase price attributed to goodwill means a company can create false reserves to release back into earnings as previously described.

A further, especially egregious version of this accounting sleight of hand is when, in *the period after an acquisition,* a company decides that the value of the assets acquired is less than originally calculated, and then creates a reserve for this decrease in anticipated, realizable value. However, instead of recognizing a charge (as discussed in the first version of this trick), in this version, in the financial statements of the period immediately following the acquisition, the other side of the entry is a false reevaluation of the portion of the purchase price that is allocated to *goodwill.* This indicates that the parent company has now decided that the net assets acquired were of less value than originally estimated. Hence, this creates the *need* for a reserve for the purported potential for the anticipated loss to be realized on those assets, and a corresponding increase is made to the allocation of the amount of the purchase price that was paid for *goodwill.*

WorldCom focused on the use of acquisitions to overstate reserves at the point of acquisition, or in the period soon after acquisition. This was achieved either by a one-time charge (expense) in the income statement, or by an allocation of a portion of the purchase price to goodwill on acquisition. WorldCom would then reverse these cookie-jar reserves in later periods by releasing them back into earnings (profits), when it opportunely "discovered" that they were no longer needed because the projected, negative events were not materializing. As the Bankruptcy Examiner stated: "It is inappropriate to record reserves unless a risk is probable and estimable. . . . WorldCom appears to have violated this principle" (*First Interim Report* 2002, 106). Furthermore, the SEC findings in its enforcement action against Sullivan alleged that "false adjustments and entries among other things, improperly reduced expenses by drawing down certain reserves" (AAER 1966, 2004).

WorldCom needed to keep on recording unnecessary reserves. Ebbers and Sullivan went after bigger and better acquisitions to create larger and larger false reserves, which would then be released into profits in future periods, in order to prop up inadequate earnings. This helped to boost the stock price, which was then used for more acquisitions—and so the Ponzi scheme's engine kept turning.

By 1997, WorldCom's acquisition frenzy became quite manic. Ebbers and Sullivan became a duo on the path to mayhem. They went on from the MFS/UUNet acquisition to acquire BLT Technologies, which supplied prepaid phone cards. Back in the office, Ebbers installed Sullivan onto the board of directors, after unceremoniously booting another member out. The turmoil was not confined to Ebbers's boardroom. Unconfirmed rumors had swirled for a while that Ebbers, the pious Sunday school teacher, had been having an affair. Whether true or not, this devout deacon of the First Baptist Church divorced his wife, Linda, and soon married Kristie Webb, who worked for WorldCom. Through it all, he managed to find time and energy to acquire ANS Communications from America Online.

One would think 1997 had been a busy enough year, but seemingly without taking a breath, Ebbers and Sullivan set their sights on acquiring a company three times bigger than their own—they decided to go after MCI.

MCI Falls under the WorldCom Spell

MCI got its start in 1963, when ex-General Electric employee John (Jack) Goeken formed a group to pursue an investment idea. Goeken had sold two-way radios for truckers to stay in touch with dispatchers and, of course, to "rap" with each other. Goeken figured out that they should put some microwave towers between St. Louis and Chicago, on the famous Route 66, to support two-way radio communications, and then sell the radios—hence the name "Microwave Communications Inc." (MCI). This was such an innovative idea that MCI immediately had to raise money to fight the legal battles launched by AT&T and General Electric to shut it down. MCI recruited William (Bill) McGowan, a Harvard law alumnus, to help raise money and fight for the fledgling company. McGowan took over from Goeken as CEO in 1974. After AT&T's breakup in 1984, MCI expanded astronomically under McGowan's leadership, developing a huge fiber-optic network that supported the long-distance phone service that we all know. After McGowan's gradual retreat from the company's affairs following heart surgery in 1987 and then his retirement in 1991, the company lost some of its focus and discipline. MCI's overhead grew disproportionately to its revenue as it made spectacular losses on its experiments with Internet business and its "Music-Now" service.

In 1996, British Telecom (BT) made an offer of $24 billion for MCI, and GTE also put in an offer. The British press generally convinced BT that they were paying too much for MCI, so BT withdrew its first offer and later offered $19 billion. Jack Grubman, the telecom analyst, added to the hype, arguing that MCI was worth the inflated price. Lynne W. Jeter's book *Disconnected: Deceit and Betrayal at WorldCom (2003)* maintained that BT needed MCI for the American market; GTE needed MCI for the overseas market; and the Baby Bells needed MCI for both the long-distance and overseas markets.

If WorldCom could snag MCI, it would thwart all these competitive efforts, and WorldCom would then be the only telecom company with a huge local service while simultaneously being the second-largest long-distance service in the United States. WorldCom already controlled half of all the domestic Internet traffic through UUNet and commanded a flabbergasting investment in bandwidth through the IDB, WilTel, and MFS acquisitions. If WorldCom could pull MCI out of the hat, it would have revenues estimated at between $28 billion and $30 billion.

In the heated competition between WorldCom, GTE, and BT for MCI, WorldCom began with a bid of $30 billion and eventually purchased MCI for approximately $42 billion. Most of this was paid for with WorldCom stock. Since BT already owned 20 percent of MCI, it had to be paid $7 billion in cash. WorldCom made this payment by taking on billions of dollars more debt.

Virtually every U.S. business magazine, newspaper, and journal was impressed with Ebbers and gushed that he was a brilliant entrepreneur. He was regarded as an ingenious visionary and a farsighted genius. Everyone repeated the chant: "Internet traffic is doubling every 100 days." Ebbers had become the Merlin of the business world, as everything he touched seemed to turn to gold.

Jack Grubman, of Salomon Brothers, did his part in spreading the WorldCom myth. In 1997, he told *Red Herring,* "WorldCom is at the intersection of everything we like—no carrier in the world can offer the integrated set of facilities that it does. The company has nothing to lose and everything to gain" (quoted in Malik 2003, 21). This was, however, the opposite of what the European press was saying after WorldCom outbid British Telecom. An editorial in *Information Society Trends* blamed the U.S. stock markets for "enabling a second-rank company such as WorldCom to become a global giant in a matter of a few years" (quoted in Jeter 2003, 81).

Meanwhile, the U.S. telecom industry was in denial. Because everyone had swallowed the fabrication that Internet traffic was doubling every 100 days, WorldCom's competitors were building up massively expensive bandwidth and data networks. Ebbers and his enchanted circle believed they had a vast capacity of a commodity that was in short supply, whereas they actually had a commodity that was in oversupply. Although they claimed that WorldCom had amazing synergy with MCI and the integration of the companies was going well, in reality the infighting festered, and the unnecessary duplications were nothing short of ludicrous. While WorldCom reported skyrocketing earnings, behind the scenes the company management was raiding the cookie-jar reserves created on acquisitions in order to meet earnings' expectations.

WorldCom's internal turmoil was so well hidden that, in 1998, Sullivan made it onto the cover of *CFO Magazine* when he was selected for an "Excellence Award" (McCafferty 1998). Ebbers the CEO, Scott Sullivan the CFO, David Myers the controller, as well as other members of WorldCom's senior personnel were the toast of the town; they had almost everyone fooled.

PART 3: PROBLEMS IN WIZARD WORLD

After the MCI merger, things started to spin out of control. However, World-Com was undeterred, and after acquiring a company more than three times its own size, it went on, in 1998, to acquire Brooks Fiber for $2.9 billion and then CompuServe for $1.2 billion of WorldCom stock. Wall Street applauded, but back home the workforce was restless. For a start, the UUNet Internet employees felt that they were the "technocrats" and far superior to the "low-tech" MCI telephone-operation proletariats. The MCI staff had already lost a lot of morale during the decline after McGowan had left, and this was exacerbated by the superior attitudes of the Internet division. To add insult to injury, WorldCom decided to do something about the cash flow problems that it faced as a result of all the debt it had incurred to pay for mergers, combined with the debt it had inherited from the merged companies. It decided to reduce MCI's hefty overhead costs with a dramatic cost-cutting program, including cutbacks like no longer flying first class, or staying in expensive hotels on business trips.

Whenever a customary company perk is withdrawn, it typically causes a negative reaction. If this is combined with a merger after a hostile bid, together with one company feeling superior to another, feelings are hurt and morale usually plunges. In fairness, Ebbers tried to get the entire WorldCom hodgepodge onto a shoestring budget—except, of course, for his own hundreds of millions of dollars of compensation, existing loans, and forgiven loans. Rumors of problems in the company began seeping into the media. It was starting to become clear that "the company's various units often operated as fiefdoms, with little communication and overlapping billing systems. The acquisition of MCI in 1998 represented the greatest failure in this respect . . . there would be multiple sales teams offering the same products, competing with each other" (Krim 2002).

In addition, as a result of the acquisition of MCI, WorldCom had two billing systems. Some employees would even switch existing customers to the other system and get an extra commission for getting a "new" account. The famous whistle-blower, Cynthia Cooper, reported in June 2001 that such switches of existing accounts purporting to be new ones had led to two over-payments of commissions of $930,000. WorldCom, however, reported publicly that the practice had been limited to just "a few bad apples" (Krim 2002).

There was such confusion between the different merged companies that a rot of inefficiency set in, and disorganization spilled over to every level. There was a great deal of double billing, as well as billing of customers for work that was not done. For example, a WorldCom internal auditor reportedly said that "two network circuits from Los Angeles to Sydney were billed and recorded even though the customer never got access to the circuits and the order was later canceled." Additionally, outside contractors billed for work that had not been done, and sometimes friends of employees were hired to do simple data-entry work at exorbitant fees. Furthermore, since the divisions were under pressure to meet sales-growth targets and the sales staff wanted commissions, often sales were made at below cost. The same article reported that "it was acceptable to sign a contract to provide a data network for $1 million even if it cost $2 million to fulfill the order." After all the acquisitions, most employees did not know what inventory WorldCom carried. Sometimes, items that WorldCom already had in inventory would be sold to WorldCom by an outside supplier for a higher cost than WorldCom had originally paid. By 2000, WorldCom had become "the aggregation of more than 60 telecommunications companies. . . . Gaining their revenue but doing little to integrate them operationally to eliminate overlapping costs." (Quotes from Krim 2002)

Ebbers ignored the gigantic turmoil, but turned his attention to insignificant and petty issues. In the subsequent CNBC interview, Robert Hudspeth, the former WorldCom vice president, explained how Ebbers had become obsessed with small and trivial details, such as "travel expenses over a certain amount, meals for employees." The interview then played an audiotape of Diana Day, head of customer service, saying, "I know this does not shock anybody that knows Bernie. He is still watching people walk out of their offices to go on their smoke break." The interviewer, David Faber, summed up the situation succinctly: "As the company he created was crashing down around him, Bernie Ebbers worried about smoking breaks." The chief wizard of WorldCom had lost his magic touch. (Quotes from Faber 2003)

While WorldCom reported immense earnings for 1999 and still greater growth in both revenues and profits for the first quarter of 2000, the bitter truth was that the company was already in dire trouble. Not only had the operating of the company become chaotic and confused with all the unco-ordinated and incongruent companies, but also the telecom industry itself was feeling the effects of having built capacity for an overestimated future growth projection. Jonathan Krim (2002) later reported that "executives discussed how the glut of network capacity was forcing down the prices that WorldCom and its rivals could charge for telephone and Internet service." The article observed how a few of the WorldCom executives had started "to confront the reality that their bubble-fueled telecommunications business was melting down. They were worried about how to characterize the health of the business in a way that didn't send investors heading for the exits."

In Pursuit of Sprint

With growing losses, slowing revenue, and debt spiraling out of control, Sullivan knew the true peril the company was in, and he knew that one way they could prolong their façade of profits—and prolong their existence—was to make yet another colossal acquisition. This would give WorldCom an additional source of false reserves to reverse back into earnings. There were only two telecommunication companies left of such magnitude: Sprint and AT&T. So they went after Sprint.

In fairness, the acquisition of Sprint would also have added an important wireless presence to WorldCom's long-distance and Internet traffic capacity to complete their all-round telecommunications clout. On October 5, 1999, a $129 billion deal was made between WorldCom and Sprint for the purchase of Sprint. Most of the price was to be paid by the issue of WorldCom shares, which were trading at $43.53 on that date. Shareholders approved the deal at their April 28, 2000, meeting. However, the deal still needed approval from regulators at the FCC in the United States, while European regulators worried that the managed companies would control too much of the long-distance and Internet traffic markets. On June 27, 2000, the U.S. Department of Justice filed a suit to put a stop to the merger of the two telecom giants.

What the world didn't know was that WorldCom's merger with Sprint was its last hope for keeping its Ponzi-type scheme going. By now, World-Com was an inefficient mess. It was a colossal, unmanageable charade, with $30 billion of debt while revenues were stalling and costs were spiraling. The end of the Sprint merger was, in effect, the end of WorldCom. The stock price began to fall. Sullivan reached desperation point in his attempts to portray the company as profitable in the financial statements.

It later emerged that "a small group of WorldCom executives, knowing that their business was eroding rapidly, discussed various accounting maneuvers that would help prop up the company's bottom line." Reportedly, on October 21, 2000, "Sullivan told then Vice Chairman Sidgemore that the company was in a 'really scary' situation of escalating costs and declining revenue growth in certain key areas . . . for instance, revenue from one of the company's biggest customers, America Online, was growing by only one percent, in part because its internet traffic growth had slowed." Sidgemore was apparently surprised to hear this and commented, "It's going to take some pretty fancy explaining." Quite magically, in WorldCom's financial report issued on October 26, "WorldCom touted 'solid' results with a 12 percent increase in overall revenue." Sullivan's later indictment maintained that October 2000 was "when he began directing finance officials to use company reserves to offset operating costs by $828 million, thereby increasing the company's earnings by the same amount." (Quotes from Krim 2002)

Then, in the first quarter of 2001, in his desperation, Sullivan began a further ploy: he directed the first of the now infamous and spectacular fraudulent transfers of line-cost expenses to asset accounts. (Of course, money spent on expenses goes into the income statement and reduces profit. However, money spent on assets is recorded in the balance sheet and does not reduce profits. Capital expenditure changes one asset, cash, into another asset.) But if Sullivan did not want to own up to the scheme that the cycle of acquisitions had been paid for with overpriced WorldCom stock based on overstated earnings, what else could he do? He could embark on a series of magical accounting manipulations.

The Bankruptcy Examiner, Thornburgh, summed up the major accounting hoaxes that Sullivan directed to falsify the financial statements:

> It appears that once income could no longer be sufficiently enhanced by the release of reserves, Mr. Sullivan and certain other WorldCom personnel directed a series of adjustments to its line costs in successive reporting periods beginning with the first quarter of 2001. (*First Interim Report* 2002, 105, 106)

PART 4: AN OVERVIEW OF WORLDCOM'S FICTITIOUS FINANCIAL REPORTING SCHEMES

At this stage, it is important to examine the two major schemes that World-Com used to overstate its earnings:

1. WorldCom artificially created unnecessary cookie-jar reserves, usually on the acquisition of companies or in the period following an acquisition, in order to reverse those reserves back into earnings in later periods. This was done to boost those later earnings and to present a false picture of financial health and growth, which inflated the price of WorldCom shares on the stock market.

2. WorldCom reclassified $3.8 billion of line-cost expenses as capital assets, thereby presenting those costs as assets on the balance sheet instead of as expenses in the income statement, in order to falsely overstate the earnings that it reported.

These two schemes were perpetrated in an unscrupulous and brazen manner, with a total disregard for veracity and accurate reporting.

Scheme #1: Improper Use of Merger Reserves

WorldCom's favored method of creating false reserves was on the acquisition of companies.

All Sullivan and his cohorts had to do was acquire numerous companies and pretend they were paying for large amounts of goodwill as they overstated the reserves and undervalued the assets. In future periods, they would then just reverse those reserves into profits as it was "discovered" that the reserves weren't really needed. This gave the impression of a financially healthy company.

The WorldCom Bankruptcy Examiner subsequently stated, "The manipulation of reserve accounts comprises a prominent part of the story of the irregularities in the WorldCom financial statements" (*First Interim Report* 2002, 106). Thornburgh reviewed the appropriateness of the following seven reserves:

- Revenue reserves
- Bad debt reserves
- Tax reserves
- Depreciation
- Purchase acquisition account reserves
- Legal reserves
- Line cost reserves (*First Interim Report* 2002, 107)

Apparently, Sullivan and his buddies had gone wild in understating the net value of assets of the companies they were acquiring and overstating liabilities while allocating large portions of the purchase price to "goodwill." Their audacity can be seen from an extract of the Examiner's schedule of the amounts allocated to goodwill, with respect to WorldCom's major acquisitions. The size of the number is hard to believe; however, what follows is not a typographical error. By December 31, 2001, WorldCom showed an asset named "Goodwill" on its balance sheet in the amount of *$50.5 billion*. Of this, $49.8 billion of goodwill was comprised of payments for acquired companies in excess of the net value of the assets of those companies, after creating the cookie-jar reserves by writing down the value of the acquired assets or by anticipating liabilities. The Bankruptcy Report provided the following goodwill allocation schedule:

Table 4.1   As of December 31, 2001, Goodwill Related to the Following Acquisitions (in billions)*

Legacy WorldCom	$ 1.9
MCI	28.2
WNS	2.2
Technologies, Telecom, MESI, MFSCC	8.3
Intermedia, PA	4.7
Other**	4.5
	$49.8 billion

*From *First Interim Report of Dick Thornburgh, Bankruptcy Court Examiner* (2002, 113).
**Includes more than twelve acquisitions

Ernst and Young estimated an impairment write-down of $15–$20 billion of this goodwill in its interim investigation in 2002. WorldCom later announced a write-off of approximately $50 billion of goodwill in its bankruptcy filing in 2002. The *Third and Final Report* (2004) on the WorldCom bankruptcy analyzed the inappropriate release of reserves to overstate earnings in two categories: first, the manipulation of line-cost accruals to boost profits by reducing reported line costs; and second, the improper release of revenue and other reserves into profits to "close the gap" between earning targets as predicted to Wall Street and the actual earnings.

Concerning the manipulation of line costs, it must be noted that, by 1999, both local and international line costs had mushroomed out of control. In order to diminish the amount of the line costs, Sullivan and his crew simply released the line-cost reserves that they had created earlier, and allocated the reversal to line-cost expenses. In accounting terminology, they "debited" the reserve on the balance sheet and made a corresponding "credit" or reduction to line-cost expense in the income statement. Since the dollar size of the debit was equal to the credit, everything still balanced, and expenses went down while profits went up. Never mind that the expenses were now understated and the earnings were overstated. Arthur Andersen never did press WorldCom for an explanation of these entries. The following such adjustments were either passed or missed by the auditors:

WorldCom Adjustments		
Fourth Quarter	1999:	$239 million
First Quarter	2000:	$369.9 million
Third Quarter	2000:	$828 million

Thornburgh stated that for the $239 million entry, "The sole support for the entry consisted of a post-it note bearing the notation '$239,000,000.'" At certain times, the reserves were released even though personnel had determined "that such reserves were needed to ensure that the company had accrued the appropriate level of reserves in relation to its liabilities." At other times, the releases were cookie-jar reserves that had been kept for when costs needed to be reduced. About $3.3 billion of reserves were released to reduce line costs inappropriately. At the close of each quarter, Sullivan's office tapped any reserve necessary to boost reported profits to "close the gap" between Wall Street expectations and actual earnings. Overall, the release of reserves accounted for the overstatement of profit before tax of approximately $3.3 billion, via the understatement of line costs. In addition, the Examiner's *First Interim Report* identified at least another $633 million in the release of reserves to satisfy Wall Street's expectations. (Quotes from *Third and Final Report* 2004, 274)

Scheme #2: Improper Capitalization of Expenses

Once they had run out of reserves to falsely reverse into earnings, the WorldCom gang turned to a much simpler, more old-fashioned ruse to inflate earnings. They merely pulled the oldest financial fraud in the world—they recorded money spent on expenses as though it had been spent on acquiring assets; i.e., as though the money was spent on acquiring capital goods that held their value into the following periods.

The Bankruptcy Examiner described the scam:

The Examiner understands that, beginning in the first quarter of 2001, Mr. Sullivan directed that hundreds of millions of line-cost expenses be capitalized, subtracting them from what otherwise would have been expenses against the company's earnings for the successive quarter, and disguising most of those reductions by transferring them as additions to the company's fixed assets. (*Third and Final Report* 2004, 278)

The entries, which were passed after the close of each quarter, amounted to $3.8 billion, mainly reducing line costs and overstating property, plant, and equipment (PPE) over the period January 2001 to March 2002. Further, "The journal entries lacked any supporting documents or explanations" (*Third and Final Report* 2004, 278). In addition, the findings of the SEC alleged that, over 2001 and 2002, WorldCom falsely portrayed its profitability:

> WorldCom did so by capitalizing (and deferring) rather than expensing (and immediately recognizing) approximately $3.8 billion of its costs: the company transferred these costs to capital accounts in violation of established generally accepted accounting principles ("GAAP"). These actions were intended to mislead investors and manipulate WorldCom's earnings to keep them in line with estimates by Wall street analysts. (AAER 1585, 2002)

The obvious question in the face of such a brazen and crude fraud is, "Where were the auditors?" According to the Examiner, the auditors—Arthur Andersen—did not demand total and simultaneous access to all of WorldCom's general ledger and journal entries. In addition, WorldCom gave Arthur Andersen misleading special "MonRevs"; namely, monthly revenue schedules that concealed the top-side journal-entry adjustments. These adjustments were used for "closing any gaps between targeted and projected actual earnings." They also spread the irregular amount over a number of months and over a number of asset accounts, so that no one amount would stand out dramatically. WorldCom also transferred the false assets out of certain accounts and into other accounts according to when Arthur Andersen planned to review the financial records: "By engaging in this shell game, those responsible for the improper entries stayed several steps ahead of Arthur Andersen in shielding these entries from the auditors." (Quotes from *Third and Final Report* 2004, 276; 283)

The combination of Arthur Andersen's restricted access to the accounting records together with the machinations by WorldCom to deceive the auditors, led to Arthur Andersen's being oblivious of these "top-side" transfers from expenses to assets. As to whether the auditors actually knew of the accounting exploits, the Bankruptcy Examiner stated:

> The evidence is not in dispute: Arthur Andersen had no knowledge of the improper capitalization of line costs or the Company's improper manipulation of

its line cost, revenue and other reserves to inflate its earnings. (*Third and Final Report* 2004, 279)

However, whether Arthur Andersen should have conducted its audit in a more conscientious manner that would have revealed irregular entries is another matter. It can be argued that WorldCom's external auditors should not have accepted so many limitations on their access to the complete general ledger at a given time.

Auditors need to demand necessary access, and if that demand is not met, they are obliged to give a disclaimer audit opinion or a qualified opinion on the financial statements. There is not much point in auditing documents if the auditors are not going to reconcile the audited documents with the financial statements that they must approve. The whole point in auditing schedules is to test their support of the financial statements. If adjustments are made to the company's documentation or accounts, or to schedules after they have been audited via massive journal entries for the preparation of the financial statements, it is quite futile to audit the underlying information in the first place.

In its discussion of the auditors, the *Third and Final Bankruptcy Report* (2004) alleged that "the company has claims against Arthur Andersen due to its responsibility for the failure to detect any aspect of the company's accounting fraud" (261).

PART 5: THE COLLAPSE OF WIZARD WORLD

Ebbers Loses Control

In addition to fraudulently misreporting its earnings and net assets, World-Com personnel also enabled Ebbers to raid the company of huge sums of money by granting or guaranteeing him loans of over $400 million. Some of these loans were unethical in that they were made at very low interest rates and there was little chance that Ebbers could repay them. Further, Ebbers did not disclose his problematic financial position to the compensation committee until 2002, and even then his disclosures were misleading.

Like most financial fraud, Ebbers's problem began with relatively small steps down the slippery slope. When WorldCom was doing well in the 1990s, Ebbers began applying for bank loans on his own behalf, or for his other business interests. The crucial point is that he dragged WorldCom interests into his private activities by pledging his WorldCom stock to secure his personal bank loans. Caught between a genuine desire to engage in philanthropy and a strong need to assuage an insatiable ego desperate for recognition, Ebbers also pledged his WorldCom stock for loans on behalf of Mississippi College. As these loans grew—and grow they did—significant amounts of Ebbers's WorldCom stock were held as security. So much so, in fact, Ebbers could argue that if he were forced to sell his WorldCom stock to pay those loans, such a large volume of selling would put considerable downward pressure on the WorldCom stock price. Astoundingly, Ebbers had pledged or guaranteed hundreds of millions of dollars of WorldCom stock.

The kicker for WorldCom was that clauses in many of these loans required Ebbers to make repayments if WorldCom stock fell below specified levels. Unfortunately, that's exactly what the stock did: it fell from a high of $64.50 per share in June 1999, to $46.07 in mid-July 2000, after the Sprint merger was called off. To pay his enormous debts, Ebbers began borrowing large amounts from WorldCom. The Bankruptcy Examiner observed that WorldCom's compensation committee alleged it was Ebbers's idea that WorldCom lend him money to avoid the sale of his WorldCom stock to repay his outside loans. Ebbers, on the other hand, disputed this, claiming that the compensation committee had asked him to borrow money from World-Com rather than sell his stock, which would put further downward pressure on the stock price. Ebbers's version makes it appear that accepting massive loans from WorldCom was a magnanimous favor he did for the company; it was a gesture of all heart. The point, of course, is that if Ebbers had not pledged vast quantities of company stock for personal loans and guarantees, neither he nor the WorldCom shares would have had to be rescued. It seemed to be lost on Ebbers that his argument of "helping" WorldCom by taking the loans was merely tautological. In fact, he appeared to favor this kind of circular logic to rationalize his actions.

The first loan of $50 million was made to Ebbers by the WorldCom compensation committee on September 6, 2000. In October, they authorized another $25 million guarantee with respect to Ebbers's personal bank loans. In January 2001, the guarantee was increased to $100 million, and then to the even more staggering amount of $150 million. (Ebbers eventually signed a note in September 2001, agreeing to repay the amounts extended under the guarantees.)

The Global Crossing bankruptcy filing, in January 2001, hit WorldCom's stock hard, putting another nail in Ebbers's coffin. That month, the stock price fell below $10 per share. Ebbers continued his desperate acquisition strategy and went after Intermedia to get control of Digex, an Internet company. The handling of this acquisition later caused special criticism by the Examiner. Ebbers was accused of withholding information from

WorldCom's board of directors as well as misleading them. The board of directors was criticized for not performing due diligence before its approval of
the acquisition. Ebbers's acquisition price of over $6 billion for Intermedia
in July 2001 was generally considered an overpayment. To make matters
worse, WorldCom became embroiled in an expensive lawsuit with Digex
shareholders. The stock price of WorldCom continued to fall, and blame was
increasingly aimed at the formerly untouchable Bernie Ebbers. In spite of
his increasing debacles, in January 2002, the compensation committee authorized another $65 million loan to Ebbers. What were they thinking?

The *Third and Final Report* shows that by April 2, 2002, the loans and
guarantees to Ebbers exceeded $379 million. On that date, in an agreement
letter, WorldCom formally protected its interest in Ebbers's WorldCom
stock as security for his loans. A couple of weeks later, on April 18, Ebbers
pledged his other personal and business interests as security. On April 29, all
Ebbers's loans and guarantees were consolidated into one promissory note of
$408.2 million—a staggering sum by any measure. The Report shows that
of this amount, $198.7 million was to satisfy loans to Ebbers for other com-
panies controlled by him; $36.5 million was for a letter of credit used to sup-
port Mississippi College; $165 million was a personal loan to Ebbers; and
$7.6 million was for interest on these loans. This, in a nutshell, is a looting
story of an ego gone wild, of an insane spending spree, and of a compensation committee that acquiesced to the CEO's wishes, rolled over, and basically shoveled WorldCom's cash to Ebbers in any amount that he requested.

Thornburgh, the Bankruptcy Examiner, faults mainly Ebbers as well as
two members of the compensation committee, for the loan fiasco. However,
since the remaining members of the board of directors "ratified compensation committee actions with virtually no data and without inquiring about
or questioning the low interest rates," the Examiner believed that claims
could be pursued against all of WorldCom's former directors (*Third and
Final Report* 2004, 18).

On March 7, 2002, the SEC finally and inevitably questioned WorldCom
formally on a wide range of items, including the loans to Ebbers, as well as
the accounting for acquisitions. On April 3, 2002, WorldCom laid off 3,700
people. The stock price continued to fall, and the pressure on Ebbers burst
through his wall of resolve to stay in charge. On April 9, 2002, Ebbers
resigned as CEO of WorldCom, and John Sidgemore was appointed in his
place. The compensation committee again did the unbelievable for their
(rather tarnished) golden-boy Ebbers, and presented him with an extremely
generous severance package that included $1.5 million per year for life and
use of the WorldCom jet for thirty hours per year.

The End of the Sullivan Era

By this time, a storm was brewing that would uncover the massive accounting fraud of Scott Sullivan and his cohorts. Business was declining; WorldCom had run out of acquisitions to falsify profits; the stock price was falling; Ebbers's loans were eating cash; and a number of suspicious events had caught the attention of WorldCom's now famous internal auditor, Cynthia Cooper.

In March 2002, John Stupka—of WorldCom's wireless division—complained to Cooper that Sullivan was taking a reserve for doubtful debts from Stupka's division to use elsewhere. Cooper noted this as suspicious, but not clearly illegal. She raised the issue with the Andersen auditors, who brushed her off. An Andersen spokesperson said that Stupka's division did not need the reserve of $400 million. Pulliam and Solomon (2002) later reported in the *Wall Street Journal* that Norton's response galvanized Cooper's determination to find out what was going on, and she assembled a team consisting of herself, Gene Morse, and Glyn Smith of the internal audit department. Morse later said: "That was like putting a red flag in front of a bull. She [Cynthia Cooper] came back to me and said, 'Go dig'" (quoted in Pulliam and Solomon 2002).

Cooper, having decided not to accept Andersen's answer, reported it to Max Bobbit, head of the audit committee, on March 6, 2002. Sullivan backed down on the issue of the reserve, but did not forget. Pulliam and Solomon reported that the next day Sullivan tracked Cooper down at her hair salon and warned her not to interfere with Stupka's business again. One day later, the SEC delivered a "Request for Information" concerning its investigation into WorldCom. That gave Cooper a little more leeway to go beyond the internal audit department's narrow operational audit and into the realm of a financial audit. In May, Sidgemore, the new CEO, appointed Cooper to head a complete investigation into WorldCom's books.

Then, on May 21, Glyn Smith, of the internal audit team, received an email from Mark Abide who was in charge of the PPE records in Texas. Abide attached an article from the *Fort Worth Weekly Online* of May 16, 2002, about Kim Emigh, a WorldCom employee in Texas who had been fired for questioning the accounting for PPE. This really caught the attention of the investigative team. The entire sham that was WorldCom may have been set in play by Ebbers following his high school basketball teammate to Mississippi College, but it was about to be unraveled by a different kind of team altogether—a team of trustworthy internal auditors. Cooper, Morse, and Smith began to "triple-team" Sullivan. The team had already come across an item of $1.4 billion in capital equipment that was suspicious. By that stage, the investigators were already suspicious about almost $2 billion of capital expenditure that "had never been authorized for capital spending" (Pulliam and Solomon 2002).

Cooper decided to call Mark Abide in Texas to see if he knew anything. Cooper's team had been told that the mysterious additions to capital assets were for "prepaid capacity." When pushed further, they were told to speak to David Myers, who was WorldCom's controller. During the call to Texas, Cooper asked Abide about "prepaid capacity" and "he too answered very cryptically, explaining that those entries had come from Buford Yates, WorldCom's director of general accounting" (Pulliam and Solomon 2002).

The team kept digging, and on May 21 they found $500 million of unsupported computer expenses that were improperly classified as capital expenditure. Cooper became convinced that operating expenses were being fraudulently booked as capital assets when she let Myers know that she had instructed Gene Smith to find out more about "prepaid capacity," and Myers tried to stop the enquiry.

Undeterred, but without full access to the accounting computer system, the internal audit team became creative and surreptitious in their search for the information they needed. Gene Morse contrived to be testing a new software program in order to retrieve the journal entry source of items in the general ledger. Initially, Morse downloaded so much data that he almost shut down the entire system. To avoid detection, he started working in the windowless audit library each day. He even started copying accounting information on CD-ROMs, in case others tried to remove the evidence by destroying the financial records. (Sullivan became suspicious and tried to find out what Morse was working on—but Morse deflected the questions.)

On June 11, Sullivan called the internal audit team into his office to ask what they were working on. Among other items, Gene Smith casually mentioned the capital expenditure audit, at which point Sullivan asked them to delay it a few months. They refused and left. Cooper and Smith then informed Bobbit, the head of the audit committee, of the $3.8 billion misallocation of operating expenses as assets. Bobbit advised them to inform WorldCom's new auditors, KPMG, who had replaced Arthur Andersen after the Enron debacle. (Interestingly, Bobbit did not mention the issue at a board of director's meeting the next day.) When KPMG asked Cooper to recheck her facts, she questioned Betty Vinson (director of management reporting) and Buford Yates about the capital expenditure entries. Vinson said that she had been instructed to make the entries but had not been given any explanations. Yates claimed that he did not know anything about them. Cooper and Smith then questioned David Myers, the controller, who "admitted he knew that the accounting treatment was wrong" (Pullman and Solomon 2002). After WorldCom's profits dropped:

> Mr. Sullivan had tried to respond by moving around reserves, according to his indictment. But by 2001 it wasn't enough to keep the company afloat. And so Mr. Sullivan began instructing Mr. Myers to take line costs, fees paid to lease portions of other companies' telephone networks, out of operating expense accounts where they belonged and tuck them into capital accounts, according to Mr. Sullivan's indictment. It was a definite accounting no-no, but it meant that the costs did not hit the company's [reported] bottom line. (Pulliam and Solomon 2002)

On June 20, Cooper, Smith, and Malone (of KPMG) told the audit committee that the line-cost transfers did not conform to GAAP. Sullivan prepared a white paper to try to provide theoretical support for the transfers, but nobody bought his arguments.

On June 24, WorldCom stock fell to below $1 on the stock exchange. The next day, WorldCom announced to the world that it had uncovered a massive fraud that had overstated profits by $3.8 billion over the last few years. That same day, the CFO, Scott Sullivan, and the controller, David Myers, were asked to resign. When WorldCom filed for bankruptcy a month later, on July 21, 2002, it attained the record for the largest bankruptcy in the United States.

PART 6: THE GATEKEEPERS WHO FAILED WORLDCOM

Over the years, the capitalization of expenses and manipulation of reserves had overstated WorldCom's profits by more than $9 billion:

> The Commission's Amended Complaint alleges that WorldCom misled investors from at least as early as 1999 through the first quarter of 2002, and further states that the company has acknowledged that during that period, as a result of undisclosed and improper accounting, WorldCom materially overstated the income it reported on its financial statements by approximately $9 billion. (AAER 1678, 2002)

This estimate of $9 billion would increase, after further investigation, to close to $11 billion.

Two of the main perpetrators, Sullivan and Myers, were arrested on August 1, 2002, and charged with securities fraud, conspiracy to commit securities fraud, and filing false statements with the SEC. On August 28, a further seven-count indictment was filed against Sullivan, charging him with conspiracy to boost earnings by hiding operating expenses. Sullivan pleaded guilty "to three fraud-related counts." Myers pleaded guilty and "helped prosecutors identify false numbers in WorldCom's financial filings from 2000–2002." The next month, Buford Yates, Betty Vinson, and Troy Normand pleaded guilty to charges of fraud, conspiracy, and securities fraud. Ebbers was later arrested and subsequently "convicted of securities fraud, conspiracy and seven counts of false filing." (Quotes from Pulliam 2005)

The responsibility for the repugnant financial reporting failure does not rest solely with the WorldCom management and staff who perpetrated the frauds, or Arthur Andersen whose audits failed to detect the irregularities. As mentioned earlier, the Bankruptcy Examiner showed how every single gatekeeping entity failed to effectively perform its function.

Concerning Arthur Andersen, the Examiner's *Third and Final Report* (2004) went further than earlier reports and concluded that allegedly Arthur Andersen failed "to carry out the kinds of substantive tests that were warranted by the risks." Even though they were "significantly deceived," Andersen lacked due "professional skepticism" (20).

Turning his attention to the board of directors, Thornburgh scrutinized the impact of the "scant involvement" of the board in the massive acquisitions. As poor as this aspect of corporate governance was, Thornburgh conceded: "In the end, however, only one acquisition ... Intermedia ... seemed truly questionable." This huge acquisition had been approved without apparent due diligence. The first Intermedia agreement, on September 1, was presented to the board of directors for its approval without "meaningful or advance data," and the directors "passively" approved the transaction. In the opinion of the Examiner, the board would probably have approved this purchase even with better information. However, the price of Intermedia increased, and by the time of the amended merger contract, in February 2001, "a vigilant and properly informed Board would have rejected the merger." Sullivan and Ebbers, without authorization, finalized the revised merger agreement and the Examiner concluded that the directors breached their "fiduciary duty of care in not learning all the circumstances concerning the merger amendment." This Report also apportioned blame (in varying degrees) to the former board of directors for the fiasco of over $400 million of loans and guarantees made by WorldCom on behalf of Ebbers, or to Ebbers, who "breached his duties of loyalty and good faith." (Quotes from *Third and Final Report* 2004, 17–21)

Certainly WorldCom's internal audit department failed to properly carry out the function that an internal audit division should fulfill and was rebuked for this by the Bankruptcy Examiner. However, the department was set up with a flawed focus and was not truly independent. It did not have sufficient resources and was geared to perform operational audits only—not financial audits. Taking this into consideration, the Examiner pointed out, "Given this focus on operational issues, it was a credit to the personnel of the Internal Audit Department that they investigated the line cost capitalization issue in 2002" (*First Interim Report* 2002, 7). The *Third and Final Report* of 2004 did not recommend that claims be pursued against the Internal Audit Department staff. Similarly, although the audit committee of the board of directors was ineffective, and the Examiner referred to "the mistaken deference" that this committee showed to senior financial management, Thornburgh did not recommend claims against the audit committee.

WorldCom's major investment bank, Salomon Smith Barney (SSB) represented yet another major gatekeeping failure. The Examiner claimed that Ebbers breached his fiduciary duties and "that SSB aided . . . and abetted those breaches" (*Third and Final Report* 2004, 17). The Report maintained that—in exchange for WorldCom's investment banking business from Ebbers— Salomon Smith Barney gave Ebbers preferential treatment in two significant ways. First, they allocated to him huge amounts of initial public offering (IPO) shares when they took other companies public; and second, they favored him by providing him with unusual financial assistance.

While the practice of investment bankers allocating some IPO shares to their best retail customers is a long established one, certain aspects of the distribution of these shares to Ebbers was strikingly unusual. For a start, when Salomon first allotted IPO shares to Ebbers, not only was he not one of their good customers, he was not a customer at all. Second, the size of the allocation to Ebbers was staggering—bigger than to any other individual customer and even bigger than the amounts offered to most institutional investors. Finally, and most incriminating of all, soon after the first allocation of valuable IPO shares to Ebbers by Salomon, Ebbers used Salomon as WorldCom's investment banker for the first time.

The first IPO stock allotted to Ebbers was for Salomon's IPO of McLeod Inc. before Ebbers was even a customer of the banking firm. Ebbers paid $4 million for 200,000 shares and sold them four months later for $6.1 million. By a startling fluke, two months after the sale of his McLeod shares, Ebbers saw to it that WorldCom employed SSB as its investment bank on its merger with MFS Communications Company. Coincidence? The Examiner did not think so: "The evidence supports the conclusion that Mr. Ebbers received his huge McLeod allocation, at least in part, because the large allocation made it more likely that Mr. Ebbers would award Salomon Investment

Banking work" (*Third and Final Report* 2004, 14, 15). Salomon earned a fee of $7.5 million from its work on the WorldCom/MFS merger.

Over the span of all WorldCom's subsequent mergers, Salomon earned over $100 million in fees, and Ebbers made over $12 million in gross profits on various IPO shares. The investment bankers attempted to justify the IPO shares, claiming that Ebbers had been one of their best customers. The Examiner, however, rejected the argument on the grounds that Ebbers had actually not traded at all on his SSB account, except for his IPO shares.

Apart from favoring Ebbers with IPO shares, Salomon Smith Barney also gave him another brand of preferential financial assistance when he could not buy any more shares because of the margin calls with respect to his personal bank loans. The bankers requested their affiliate, Citibank, not to sell any of Ebbers's stock that Citibank held as security for their $40 million loan to him. SSB also guaranteed Ebbers's loan to Citibank. One week after Ebbers resigned as CEO of WorldCom and had no more business to extend to the banks, SSB sold—at a loss—the stock that had been held as security for his loan.

The following table shows the interrelationship between Ebbers's IPO allocations and SSB's investment-banking work for WorldCom:

Table 4.2   Summary of Salomon's IPO Allocations to Mr. Ebbers and Investment Banking Activity for WorldCom in 1996 and 1997*

- *June 10, 1996.* Salomon first allocates IPO shares to Mr. Ebbers—200,000 shares in the McLeod IPO. He realizes profits of $2,155,000.
- *August 14, 1996.* Salomon is engaged for the first time by WorldCom on the Company's acquisition of MFS, receiving fees of $7,500,000.
- *November 15, 1996.* Salomon allocates 89,286 shares to Mr. Ebbers in the McLeod Secondary Offering. He realizes profits of $390,172.
- *March 18, 1997.* Salomon is engaged by WorldCom on its issuance and sale of $2 billion in senior notes, receiving fees of $8,330,600.
- *May 15, 1997.* Salomon is engaged by WorldCom on its exchange offering for MFS Bonds, receiving fees of approximately $1,500,000.
- *June 23, 1997.* Salomon allocates 205,000 shares to Mr. Ebbers in the Qwest IPO. He realizes profits of $1,957,475.
- *September 26, 1997.* Salomon allocates 200,000 shares to Mr. Ebbers on the Nextlink IPO. He realizes profits of $1,829,869.
- *September 29, 1997.* Salomon is engaged by WorldCom on the MCI transaction, receiving fees of more than $48 million, including fees from a related investment-grade debt offering.
- *October 26, 1997.* Salomon allocates 100,000 shares to Mr. Ebbers in the MFN IPO. He realizes profits of $4,558,711.

---

*From: *Third and Final Report* of Dick Thornburgh, Bankruptcy Court Examiner. January 26, 2004.

All of this happened while SSB's "independent" star telecom analyst, Jack Grubman, wined and dined and shot pool with Ebbers. Grubman also touted WorldCom stock, attended WorldCom board meetings, and echoed the absurd "demand for broadband is doubling every 100 days" line. SSB earned $100 million in investment-banking fees as WorldCom's stock skyrocketed and then plunged. Grubman steadfastly refused to give the stock a "sell" rating. In his analysis of Ebbers's relationship with SSB, the Bankruptcy Examiner stated:

> The Examiner believes that Mr. Ebbers breached his fiduciary duties of loyalty and good faith by putting his personal interest ahead of those of the Company. The Examiner also believes that SSB aided and abetted those breaches . . . . Indeed, SSB is jointly and severally liable along with Mr. Ebbers for these breaches. The recoveries could include ... disgorgement for the fees WorldCom paid to SSB. (*Third and Final Bankruptcy Report* 2004, 17)

So it was that each of the institutional gatekeepers failed in their corporate governance duties. Even after Arthur Andersen was dismissed as the independent auditor following its Enron catastrophe, KPMG, in its capacity as taxation consultant, bungled as well. The Examiner commented on KPMG's aggressive plan to minimize state taxes as follows: "To the extent that state taxing authorities bring actions and prevail . . . WorldCom has claims against KPMG" (*Third and Final Bankruptcy Report* 2004, 13).

The particular part of the tax scheme that was aggressive and vulnerable pertained to a transfer-pricing scheme, whereby KPMG advised WorldCom to categorize "the foresight of top management" as an intangible asset and to charge a royalty expense to subsidiaries for the "use" of this privilege. This "expense" would reduce tax liabilities in high state tax areas, and the royalty "received" would be given favorable state tax treatment. Furthermore, KPMG was not shy in its advice on how to pursue this nonsense. Of the $20 billion that WorldCom received in royalties from its subsidiaries, the majority of this amount was for the use of "the foresight of top management." (Quotes from *Third and Final Bankruptcy Report* 2004, 12)

Management, at this stage, was actually running the company with the opposite of foresight—it was running it into the ground with shortsightedness and denial. The "management foresight" that KPMG sought to license as an "intangible asset" was, in fact, an intangible liability. Further, the Examiner stated that "instead of explicitly disclosing that the cornerstone of the programs was the classification of 'management foresight' as an intangible asset, the applications indicated that the royalty income would be the result of the licensing of traditional intellectual property, such as trademarks, trade names and service names. . . ." Astoundingly, royalties received from subsidiaries "exceed[ed] WC's consolidated net income for that period." Since the alleged "management foresight" does not represent an intangible asset that can be transferred to a third party, accounting rules do not support it being capable of attracting royalty income. With this brazen and highly irregular tax advice, the full circle of WorldCom shareholders, lenders, employees, and consultants were betrayed by every single category of gatekeeper—a spectacular corporate-governance failure on every dimension. (Quotes from *Third and Final Report* 2004, 12–13)

PART 7: SIGNALS OF THE WORLDCOM FRAUD

Signals of WorldCom's Fictitious Reporting Scheme #1:

- Improper Use of Merger Reserves

Signal #1: The prospective investor should be on the lookout for large amounts allocated to goodwill on the acquisition of other companies. This is an indication that false cookie-jar reserves may have been created and released back into earnings in order to falsely boost post-acquisition profits.

WorldCom had $49.8 billion of goodwill recorded as amounts paid in excess of net asset values on acquisitions, as reported earlier in this chapter. Of this colossal amount, $28.2 billion was related to its acquisition of MCI. In subsequent restatements of WorldCom's financial statements, virtually all of the $49.8 billion was written off as valueless. Whenever goodwill increases dramatically over time as a percentage of earnings, it should be taken as a sign to be very skeptical about a company's financial statements.

Signal #2: When the goodwill, on an acquisition, relates to a company that does not have or is not very likely to have a supernormal return on assets, it is a signal that the goodwill may be false since, in economic terms, goodwill is an ability to earn supernormal profits. If the parent company is not paying for supernormal profits, what is it paying for when it pays more for a company than the value of its net assets? One should keep a skeptical watch to see whether these profits materialize.

Signal #3: When a company that makes a number of acquisitions also creates significant reserves, it is a signal that the company may be creating false reserves to boost later periods' earnings. WorldCom created a number of reserves that later became the subject of the Bankruptcy Examiner's inquiry.

Moreover, according to the Bankruptcy Report, the reserves that were related to restatement entries, as announced on August 2002, had the effect of reducing EBITDA (earnings before interest, taxation, depreciation, and amortization) by the amount of $2.3 billion.

Signal #4: Investors should be wary of large one-time charges in the income statement, especially around the acquisition period, because these are often signals that the company could be creating false reserves to boost later earnings.

Signal #5: Adjustments that increase goodwill in a later period, with respect to an acquisition, are further signs that a company may be creating false reserves. Sometimes companies want additional false reserves, in excess of the reserves created at the time of the acquisition. The parent company may even wish to avoid taking a large one-time charge in its income statement in order to acquire the cookie-jar reserve. In such a case, the company may reopen the value placed on goodwill at acquisition by creating false reserves in a later period, and increasing the goodwill paid for an acquisition by a complementary amount. These later adjustments increasing goodwill are a huge red flag that false reserves are being created to boost later profits.

Signals of WorldCom's Fictitious Reporting Scheme #2:

• Understating Expenses via improper capitalization of expenses

This fraud overstates earnings reported on the income statement and also inflates assets on the balance sheet. In addition, this fraud overstates the cash flow from operations (CFFO), and inflates the amount reported as "cash used in investing activities" in the statement of cash flows.

WorldCom, of course, fraudulently reallocated billions of dollars out of its "line-cost" expense and into the asset designated as PPE.

Signal #1: The first signal of this kind of fraud is often a decrease in the ratio of sales to assets (i.e., the asset-to-turnover ratio). Ultimately, the reason that a company invests in assets is to generate revenue with those assets. Obviously, a fictitious asset cannot produce revenue. Since one of the most common assets chosen for fraudulent companies to misclassify expenses is PPE, the first way to identify this fraud is to check the ratio of sales to PPE.

In Table 4.3 we see that over the period during which WorldCom manipulated its financial statements by understating its "line costs" in its income statements—and allocating the amounts spent to PPE instead—its revenue as a percentage of PPE assets grew smaller and smaller. In the second quarter of 2000, revenue was 59.2 percent of PPE and it fell steadily to 44 percent by the second quarter of 2001. Then, as WorldCom increased its fraudulent transfers from line costs to PPE, we see that revenue as a percentage of PPE dropped precipitously to only 35.6 percent in the fourth quarter of 2004, and to just 32.2 percent in the first quarter of 2002.

Table 4.3   WorldCom: A Selection of Ratios
Third Quarter 2000—First Quarter 2002*

	2000 06/30	2000 09/30	2000 12/31	2001 03/31	2001 06/30	2001 09/30	2001 12/31	2002 03/31
Line-costs/ Revenues	40.73%	38.49%	42.53%	42.26%	41.86%	41.77%	42.09%	42.84%
Sales/Total Assets	10.47%	10.06%	9.71%	9.76%	8.74%	8.55%	8.16%	7.82%
Sales/PPE	59.2%	55.1%	47.4%	45.5%	44.1%	40.7%	35.6%	32.2%

*Derived from SEC Filings

Table 4.4   WorldCom: Extracts from Quarterly Statements and Balance Sheets
(in Millions) Third Quarter 2000—First Quarter 2002

	2000 06/30	2000 09/30	2000 12/31	2001 03/31	2001 06/30	2001 09/30	2001 12/31	2002 03/31
Revenues	10,193.	10,047.	9,607.	9,720.	8,910.	8,966.	8,478.	8,120.
Line Costs Originally Reported	4,152.	3,867.	4,086.	4,108.	3,730.	3,745.	3,568.	3,479.
Improperly Capitalized Line-costs	292.	292.	292.	1,063.	902.	1,035.	1,223.	1,089.
Less Tax Shield	119.	117.	107.	419.	352.	403.	474.	390.
Total Assets	97,373.	99,893.	98,903.	99,580.	101,944.	104,902.	103,914.	103,803.
Goodwill	46,670.	46,594.	46,594.	46,113.	50,820.	50,820.	50,531.	50,607.
PPE	17,226.	18,243.	20,288.	21,381.	20,191.	22,053.	23,814.	25,219.
Accumulated Depreciation	6,104.	6,707.	7,204.	7,770.	8,241.	9,061.	9,852.	10,807.

Signal #2: When the PPE amount on the balance sheet increases while revenue actually decreases, this is a double red flag that something is likely to be seriously wrong with the company. This signal is, of course, based on the same logic and dynamics as Signal #1, but it is a more pronounced signal and very easy to spot. Without even calculating a percentage, the prospective investor reading the financial statements can simply check to see that revenue does not decrease over time while the amount reportedly invested in PPE increases.

From an examination of Table 4.4, we see that in WorldCom the amount of dollars reportedly invested in PPE grew steadily from $17.2 billion in the second quarter of 2000, to $20.1 billion in the second quarter of 2001, and jumped to $25.2 billion in the first quarter of 2002, at the height of the fraud. Over that same time, revenues dropped from $10.1 billion, to $8.9 billion, to $8.1 billion.

The logic behind this signal, of course, is that companies invest their cash in PPE to *increase* their capacity to produce goods and services and earn revenue with these goods and services. A company cannot continue for an extended period of time increasing its cash spent on production capacity while reducing the revenue it gets from that capacity. If such a trend *continues over time,* at least one of two things has happened, and they are both bad. Either the company is falsely reporting some of its cash spent on operating expenses as cash invested in the fixed assets of PPE, or it is reporting honestly and its business model has serious problems. In the latter case, the investment in PPE assets is not producing the revenue for which the investment was made in the first place. In the absence of clearly understandable explanations in the Management Discussion and Analysis (MD&A) section of the company's annual report, or in coherent press releases, either of these signals in the financial statements is a strong alert for an investor to consider a downgrade of the stock.

In the case of WorldCom, these two signals could have easily been revealed by simply going to *www.sec.gov/edgar.shtml* and perusing WorldCom's income statement and balance sheet in the 10-Q and 10-K filings, and then comparing the amount reported as revenues to the amount reported as PPE over time. It would have been evident that something was going very wrong.

Over a period of time, WorldCom's comparison of sales to PPE produced a strong signal of overstatement of PPE, because so much of the misallocation of the line-cost expense went specifically into PPE. The misallocation of expenses could also go to other assets. Thus it is useful to test each of the following ratios, looking for the same trend of sales declining as a percentage of assets:

- Ratio of sales to each fixed-asset category on the balance sheet
- Ratio of sales to total fixed assets
- Ratio of sales to total assets

Signal #3: When an expense that has a fixed-cost component remains a constant percentage of sales revenue as revenue decreases, it is a signal that the expense is being understated. When revenues decrease over time, test all expenses that have a fixed-cost element against sales revenue, checking for such expenses that have not increased as a percentage of sales.

When revenues decrease over time, variable costs can usually be cut back proportionately. However, fixed costs, by definition, do not respond to changes in scale of operation, and hence the fixed cost becomes a greater percentage of the shrinking sales revenue amount. (For example, if a company produces and sells less, the landlord charges them the same amount of factory rent and so the rent expense becomes a greater percentage of the sales revenue amount.)

In the case of WorldCom, the "line-cost" was a very significant expense that had a fixed-cost element as well as a variable-cost element. Looking at Table 4.4, we see that revenue declined from $10.1 billion in the second quarter of 2000, to $8.9 billion in the second quarter of 2001, and to $8.1 billion in the first quarter of 2002. However, in Table 4.3 we see that the "line-cost" expense remained amazingly close to 41 percent throughout the period. It would have looked very suspicious if so much had been reallocated out of line costs that the expense actually declined as a percentage of sales. Nobody had checked to see why this expense with a fixed-cost element had remained suspiciously constant as sales revenue declined. We now know that WorldCom was calculating how much it needed to reduce expenses in order to hit profit targets. If necessary, the company would understate line costs down to the constant amount of close to 41 percent of sales revenue each quarter.

In fact, whenever any expense either fluctuates too wildly as a percentage of sales or keeps at a very constant percentage of sales, quarter after quarter, it is cause for some suspicion. When the expense that keeps constant to within a percentage of sales has a fixed-cost component, it becomes much more suspect that perhaps part of the expense is being recorded as an asset. When, in addition, the assets are growing at a faster rate than sales, it becomes probable that some expenses are being reported as assets. The signals combine to create a siren when, simultaneously, assets (like PPE at World-Com) grow, while sales actually decline, and expenses (like line costs at WorldCom) hold constant or decline as a percentage of sales. At WorldCom, these signals indicated that the line-cost expense was being misallocated as the asset PPE.

Signal #4: A fourth signal of misclassifying expenses as assets occurs when the notes to the financial statements indicate that the company is cap-italizing costs that other companies—in the same industry—expense. One can browse through a company's accounting policy note to look for such ev-idence. Although WorldCom's note did not reveal much, often the note will indicate that the company is capitalizing questionable costs. In general (although not in the case of WorldCom), these kinds of aggressive capital-izations of expenses occur in the areas of:

• Direct response advertising costs
• Customer acquisition costs and subscriber acquisition costs
• Software development costs
• Capitalized interest costs (which occur when interest is incurred on amounts invested in assets under construction). The interest must relate to the period beginning with construction costs and ending when the asset is complete and ready for service.

Signal #5: If a company changes its accounting policy to begin capital-izing a cost as an asset that was previously classified as an expense, it should alert the reader to the possibility of an aggressive capitalization policy, and to use all the signals in this chapter to test whether an expense has been mis-classified as an asset.

Signal #6: If, in the past, the company had a special charge in the income statement writing off a previously capitalized cost, this should be seen as a signal that the company could be aggressive in its approach to the classifica-tion of items as assets rather than expenses. (In 1989, Cendant Corp. had written off previously capitalized membership acquisition costs, long before the company's spectacular problems in 1997. In 1999, American Software had to write off previously capitalized software costs.)

It is important to note that for this particular fraud of misallocating ex-penses as fixed assets, CFFO lagging operating income is usually not as help-ful as it is in uncovering other frauds. The reason is that in the statement of cash flows, the fraud simultaneously overstates CFFO and the amount of cash used in investing activities. Therefore, this fraud makes it look as though the company did generate cash in its operating activities, but that it spent that cash on investing in fixed assets, like PPE. Thus, we have to rely more on the previously mentioned signals for this scam.

Are They Living Happily Ever After?

≈ **Bernard Ebbers,** former WorldCom CEO, was convicted of securities fraud, conspiracy to commit securities fraud, and false filings on March 17, 2005. He was sentenced to twenty-five years in prison. Ebbers was released on bail, pending appeal ("Enron Trial . . ." 2005). The appeals process commenced in November 2005 ("An Appeals Court . . ." 2005). As of May 2006 the appeal was still in progress.

≈ **Jack Grubman** "accepted a lifetime ban from the securities industry and paid a $15 million fine" (Guyon 2005). Grubman was never charged with any criminal misconduct relating to WorldCom.

≈ **David Myers,** former WorldCom controller, pleaded guilty to one count of conspiracy to commit securities fraud. In August 2005, he was sentenced to one year plus one day in prison and is currently at a medium-security facility in Mississippi ("WorldCom Ex-Controller . . ." 2005; *Bureau of Prisons* 2005).

≈ **Scott Sullivan,** former WorldCom CFO, pleaded guilty to three fraud-related counts on March 2, 2004. He was the chief witness for the prosecution in the trial of Bernard Ebbers. Sullivan reportedly admitted "that he repeatedly lied to the board about the company's financial plight and its fraudulent accounting maneuvers" ("WorldCom's Finance Chief . . ." 2005). Sullivan was sentenced to five years in prison, with his sentence commencing in November, 2005 ("Sullivan Gets Five Years . . ." 2005).

≈ **Betty Vinson** pleaded guilty to one count of conspiracy to commit securities fraud and one count of securities fraud. She was sentenced to five months in prison and five months home detention ("Ex-WorldCom Executive Sentenced . . ." 2005).

≈ **Buford Yates, Jr.,** pleaded guilty to one count of conspiracy to commit securities fraud. He was sentenced to one year plus one day in prison, with his sentence commencing in October 2005. He also received a fine of $5,000 ("Ex-WorldCom Exec Gets a Year . . ." 2005).

≈ **WorldCom** emerged from bankruptcy in April 2004, doing business as MCI. On January 6, 2006, Verizon Communications Inc. completed its merger with MCI. The new business unit is named Verizon Business ("Verizon Business"). The WorldCom Bankruptcy remains the largest bankruptcy in the history of the United States.

References

AAER 1585. *U.S. Securities and Exchange Commission* Accounting and Auditing Enforcement Release, June 27, 2002. www.sec.gov

AAER 1678. *U.S. Securities and Exchange Commission* Accounting and Auditing Enforcement Release, November 26, 2002. www.sec.gov

AAER 1966. *U.S. Securities and Exchange Commission* Accounting and Auditing Enforcement Release, March 2, 2004. www.sec.gov

AAER 1977. *U.S. Securities and Exchange Commission* Accounting and Auditing Enforcement Release, March 17, 2004. www.sec.gov/litigation/admin/33-8402.htm

"An Appeals Court is Urged to Uphold Ebbers Conviction," *New York Times,* November 12, 2005. www.nytimes.com

Bureau of Prisons Website. October 18, 2005. www.bop.gov

"Enron Trial to Highlight 2006 Corporate Scandal Cases," *Chicago Sun Times,* December 26, 2005. Available online via ProQuest database.

"Ex-WorldCom Exec Gets a Year in Prison," *Associated Press,* August 9, 2005. www.msnbc.com

"Ex-WorldCom Executive Sentenced to Prison," *Reuters,* August 5, 2005. www.msnbc.com

Faber, David. 2003. "The Big Lie: Inside the Rise and Fraud of WorldCom," *CNBC News Transcripts,* September 9. Available online via LexisNexis database.

First Interim Report of Dick Thornburgh, Bankruptcy Court Examiner. November 4, 2002. United States Bankruptcy Court Southern District of New York in re: WorldCom Inc. Case No. 02-13533 (AJG).

Guyon, Janet. 2005. "Jack Grubman Is Back. Just Ask Him." *Fortune,* May 16. www.money.cnn.com/magazines/fortune

Jeter, Lynne W. 2003. *Disconnected: Deceit and Betrayal at WorldCom.* Hoboken, New Jersey: John Wiley & Sons.

Krim, Jonathan. 2002. "Fast and Loose at WorldCom: Lack of Controls, Pressure to Grow Set Stage for Financial Deceptions," *Washington Post,* August 29.

LR 17753. *U.S. Securities and Exchange Commission* Litigation Release. September 26, 2002. www.sec.gov/litigation/litreleases.shtml

LR 17829. *U.S. Securities and Exchange Commission* Litigation Release. November 1, 2002. www.sec.gov/litigation/litreleases.shtml

LR 18277. *U.S. Securities and Exchange Commission* Litigation Release. August 7, 2003. www.sec.gov/litigation/litreleases.shtml

LR 18605. *U.S. Securities and Exchange Commission* Litigation Release.
March 2, 2004. www.sec.gov/litigation/litreleases.shtml

Malik, Om. 2003. *Broadbandits: Inside the $750 Billion Telecom Heist.*
Hoboken, New Jersey: John Wiley & Sons.

McCafferty, Joseph. 1998. "Scott Sullivan—WorldCom, Inc.," *CFO
Magazine,* September 1. www.cfo.com

"New York Judge Grants Ebbers Bail," *Associated Press,* September 7, 2005.
www.msnbc.msn.com

Pulliam, Susan, and Deborah Solomon. 2002. "Uncooking the Books,"
Wall Street Journal, October 30. Available online via ProQuest database.

Pulliam, Susan. 2005. "Crossing the Line: At Center of Fraud, WorldCom
Official Sees Life Unravel," *Wall Street Journal,* March 24.

Reaves, Gail. 2002. "Accounting for Anguish," *Fort Worth Weekly Online,*
May 16. www.fwweekly.com

Second Interim Report of Dick Thornburgh, Bankruptcy Court Examiner. June 9,
2003. United States Bankruptcy Court Southern District of New York
in re: WorldCom Inc. Case No. 02-13533 (AJG).

"Sullivan Gets Five Years for WorldCom Fraud," *Associated Press,* August 11,
2005. www.msnbc.com (accessed October 18, 2005).

Third and Final Report of Dick Thornburgh, Bankruptcy Court Examiner.
January 26, 2004. United States Bankruptcy Court Southern District of
New York in re: WorldCom Inc. Case No. 02-13533 (AJG).

United States of America v. Bernard J. Ebbers, Indictment S3 02 Cr. 1144
(BUS). www.usdoj.gov

"WorldCom Ex-Controller Gets a Year in Prison," *Associated Press,* August
10, 2005. www.msnbc.com

"Verizon Business," *News Release,* January 23, 2006.
http://newscenter.verizon.com

"WorldCom's Finance Chief Says He Lied," *The Los Angeles Times,*
February 20, 2005.

Chapter 5

Abracadabra

This chapter presents the unfortunate tales of:
- **Livent**
- **Rite Aid**
- **Allegheny (AHERF)**
- **Lockheed**

Livent: Phantom of the Finances

> Livent is presented mainly as an example of Improper Expense Recognition via:
>
> - Failure to record expenses
> - Improper deferral of expenses

Introduction

Livent Inc. was a Canadian theater company that originated in Toronto toward the end of the 1980s. It expanded quickly, and within a few years traded its stock on NASDAQ in the United States. Two of the main performers in the dramatic saga of Livent were its founders, Garth Drabinsky and Myron Gottlieb, who staged many large and lavish shows, such as *Ragtime, Showboat,* and *Phantom of the Opera.* Not satisfied with creating grand fantasies on stage, it seems they may have, according to the SEC, also performed some creative artifice on the company's financial statements.

In 1998, Livent was purchased by a U.S. consortium headed by Michael Ovitz, the well-known Hollywood icon. However, it did not take long before "the new owners said that they had uncovered accounting irregularities." Toward the end of 1998, Livent declared bankruptcy in both the United States and Canada. In January 1999, Drabinsky and Gottlieb were indicted in the United States "on 16 counts of fraud and conspiracy," but because they refused to face these charges in the United States and remained in Canada, they have been regarded as "fugitives" in the United States. In October 2002, "The

Royal Canadian Mounted Police said it filed 19 charges of fraud against the two men." The Royal Canadian Mounted Police also filed charges against two other Livent executives. Drabinsky and Gottlieb have denied both the U.S. and Canadian charges. (Quotes from Simon 2002)

Livent's alleged frauds are particularly interesting because they were implemented not only to present a better-looking overall income statement and balance sheet, which inflated the stock price, but the executives allegedly had reasons for wishing to make particular shows appear to be more successful than they really were. For instance, if *Ragtime*'s ticket sales fell below $500,000, the Schubert Theater (in Los Angeles) could evict the company. Further, if *Ragtime* was evicted, according to the SEC, this would have undermined its "later planned opening on Broadway" (AAER 1095, 1999). It therefore became important for Livent to report high ticket sales, even if the seats were not filled.

The Livent case is presented here because it contains some clear examples that alert the reader to the frequently committed, old-fashioned fraud of omitting expenses, and the corresponding liabilities, by simply failing to record invoices in the ledger during the correct period. This understates both expenses and liabilities and overstates earnings. Livent is also presented as a good example of the scheme of improperly deferring expenses via transferring costs from their correct accounts to other accounts in order to delay amortization.

The SOX Report's study of SEC enforcement actions found that the most common method of misstating financial reports was improper expense recognition via a "lack of accrual" of expenses and their corresponding liabilities. This is a subset of the SEC category described as "Failure to Record Expenses or Losses via Improper Capitalization/Deferral or Lack of Accrual" (SOX Report 13), which can actually be broken down into the following three components:

1. Failure to Record Expenses or Losses
2. Improper Deferral of Expenses or Losses
3. Improper Capitalization of Expenses or Losses

While WorldCom represents the leading and largest case of the "Improper Capitalization" part of this category, Livent is presented to complete the category in that it contains an interesting and illustrative example of the first and second components listed above. Livent's financial statements also contained some examples of the third component.

As is usually the case, the SEC findings also alleged other overlapping irregularities in Livent's financial reporting. The company understated some expenses by capitalizing them as assets, and moved expenses to different periods by transferring the expenses to different assets or theatrical shows, in order to amortize them more slowly and defer recognition of the expense. The SEC also found that Livent employees recorded revenues before they should have, by recognizing revenues that were subject to side agreements. In addition, they recorded fictitious ticket sales. Furthermore, the SEC found that Livent management was involved in a "kickback scheme designed to misappropriate funds for their own use" (AAER 1095, 1999).

An Overview of Livent's Fictitious Financial Reporting Schemes

Livent's manipulations were carefully orchestrated by senior management. After two controllers produced the general ledger each quarter, they gave the information to Gordon Eckstein, the former vice president of finance and administration, who summarized the information. The SEC alleged that Eckstein then met with Livent's top executives. At these meetings, they "agreed on the approximate nature and quantity of adjustments to be made . . . in order to achieve a predetermined false financial picture" (AAER 1095, 1999).[1] After the adjustments were completed, Eckstein met again with top management, with an adjusted general ledger, and further specific adjustments were directed.

The SEC states that senior management provided "approximate dollar adjustments that they were required to make to various accounts in the balance sheet and income statement, including expense categories, specific shows and fixed-asset accounts." In addition, the SEC found that Drabinsky, Livent's former CEO, and Gottlieb, the company's former president, ". . . from at least 1994 through the first quarter of 1998 . . . engaged in a deliberate manipulation of Livent's books and records." As a result of these manipulations, which were orchestrated together with other officers and employees of the company, expenses were understated for the purpose of inflating profits. There were many adjustments that they could not enter, however, because such adjustments "would have left a trail of 'red flags' for the auditors." Therefore, senior company officials had a special computer program designed that would enable accounting personnel to "override the accounting system without a paper or transaction trail." The Commission also maintained, "This process had the effect of falsifying the books, records and accounts of the company so completely that the adjustments appeared as

---

[1] Livent submitted an offer of settlement and consented to the entry of the order without admitting or denying the findings. As set out in AAER 1095, 1999.

original transactions, and no trace of the actual original entries remained in the company's general ledger." (Quotes from AAER 1095, 1999)

By means of the previously mentioned schemes, Livent's financial statements understated expenses in three ways, namely:

- They transferred production costs to fixed assets.
- They erased expense invoices from the accounting system.
- They deferred expenses by transferring costs from a current theatrical show to other shows, to defer amortizing the assets.

Scheme #1: Understatement of Expenses via Removing Invoices from the Records

Of particular interest for the financial reporting ploy of "failure to record expenses" was Livent's erasure of expense invoices. The SEC findings described the company's actions as follows:

> . . . at the end of each quarter, Livent simply removed certain expenses and the related liabilities from the general ledger, literally erasing them from the company's books. In the succeeding quarter, the expenses and related liabilities would be re-entered in the books as original entries. This blatant accounting manipulation violated the basic tenets of GAAP. The amount of expenses moved from current periods to future periods was tracked at Livent as the "Expense Roll." This manipulation permitted significant redirection in show expenses while also increasing profits. For example, the total expenses rolled from the first to the second quarter of 1997 was approximately $10 million. (AAER 1095, 1999)

Specific invoices were periodically identified as part of the effort to adjust reported profits. Then, on an "invoice-by-invoice basis," they were deleted from the accounting system. This understatement of expenses and liabilities of $10 million for the first quarter of 1997 was a significant part of the financial misstatements. The Commission found that, for 1997, Livent reported a pretax loss of $62.1 million, when its actual loss was a minimum of $83.6 million.

Scheme #2: Improper Deferral of Expenses

Livent also represents an example of the failure to record expenses or losses by means of improper deferral. In this instance, as is often the case, Livent achieved the deferral of expenses by moving the cost from one asset account to another one where the amortization could be delayed. This is a prevalent method of moving expenses from current periods to future periods. According to the SEC:

> . . . Livent transferred costs from one show currently running to another show that had not yet opened or that had a longer amortization period. This accounting manipulation increased profits in a particular quarter by reducing the charge for amortization of preproduction costs, since amortization is only appropriate once a production has begun. For example, in 1996 and 1997, approximately $12 million relating to seven different shows and twenty-seven different locations was transferred to the accounts of approximately thirty-one different future locations and ten other shows then in process. (AAER 1095, 1999)

Livent internally tracked the amortization moved in this manner from current periods to future periods under the clandestine label of the "Amortization Roll."

Variations on this scheme of deferring current expenses to later periods include extending the time period over which assets are amortized, and changes in accounting policies regarding the capitalization of costs. Two possible manipulations to look out for are changes regarding policies for the capitalization of software costs and the capitalization of pre-opening costs.

Scheme #3: Improper Capitalization of Expenses

Further, as an example of improper capitalization of expenses, Livent also "transferred preproduction costs for shows to fixed asset accounts such as the construction of the theaters." The WorldCom chapter in this book gives a detailed example of the leading fraud of this nature, namely, the capitalization of expenses as assets, which overstates a company's assets on the balance sheet and understates its expenses. Livent's preproduction costs should have been expensed through amortization once the shows began, over the life of the shows up to a period of not more than five years. However, fixed assets were amortized over periods up to forty years. In 1997, Livent transferred preproduction costs and operating expenses "totaling $15 million from six different shows in thirty locations to three different fixed asset accounts." (Quotes from AAER 1095, 1999)

Miscellaneous Schemes

In addition to finding that Livent understated expenses in the previously noted matters, the SEC also found that Livent misstated revenues. During 1996 and 1997, Livent recognized $34 million of revenue on transactions that utilized side agreements that required Livent to repay the revenues that it received. (This is an example of either improperly timed revenue if a later transaction with full economic substance materializes, or fictitious revenue if there is no intention of finalizing a proper transaction later on.)

Further, in an effort to make the Los Angeles production of *Ragtime* look more successful, senior management of Livent arranged for outside associates to purchase approximately $381,000 of tickets on personal credit cards, and to make future ticket purchases using personal checks. The amounts were reimbursed to these individuals' companies and recorded as Livent's payments for fixed assets. This is a clear example of both reporting fictitious revenue as well as overstating assets. Also, even before Livent was a listed company in the United States, the SEC alleged that "between 1990 and 1994, Drabinsky and Gottlieb received approximately $7 million through [a] kickback scheme" where they got outside individuals to inflate invoices to Livent, which Livent paid, and for which approximately $7 million was kicked back to Drabinsky and Gottlieb (AAER 1095, 1999).

All in all, as a result of an independent investigation by KPMG Peat Marwick, Livent restated its financial statements for the years 1996 through the first quarter of 1998, and these restatements resulted "in a cumulative adverse effect on net income in excess of $98 million (Canadian). When trading briefly resumed following restatement, Livent stock plummeted over ninety-five percent from $6.75 (US) per share to approximately $ .28 cents per share and a loss of $100 million (US) in market capitalization" (AAER 1095, 1999). The Commission further claimed that for each of Livent's years as a U.S. public company, Livent either reported inflated pretax earnings or understated it pretax losses:

> For fiscal 1995, Livent reported pre-tax earnings of $18 million. In fact, the company's true earnings were approximately $15 million. For fiscal 1996, Livent reported pre-tax earnings of $14.2 million. In fact the company earned a loss of more that $20 million in that year. For fiscal 1997, Livent reported a pre-tax loss of $62.1 million. In fact the company's true loss in fiscal 1997 was at least $83.6 million. (AAER 1095, 1999)

Signals of Livent's Fictitious Reporting Scheme #1:

- Understating Expenses and the Corresponding Liabilities via Lack of Accrual by simply omitting the recording of the expenses in the current period.[2]

---

[2] Since signals for Improper Recognition of Revenue are thoroughly discussed in Chapter 2, 'The Sizzling Saga of Sunbeam," this section will focus on the signals of the Understatements of Expenses and Liabilities.

Signal #1: As with any understatement of expenses, test each category of expense as a percentage of sales to see whether it represents either a decreasing percentage compared to previous quarters or periods, or whether the expense is a smaller percentage of sales than the average for the industry. Also, if a category of expense has a significant fixed-cost element, and the expense remains the same percentage of sales as sales decrease, it is an indication that some of the fixed expenses may not be recorded. Fixed costs increase as a percentage of sales when sales volume declines.

Signal #2: When the company first omits recording expenses and current liabilities, this omission will decrease the company's current liabilities as a percentage of current assets and as a percentage of sales. Such a change could, of course, be the result of an improvement in efficiency or of legitimately paying off current liabilities earlier, for example, by obtaining a long-term loan. However, if the decrease in current liabilities does not seem to be explained by efficiency or by a form of longer-term financing on the balance sheet and Signal #1 is also in force—that is, expenses show a decrease as a percentage of sales—the warning signs get stronger.

The existence of both signals could be a strong alert that there has been a failure to record expenses and the corresponding liabilities. With these frauds, attempts should be made to locate these signals early on. Although the initial omissions of the expenses decrease reported expenses and liabilities, it must be remembered that the expense is "rolled" forward to later periods, with the result that later periods' expenses will not appear small, relative to sales, to the extent that they include the previous period's omitted expenses.

Signal #3: If one has access to the company's internal records, lack of accrual can be tested by selecting vendors that the firm does business with, checking that they are on the list of accounts payable, and then reconciling the amount accrued with the vendors' statement of amounts owing. To test for an unrecorded liability, it is pointless to start with the list of current liabilities recorded by the firm and simply checking those amounts. It is vital to remember that the test is for understatement, and so it has to begin from the origin—for example, choosing a known vendor and tracing that vendor to the list of accounts payable that supports the amount listed on the final record, which is the balance sheet.

If one does not have access to the company's internal records, one has to rely on alerts, such as the signals mentioned earlier, from the published financial statements. However, when a firm omits recording its expenses and liabilities, it often also understates expenses by capitalizing them as fixed assets and deferring them to later periods. Therefore, being alert to the signals of those misstatements will strengthen the overall alert for this method of understatement of expenses.

Signals of Livent's Fictitious Reporting Scheme #2:

• Understating Expenses via Deferral of the Expenses.

Signal #1: If deferred costs or prepaid expenses increase significantly as a percentage of total assets, it could be a sign that operating expenses are being capitalized.

Signal #2: As with Scheme #1 (omitting expenses), if a category of expense decreases as a percentage of sales compared to the industry, or compared to previous periods, it is an alert that part of the expense may be deferred to future periods.

Signal #3: If an accounting policy note to the financial statements indicates that an asset is being depreciated or amortized over a longer period than in the past, or over longer periods than the average for the industry, it is a red flag that the company may be aggressive in deferring the current cost to future periods.

Signal #4: When there is a worry about the possibility of aggressive deferral of expenses by means of recording them as assets (e.g., preproduction costs recorded as assets), test the ratio of the deferred assets to sales in comparison to companies in a comparable situation, taking into account the stage in the life cycle of the companies and the logic of the deferment as described in the accounting policy notes.

Signals of Livent's Fictitious Reporting Scheme #3:

• Understating Expenses via Capitalization of the Expenses.[3]

Signal #1: Compare the asset-turnover ratio and the fixed-asset turnover ratio of the company to that of the industry, and to that of the company in

---

[3] For a thorough discussion of the signals for this fraud, see the discussion in Chapter 4, "WorldCom Wizardry." WorldCom is the leading example of this kind of fraud.

previous periods. If the ratio is lower than that of the industry average, or if it is decreasing, it is an indication that some expenses may be recorded as assets, or that the investment in assets is not efficient in that it is not producing sufficient revenue.

Signal #2: Be on the alert for notes to the financial statements that indicate that there has been a change in policy regarding the capitalization of costs. (This signal was not present in the case of Livent, since the SEC found that Livent contradicted its own accounting policy description when it miscapitalized costs.) However, a note regarding a change in capitalization policy is often a blatant signal regarding an aggressive accounting change to decrease recorded expenses.

Signal #3: One must definitely be on the alert for aggressive capitalization of costs when a company writes off costs that were formerly capitalized. (According to Mulford and Comiskey (2002), a good example of possible aggressive accounting with regard to capitalization policies is American Software, which capitalized the majority of its software costs in 1997, wrote down a large amount of capitalized software costs in 1999, and then increased the percentage amount capitalized again in 2000.)

Signal #4: Read the notes to the financial statements to compare the company's capitalization policy to the capitalization policy of other companies in the same industry. If a company capitalizes costs that other companies in the industry do not capitalize, it could be an alert that the company may be aggressive in capitalizing expenses.

Are They Living Happily Every After?

≈ **Garth Drabinsky and Myron Gottlieb** were ordered to pay $23 million in damages in a civil ruling issued in New York on February 4, 2005. According to news reports, the two men have a strong motivation to stay in Canada: "If they were to enter the U.S. the pair would find themselves in more hot water. They also have 16 outstanding fraud and insider trading charges . . ." (Tillson 2005). In addition, the Royal Canadian Mounted Police have charged the Livent executives with fraud. A Canadian trial is scheduled to begin only in March 2007 (Heinzl 2005).

RITE AID: "THE KEYS TO THE KINGDOM"

> Rite Aid is presented mainly as an example of Overstating Ending
> Inventory Values to reduce cost of goods sold.

Introduction

Founded by Alex Grass in 1962 in the town of Scranton, Pennsylvania,
Rite Aid grew from a single drugstore to one of the biggest pharmacy conglomerates in the United States, operating over 3,500 stores across the country. In February 1995, Alex Grass handed what he reportedly called "the
keys to the kingdom" to his eldest son, Martin Grass, who became CEO of
Rite Aid. Several years earlier, Martin's younger brother, Roger, had resigned
from his position as a senior vice president at Rite Aid because "he recognized that the top job would go to a brother he considered incompetent."
(Quotes from Berner and Maremont 1999)

Less than five years after taking charge of Rite Aid, Martin Grass was
fired, and that same week, an article in the *Wall Street Journal* remarked:
"With his departure, the eldest son of company founder Alex Grass leaves
behind a legacy that is just short of disastrous" (Berner and Maremont 1999).

According to the grand jury, Rite Aid was riddled with "massive accounting fraud, the deliberate falsification of financial statements, and intentionally
false SEC filings" (quoted in "8-Year Sentence" 2002). Documents from the
SEC alleged that for over two years—from the fiscal year 1998 through the
first quarter of 2000—Rite Aid overstated its net income, and former senior
management failed to disclose material information, including related-party
transactions in 1999 (AAER 1579, 2002). The SEC maintained that Rite
Aid's resulting restatements in July and October of 2000—in which the company restated reported cumulative pretax income by a total of $2.3 billion and
restated cumulative net income by $1.6 billion—represented "the largest
financial restatement of income by a public company" at the date of that
report (AAER 1579, 2002). (Note that since then, WorldCom's restatement
has substantially dwarfed Rite Aid's restatement.)

While Rite Aid did understate various expenses, most of its understatement of expense, by far, was its understatement of cost of goods sold. Rite
Aid represents a leading example of overstating earnings via understating
cost of goods sold. It manipulated cost of goods sold through a number of
mechanisms.

Rite Aid's Fictitious Financial Reporting Schemes
Scheme #1: Overstating Ending Inventory Values to Reduce Cost of Goods Sold

One of the three most significant methods that Rite Aid used to understate its cost of goods sold amount was that it overstated its ending inventory by failing to write-down its inventory amount for the full amount of the "shrinkage" that it suffered. This method did not account for the largest dollar amount in its understatement of cost of goods sold, but it is presented first, because understating cost of goods sold by overstating ending inventory values is a very prevalent financial-reporting fraud. The SOX Report found that this method of improper expense recognition accounted for twenty-five SEC enforcement matters in the study period.

Rite Aid conducted periodic physical inventory counts at many of its stores. To the extent that the physical count revealed less inventory on hand than reflected in its records, Rite Aid's official policy, of course, was to write-down its inventory amount in its records via a "shrink" expense on the assumption that the difference was due to theft or loss. The Commission's findings alleged: "In FY [fiscal year] 1999, Rite Aid failed to record $8.8 million in shrink." For those stores in which Rite Aid did not conduct a physical inventory count, Rite Aid's policy was to estimate a shrink amount and accrue that amount. The Commission further alleged:"In FY 1999, Rite Aid improperly reduced the accrued shrink expense for 2,000 stores resulting in an aggregate increase to income of $5 million." Thus, in total, pretax income for 1999 was allegedly overstated by $13.8 million, due to overstating ending inventory by not recognizing the full amount of its shrinkage.

Scheme #2: Adjusting Gross Profit Entries to Reduce Cost of Goods Sold

Of all its manipulations to cost of goods sold and net income, Rite Aid's manipulation of cost of goods sold via adjusting "gross profit" journal entries represented the biggest dollar amount of its distortions by far, and also its most brazen. Rite Aid simply would put through journal entries decreasing cost of goods sold, and decreasing accounts payable by a corresponding amount. These entries were known internally as "gross profit entries," and according to the SEC, they were "determined by one person without input or review by anyone and were completely unsubstantiated."[4] The size of these adjustments was staggering. The most egregious entries were in the

---

[4] Rite Aid consented to the issuance of the order without admitting or denying the findings contained herein. As set out in AAER 1579, 2002.

second quarter of the 1999 fiscal year, and the SEC found that Rite Aid allegedly "improperly reduced cost of goods sold and accounts payable by approximately $100 million." It is interesting to note that in each of the years that Rite Aid adjusted its cost of goods sold in this way, it did this for the first three quarters of the year, and then always reversed the entries in the fourth quarter of each year. The reversal led Rite Aid to find new adjustments in the fourth quarter to offset the reversal. One of these adjustments was the misstatement of the inventory "shrink," discussed previously, and another was Rite Aid's treatment of vendor rebates. (Quotes from AAER 1579, 2002)

Scheme #3: Improper Recognition of Vendor Rebates to Reduce Cost of Goods Sold

Rite Aid was entitled to receive rebates on amounts owing to certain vendors, contingent upon Rite Aid's sales of the vendors' products. Of course, in its income statement, Rite Aid should have applied the rebate only to purchases relating to goods that it had already sold. The SEC stated that, regarding $77 million of such refunds that Rite Aid recognized for the 1999 fiscal year, the sales had not yet occurred. Additionally, the purchasing agreements had not yet been legally finalized. Nevertheless, on the last day of the 1999 fiscal year, Rite Aid reduced cost of goods sold and accounts payable by $42 million, and in the same way reopened its books to recognize the other $33 million of these rebates after the close of the 1999 fiscal year. The Commission noted quite pertinently that, at that particular stage, it "was readily apparent that the Company's results would fall short of Wall Street analysts' projections. These entries violated GAAP because the credits were unearned as of FY 1999" (AAER 1579, 2002).

Other Rite Aid Manipulations

According to the SEC, Rite Aid also employed a number of other methods to overstate its reported income. One ploy it used was that it failed to write off capitalized costs, like legal services and title searches in respect of possible new stores, when it determined not to construct such stores. Another alleged Rite Aid ruse, according to the Commission, was regarding the company's "will call" accounts payable. A number of prescription medications had been ordered but not collected by Rite Aid customers. Rite Aid, however, had been paid for these medications by the customers' insurance carriers. Instead of returning the payments to the insurance companies, Rite Aid reversed the accounts payable into profit "without sufficient justification or basis in violation of GAAP. Ultimately, the accrual was re-established and the $6.6 million attributable to the will-call payable was repaid to the insurance carriers" (AAER 1579, 2002).

The SEC also found that Rite Aid allegedly failed to properly accrue an expense each quarter with respect to the stock appreciation rights (SARS) that the company granted to certain field managers. Each quarter, Rite Aid should have accrued an expense based on the market price of its stock at the end of the quarter. The Commission found that in fiscal years 1998 and 1999, Rite Aid allegedly "should have recorded an accrued expense of approximately $22 and $33 million respectively" (AAER 1579, 2002).

The SEC's summary of Rite Aid's overstatement of pretax income is presented in Table 5.1.

Table 5.1 Summary of Rite Aid's FY 1998, FY 1999 and 1st Quarter FY 2000 Overstatements of Pre-tax Income*

The quantifiable effect of Rite Aid's practices in the above-described areas on Rite Aid's reported pre-tax income are summarized below:

	1st Q FY 1998	2nd Q FY 1998	3rd Q FY 1998	FY 1998	1st Q FY 1999	2nd Q FY 1999	3rd Q FY 1999	FY 1999	1st Q FY 2000
Reported Pre-tax Income	114.3	101.5	113.7	530.0	151.3	135.2	144.7	199.6	141.1
Adjustments									
Corporate Entries									17.5
Retail Entries	0.0	9.0	(4.0)		1.0	12.2	1.7		8.0
Gross Profit Entries	25.3	26.2	5.9		47.1	100.4	39.6		23.8
Undisclosed Up-charge	2.6	1.7	1.5	7.6	5.9	6.5	7.0	27.8	
Undisclosed Markdowns								29.7	
Vendor Rebates								75.6	
Litigation Settlement								17.0	
Dead Deals								10.6	
SARS	3.4	3.6	12.6	22.1	9.0	13.7	21.9	33.2	
Will-Call Payables								6.6	
Inventory Shrink								13.8	
Depreciation				14.6					
Total Adjustments	31.3	40.5	16.0	44.3	63.0	132.8	70.2	214.3	49.3
Corrected Pre-tax Income/(Loss)	83.0	61.0	97.7	485.7	88.3	2.4	74.5	(14.7)	91.8
Overstatement Percentage	38%	66%	16%	9%	71%	5533%	94%	N/A	54%

*From AAER 1579, 2002.

Signals of Rite Aid's Fictitious Reporting Schemes #1–#3:

- Reducing Cost of Goods Sold

Rite Aid's three methods of understating cost of goods sold all produce similar signals. Overstating inventory to reduce cost of goods sold, as well as other methods of understating cost of goods sold, affects similar key ratios. For instance, inventory as a percentage of cost of goods sold increases when cost of goods sold is understated, and this occurs whether the reduction of cost of goods sold is achieved by the overstatement of inventory or by another means. The ratio is, of course, distorted by an even greater amount if ending inventory is overstated. Therefore, the signals for the various methods of understating cost of goods will be considered together.

Signal #1: When inventory increases as a percentage of cost of goods sold (COGS), it is an indication that inventory could be overstated, and COGS could be understated. This measure is calculated or presented in a number of different ways. The inventory turnover ratio is a common measure, and is calculated as follows:

$$COGS \div \text{average inventory}$$

Another frequently used measure is the number of "days sales in inventory," which is calculated as follows:

$$365 \div \text{inventory turnover ratio}$$

If the inventory turnover ratio decreases, or if days sales in inventory increases, it is an indication of possible overstatement of inventory and understatement of COGS. If this ratio increases significantly, even if the cause is not the actual overstatement of inventory, it is an alert to the fact that sales are not keeping up with production.

Signal #2: Sudden, significant decreases in gross margin as a percentage of sales are indications of possible overstatements of inventory and understatement of COGS. Sudden changes (either increases or decreases) should be accompanied by simple, logical explanations, such as, for example, a new manufacturing technique, or a change in the selling price. The Management Discussion and Analysis (MD&A) section of the Annual Report ought to explain significant changes in the gross-margin percentage measure. Without clear explanations, suspicion and skepticism should be aroused.

Signal #3: When the reserve for the obsolescence or shrinkage of inventory decreases as a percentage of inventory, it is a signal that the company may be overstating its inventory by understating its reserve for obsolescence or shrinkage. (According to Schilit (2002), Lucent Technologies represents a major example of this signal. Its inventory grew by over 40 percent between 1997 and 1999; however, the amount of its reserve for obsolescence of inventory actually declined over the same period.)

Signal #4: As is so often the case, cash flow from operations (CFFO) falling below operating income or net income is always a useful signal that profit may be misreported. In the case of Rite Aid, CFFO changed from being *greater* than net income in 1997, to significantly *less* than net income in 1998. In fact, after adjustments for nonrecurring charges, Rite Aid's net income for the first quarter of the 1998 fiscal year was $81.2 million, while it's CFFO for that same quarter was *negative* $77.5 million. This signal, in itself, ought to have broadcast a warning to anyone examining that set of Rite Aid's financial statements.

Are They Living Happily Ever After?

≈ **Martin Grass,** former CEO of Rite Aid, pleaded guilty to a conspiracy charge, and in May 2004, Judge Sylvia Rambo sentenced him to eight years of imprisonment ("8-Year Sentence" 2004). He is serving his sentence in federal prisons in Florida. In August 2005, Judge Rambo reduced his sentence by one year. According to reports, Grass is a model prisoner (Scolforo 2005).

≈ **Franklin C. Brown,** former vice chair and chief counsel, was found guilty of playing a major role in the Rite Aid case and sentenced to 10 years of imprisonment (Scolforo 2005). Citing Brown's advanced age, 76, his attorneys described the sentencing as "a de facto death sentence" (Scolforo 2004).

≈ **Several other Rite Aid executives** received lesser sentences.

ALLEGHENY (AHERF): TRICK OR TREATMENT?

Allegheny (AHERF) is presented mainly as an example of Understating Reserves for Bad Debts.

Introduction

The Allegheny Health Education & Research Foundation (AHERF) was described by the SEC Enforcement Files as a collection of non-profit acute-care hospitals, with a medical university, physicians groups, and other affiliated entities. AHERF grew very rapidly from its inception, in Pittsburgh in 1983, to the largest nonprofit health-care provider in Pennsylvania, before its sudden decline and bankruptcy in July 1998. The SEC subsequently found that AHERF and some of its subsidiaries, collectively known as Delaware Valley, allegedly "issued annual financial statements and municipal disclosure reports that materially misrepresented, among other things, AHERF's and Delaware Valley's net income" (AAER 1283, 2000).

AHERF's swift growth came at the expense of large debt, and along with the debt came the pressure to appear financially stable. When a company appears to be in a financially stressful situation, this can instigate a vicious circle of driving up interest rates for future borrowing and difficulty in obtaining future financing. This, in turn, can increase the likelihood of debt repayments being demanded, which can eventually lead to bankruptcy. Due to such an environment of high debt, the SEC concluded that "AHERF, through certain of its senior officers, and in violation of applicable accounting principles, misstated its financial statements and schedules" (AAER 1283, 2000).

As a holding company, AHERF did not assume liability for the preexisting debt of its acquired entities. The obligation to repay debt was placed on the non-profit "obligated groups" known collectively as Delaware Valley. AHERF's obligated groups were responsible for over $900 million of debt by the time of the bankruptcy in 1998. The misstated reports, in this case, went beyond annual financial statements and included municipal securities disclosure reports known as Nationally Recognized Municipal Securities Information Repositories. In a speech to the AICPA National Healthcare Industry Conference in August 2000, SEC attorney Stephen Weinstein pointed out that "the Disclosure Reports were made available to the public through the Repositories and were the most easily accessible source of information for investors and potential investors in AHERF bonds."

AHERF's Fictitious Financial Reporting Scheme of Understating Bad Debts

According to the SEC, during 1996 AHERF's senior management became aware that there were significant problems with the collection of Delaware Valley's patient accounts receivable. They were also aware of the considerable growth in the amount of these accounts receivable, and they attempted to solve the problem with changes in management. However, the SEC found that, as early as October 1996, "AHERF decided to write off approximately $81 million in Delaware Valley patient accounts receivable."[5] To do this, the company needed to increase the bad debt reserve on the June 30, 1996, financial statements in which the reserve was short of this amount by approximately $40 million. It should have increased that reserve by $40 million, and recognized the expense of $40 million in the income statement. However, AHERF did not adjust its 1996 financial statements, and instead, decided to write off the uncollectible accounts receivable in quarterly installments. The SEC found that in the audited financial statements as well as the Disclosure Report distributed by AHERF to the public, properly adjusting the bad debt reserve of Delaware Valley would have "reduced its reported net income of $27 million before extraordinary item and change in accounting principle by approximately $40 million and similarly reduced its reported net accounts receivable figure of $253 million by approximately $40 million." Furthermore, the MD&A section of the AHERF Disclosure Report "implied that the $72.2 million increase in Delaware Valley accounts receivable during fiscal year 1996 was a temporary phenomenon that would resolve itself." (Quotes from AAER 1283, 2000).

AHERF'S Other Fabrications

The SEC also found that AHERF inappropriately transferred $99.6 million of reserves from the various hospitals to Delaware Valley in 1997, to avoid recognizing the expense in its income statement when it had to write off accounts receivable and did not have a sufficient bad debt reserve. Also in 1997, AHERF overstated its reported consolidated net income by incorrectly recognizing over $54 million of irrevocable trusts' income as its own income.

Signals of AHERF's Fictitious Reporting Scheme of:

• Understating Bad Debts.

Signal #1: When a company fails to recognize its bad debts by failing to increase the reserve for bad debts, the net accounts receivable is larger than it should be. This is likely to show up in ratios that measure accounts receivable as a percentage of sales, for example, an increase in days' sales outstanding (DSO).

Signal #2: When the reserve for bad debts decreases as a percentage of accounts receivable, it is an indication that the company may be understating

---

[5] AHERF consented to the entry of the findings and the issuance of the order without admitting or denying the findings. As set out in AAER 1283, 2000.

its bad debt reserve. If the reserve or allowance for doubtful debts decreases while the gross amount for receivables increases, consider that a red alert.

Signal #3: When net accounts receivable increase as a percentage of total current assets, it could be a signal that the company is not writing off bad debts, or is not appropriately determining its reserve for doubtful debts.

Signal #4: When a company does not appropriately recognize an expense, the CFFO lags behind operating income or net income. Bad debts that are not written off represent operating profit that was recognized in the income statement but should be expensed out because the profit will not be liquidated—that is, the accounts receivable asset will not be paid and will not turn into a cash asset. Therefore, this will show up in the form of CFFO being less than operating profit if it is not disguised by some further misstatement in the statement of cash flows.

Are They Living Happily Ever After?

≈ **Sherif Abdelhak,** former CEO of AHERF, "pleaded no contest" to charges of raiding the company's charitable endowments in order to bolster AHERF's deteriorating health-care system. In August 2002, he received up to twenty-three months in prison (Becker 2002). After serving three months of his sentence, Abdelhak was released on parole (Becker 2003).

≈ **David McConnell,** former CFO of AHERF, was placed on twelve months' probation in September 2001. He was also given 150 hours of community service and ordered to pay $16,700 in compensation for "spending AHERF funds on a luxury box at Three Rivers Stadium in Pittsburgh" ("Pennsylvania Attorney General" 2002).

LOCKHEED: SKY HIGH[6]

> Lockheed is presented mainly as an example of Failing to Record Impairments of Assets.

Introduction

As jet-travel boomed in the sixties, there was such a demand by the airlines for larger, wide-bodied jets to carry more passengers that two large

---

[6] Background information in this section is mainly from "Lockheed L-1011 TriStar," "Lockheed L-1011 TriStar History" (2003), Mondout and Willatt (1970), and Schilit (2002).

airline manufacturing companies, McDonnell Douglas and Lockheed, went ahead with plans to design similar aircrafts with similar ranges and load capacities. While McDonnell Douglas launched its DC-10 project, Lockheed began its design and production of the TriStar. Although pilots and aviator enthusiasts still rank the TriStar's performance and safety record highly, the ambitious and costly TriStar program was dogged with financial problems almost from its outset.

As gas prices soared in the seventies, and demand for air travel fell, it became clear that there was only enough traffic for one of the new plane designs. By this time, however, too many sunk costs had already been invested in the production of the aircrafts. As Patrick Mondout summed it up: "Even if the L-1011 [TriStar] was 'technically superior' to the DC-10, it cost more to purchase and more per passenger mile than its competitor." Furthermore, Lockheed's initial estimates were that the break-even point on the TriStar would be sales of 300 aircraft. However, with cost overruns, the break-even point required, in fact, sales of 500 aircraft.

Lockheed's problems with the TriStar originally began with its choice of the British Rolls-Royce RB-211 engine for its new plane. Interestingly, David Huddie, head of Rolls-Royce's Aero Engine Department at that time, later received a knighthood from the Queen of England for securing the contract to supply the engine for the TriStar. However, the Rolls-Royce engine was itself still in the design stage, and the costs for this engine skyrocketed long before it was ready to propel an aircraft. Lockheed therefore had to carry a share of the climbing Rolls-Royce costs, while its own development costs were growing well over budget.

In December 1970, the TriStar took off from Palmdale, California, on its very first flight. That same year, Rolls-Royce was driven into quasi-bankruptcy which, according to some sources, was a result of the TriStar project. The entire venture was now in jeopardy, and for the program to continue, it took the combined efforts of the British government taking over Rolls-Royce, as well as the United States providing a federal guarantee for Lockheed to receive a $250 million line of credit.

Ultimately, Lockheed's accounting tale is the story of misstating earnings by failing to write off an "impaired" asset, which was the development cost of its TriStar L-1011 wide-body jet. This evidently inadvertent accounting failure certainly drew the attention of the shareholders when the company suddenly wrote off over $700 million of the TriStar's development costs in 1981, after the program had been losing a fortune for years.

Lockheed's Failure to Account for Asset Impairments

Lockheed had an accounting policy in which it capitalized TriStar's development costs, with the intention of writing them off as the planes were sold. The company estimated the total development costs as well as the total number of TriStar aircraft that it would sell, and then calculated an average development cost per airplane. As each aircraft was sold, this average development cost was expensed, and a corresponding amount was written off the development-cost asset.

By late 1975, Lockheed had capitalized $500 million in TriStar development costs (Schilit 2002). The TriStar program was making losses and continued to do so. It became clear that the future sales were not going to be made at a profit, and that this "asset" was impaired and needed to be written off. However, instead of writing off the entire $500 million, Lockheed wrote off the amount in installments of $50 million annually. The TriStar program lost over $900 million up to 1981, when Lockheed finally wrote off the remaining amount of this impaired asset in one lump sum of $400 million (Mondout, "Lockheed L-1011"). By the end of 1983, when Lockheed ceased production of the TriStar, only 250 planes had been built, far short of the break-even point of approximately 500 aircraft ("Lockheed L-1011 TriStar").

Lockheed's delay in writing off the impaired asset caused both assets and earnings to be overstated for the duration of the delay.

Signals of Lockheed's Failure to Record Asset Impairments

Signal #1: When the development of a product or a program is accompanied by the recording of a material, intangible asset such as development costs or start-up costs, and the product or program hits scheduling problems and runs at a loss, it is a strong indication that the associated asset is impaired and should be written off. The indication that a product or program associated with the intangible asset is making a loss can often be found in press articles, in notes to the financial statements, in the segmented income statement, or in the Management Discussion and Analysis (MD&A). In Lockheed's case, press articles pointing toward the losses of the TriStar program were abundant, and the capitalization of significant development costs for the program were clearly indicated on the balance sheet and on notes to the financial statements. This signal ought to have alerted users of the financial statements to the possibility that, eventually, Lockheed would have to recognize a huge expense to write off this asset.

Signal #2: When there are material intangible assets and a company is making a loss overall, it is an indication that the intangible assets are impaired. Although this signal is not always clear as to which assets are impaired, it is logical to assume that the purpose of assets overall is to produce future profits, and if they are not producing profits currently, it is an indication that they might not produce them in the future. It can even be argued that if a company is not likely to produce a super-normal return on its tangible assets, the net value of all its intangible assets is zero. Certainly a company cannot continue to make losses indefinitely, and if it goes into bankruptcy, or scraps a segment, certain intangible assets—like development costs, start-up costs, and goodwill—will not be saleable.

Signal #3: When a company's asset-turnover ratio declines, either for a category of assets or for total assets, it is an indication that the assets may be impaired. When the sales-to-total-assets ratio declines, or the ratio of sales to a specific asset declines, the user of financial statements should be alert to the possibility that either some assets are failing to achieve their objectives (and the assets may be impaired), or that the assets should not have been capitalized in the first place.

Signal #4: Accounting policy notes to the financial statements that indicate the company has a policy that is slower than other companies in the industry to write off assets—such as development costs, or start-up costs—should alert the reader to the possibility that the company is aggressive in its efforts to overstate the value of assets. Such aggressive policies often include the failure to record the impairment of assets.

Signal #5: Restructuring charges in a current period can indicate that the company failed to recognize impairments of assets in previous periods. Always carefully scrutinize the notes explaining restructuring changes. If there is an indication that the company failed to write off assets that were impaired previously, it may be an indication that the company is in the habit of being aggressive in overstating its earnings by failing to recognize the impairment of its assets.

Are They Living Happily Ever After?

≈ **Lockheed** was embroiled in a minor scandal in 1985 when Congress learned that the Department of Defense had purchased new toilet seats for some of its planes and Lockheed had charged $640 for each seat ("Flying by Their Seats" 1985).

≈ **Lockheed** merged with Martin Marietta Corp. in 1995 to form one of the largest aerospace companies in the world.

≈ **Lockheed Martin** was ranked 47th in the 2005 list of *Fortune* 500 companies (Lockheed Martin website).

References

"8-Year Sentence for Rite Aid Exec," *CBSNEWS.com*, May 27, 2004. www.cbsnews.com

AAER 1095. *Securities and Exchange Commission.* Accounting and Auditing Enforcement Release, January 13, 1999. www.sec.gov

AAER 1283. *Securities and Exchange Commission* Accounting and Auditing Enforcement Release, June 30, 2000. www.sec.gov

AAER 1579. *Securities and Exchange Commission* Accounting and Auditing Enforcement Release, June 21, 2002. www.sec.gov

Becker, C. 2002. "No Contest for Ex-AHERF Chief: Sherif Abdelhak Defends Himself, Stating He Intended to Keep the Healthcare System Open for Patients and Employees," September 2. www.ncbi.nlm.nih.gov

Becker, Cinda. 2003. "Early Release: Abdelhak Wins Parole after Serving 3 Months," February 3. *Modern Healthcare.* www.modernhealthcare.com

Berner, Robert, and Mark Maremont. 1999. "Lost Heir," *The Wall Street Journal* (Eastern edition), October 20, A1. Available online via ProQuest database.

"Flying by Their Seats," *The Wall Street Journal,* July 29, 1985. Available online via ProQuest database.

Heinzl, Mark. 2005. "Slow Canada: Fraud Cases Can Drag On," *The Wall Street Journal,* October 27. Available online via ProQuest database.

Levitt, Arthur. 1998. "The Numbers Game." Remarks at NYU Center for Law and Business, New York, N.Y. September 28.

"Lockheed L-1011 TriStar," *Airliners.net.* www.airliners.net/info/stats.main?id=271

"Lockheed L-1011 TriStar History," *GlobalSecurity.org,* August 25, 2003. www.globalsecurity.org

Lockheed Martin website. www.lockheedmartin.com

Massey, Steve. 1999. "Anatomy of a Bankruptcy. Part I: Wake Up to Break Up," *Post-gazette.com*, January 17. www.postgazette.com

Mondout, Patrick. "Lockheed L-1011," *Super70s.com.* www.super70s.com

Mulford, Charles W., and Eugene E. Comiskey. 2002. *The Financial Numbers Game: Detecting Creative Accounting Practices.* New York: John Wiley & Sons.

"Pennsylvania Attorney General Fisher: Former AHERF Official Pleads to Raiding Endowments; CEO Sentenced to 11 1/2—23 Months," August 29, 2002. www.biobn.com.

Schilit, Howard. 2002. *Financial Shenanigans.* 2nd edition. New York: McGraw Hill.

Scolforo, Mark. 2004. "Former Rite Aid Vice Chairman Sentenced to 10 Years in Fraud Case," *The Daily Item,* October 15. www.dailyitem.com

Scolforo, Mark. 2005. "Judge Cuts a Year from Rite Aid Chief Grass' Sentence," *The SanDiego Union Tribune,* August 11. www.signonsandiego.com

Simon, Bernard. 2002. "Theater Founders are Charged with Fraud," *New York Times* (Late edition East Coast), October 23, C2. Available online via ProQuest database.

SOX Report. *Report Pursuant to Section 704 of the Sarbanes-Oxley Act of 2002.* www.sec.gov/news/studies/sox704report.pdf

Tillson, Tamsen. 2005. "Legit Plot Twist: Judge Rules Livent Duo Must Pay 23 Mil." *Daily Variety*, February 10. Available online via InfoTrac database.

Weinstein, Stephen. 2000. "Understanding AHERF: Observations of the Recent Settlements Involving Allegheny Health, Education and Research Foundation." Speech before the AICPA National Healthcare Industry Conference, Washington, D.C. August 1.

Willatt, Norris. 1970. "Out of the Spin?" *Barron's National Business and Financial Weekly*, December 21. Available online via ProQuest database.

CHAPTER 6

ENRON AND THE TALE OF THE GOLDEN GOOSE[1]

- Enron is presented here mainly as an as example of:
  1. The abuse of mark-to-market accounting
  2. The improper use of off-balance sheet entities which it used to:
     - Understate debt
     - Overstate earnings via:
       - Related-party sales
       - Loans disguised as sales
       - Related-party management fees
       - Contrived put options purporting to lock in profits on investments in shares
       - Mark-to-market revaluations of assets via references to contrived sales to these contrived entities
       - Recognition of profits on its own stock that was issued to off-balance-sheet entities
  3. Misclassification of "prepays" as sales

PART 1
HATCHING THE GOOSE: THE START OF ENRON

Enron. The company that once represented the pinnacle of corporate success—and the company that became the golden goose for so many—is now a symbol of all that can go horribly wrong in the corporate world. In August 2000, Enron's stock was at an all-time high, trading at $90 a share. By November 2001, an Enron share was worth less than $1. What happened? And why was it allowed to happen? How did the golden goose become the cooked goose?

The real story of Enron goes back to May 1985, when InterNorth— the company that owned the biggest and best gas-pipeline network in the

---

[1] General background information in this chapter is from *Bankruptcy Report #1* (2002), *Bankruptcy Report #2* (2003), *Bankruptcy Report #3* (2003), Bryce (2002), Eichenwald (2005), "Enron Timeline" (2005), Gruley and Smith (2002), McLean and Elkind (2004), Powers Report (2002), and Swartz and Watkins (2003).

United States—merged with Houston Natural Gas (HNG), whose ancestry went right back to the Houston Oil Company that had been formed in 1901. Twenty-four years later, in 1925, Houston Oil entered the gas business and formed two companies: the Houston Pipeline Company (to pipe natural gas) and Houston Natural Gas (to distribute the gas). By the early 1980s, Houston Natural Gas owned hundreds of gas wells and had annual revenue of $3 billion. Around this time, the HNG board of directors started searching for a dynamic chief executive officer (CEO), and they believed that they had found such a man in Kenneth Lay, who was appointed CEO of Houston Natural Gas in 1984. Both HNG and InterNorth were first-rate companies with impeccable credentials—and both were targets for hostile takeovers. In an attempt to avoid such takeovers, HNG merged with InterNorth in 1985, and Lay became CEO of the new conglomerate, which took the name of "Enron."

So perhaps the real story of Enron starts with the story of Kenneth Lay . . .

Kenneth Lay: The Duckling Who Wanted to Be a Swan

Born in Missouri in 1942, Kenneth Lay was the son of respectable, down-to-earth parents who constantly struggled to make ends meet. At one stage in Lay's early childhood, after his parents' feed store had gone bankrupt, Kenneth and his family "bounced around Missouri and Mississippi. Thanksgiving dinner that year was lunch meat with bread" (Gruley and Smith 2002). The family was then taken in by in-laws who lived on a small, meager farm. After that, the Lays never really regained their financial footing. There are several accounts of Kenneth Lay sitting on a tractor as a child and gazing at the downtown buildings he saw in the distance, daydreaming about inhabiting that sophisticated world which seemed so elusive.

As so many before him, Kenneth Lay's route out of poverty was higher education. After high school, he attended the University of Missouri where he studied economics, and apparently became "captivated by theories of how markets and companies work." He went on to complete a master's degree in economics in 1965, and later earned a doctorate from the University of Houston. Lay had married his college sweetheart, Judith, in 1966, and within a few years they were the proud parents of a son, Mark, and a daughter, Elizabeth. A couple of years after his marriage, Lay enrolled in the U.S. Navy. Lay's undergraduate economics professor, Pinkney Walker, wrote a letter of recommendation to procure a Pentagon position for Lay during the Vietnam War. In 1971, President Nixon appointed Professor Walker to the Federal

Power Commission, and Walker selected Lay as his chief aide. During this time, Lay wrote speeches for Walker that "shook up Washington with their fervor for deregulation." Washington was impressed, and Lay was appointed interim deputy undersecretary for energy. (Quotes from Gruley and Smith 2002)

As steep as his ascent had been from underprivileged farm boy to deputy undersecretary, nobody observing the likeable, unfailingly courteous Lay would have guessed at the ambition that brewed inside him as he surveyed the country's energy sector, much as he had yearned for those distant city buildings in his younger days. His attention was particularly riveted on the natural-gas segment of the energy sector. Lay saw a highly regulated business where the price of gas was mandated. Pipeline companies paid regulated amounts to the gas producers, and in turn received regulated prices from industrial customers and gas utilities for piping the gas to them. Lay believed in free markets. He was certain that deregulation would eventually come to the gas industry and that it would unleash vast opportunities for making a fortune from natural gas. Adhering to this belief, he left the public sector, and with the help of another letter of recommendation from Walker, he landed a job in the corporate planning office of Florida Gas in 1974. By 1979, he was president of the company, and by anybody's standards, the once poor farm boy was rich. The duckling had become a swan.

Soon, however, the new president of Florida Gas became restless. He didn't want to be a big bird in a small pond—he wanted a much bigger pond. Lay's restlessness was reflected in his personal life, which was in disarray. He was in the midst of a divorce from his wife and a very public affair with his secretary, Linda Phillips. The impending divorce affected Lay's wife, Judie, so badly that she suffered a "psychotic episode," and at her doctor's recommendation Lay signed "papers to have his estranged wife involuntarily committed" (McLean and Elkind 2004, 7, 8). Wanting to escape from Florida and the conflict in his personal life, Lay telephoned an old contact of his, Jack Bowen, the chief executive officer of Transco Energy, which was based in Houston. That must have been some phone call, because in 1981 Lay was appointed president of Transco and he moved to Houston with Linda, whom he then married. Now Lay had a new wife, a new job, and lots of money. But he was still restless.

In 1984, when Houston National Gas (HNG) came looking for a new chief executive officer, Lay jumped at the opportunity to become CEO and chairman of this old and highly respected Houston gas-production company. Lay was 42 years old and he had arrived. Finally the pond was big enough . . . or was it?

Lay soon began fretting that HNG did not have a large enough network of pipelines. Quite coincidentally, he received an unexpected, yet timely, call from Sam Segnar, the CEO of InterNorth, asking if Lay was interested in a plan for InterNorth to acquire HNG. Segnar was keen to shut out the chance of a hostile takeover by a corporate raider and felt that all the debt InterNorth would incur by buying HNG would make it immune to a future takeover. In May 1985, InterNorth acquired HNG for $2.3 billion.

Although InterNorth was three times the size of HNG, the deal was done on terms that were unusually favorable to HNG. The agreement included paying HNG $70 per share for shares that were trading at $48 at the time of the amalgamation of the two companies. Also, according to the contract, after eighteen months Lay would replace Segnar as CEO of Inter-North. The InterNorth board soon regretted the merger and blamed Segnar for persuading them to agree to it. As a result of the inexplicably poor terms and other difficulties with the merger, the board of the merged companies decided to replace Segnar sooner rather than later, and in November 1985, it appointed Kenneth Lay as the chief executive officer of the new conglomerate.

Lay was now CEO of a huge company that, with over 37,000 miles of pipeline, controlled "the largest gas-distribution system in the country, running from border to border, coast to coast" (McLean and Elkind 2004, 10). It also had natural gas exploration plants, productions plants, hundreds of gas wells, and other energy businesses. Lay himself had a lot to offer the new company. In addition, he was good at cajoling politicians and on friendly terms with the future governor of Texas, Ann Richards. Lay's support was also courted by then Governor George W. Bush. Yet in spite of Lay's talents, and the power and reach of this awesome combination of companies, the merger had a strange and difficult start.

After InterNorth's bout of merger remorse, the next blunder—minor, yet indicative of a troubled future—involved the naming of the new company. The board of InterNorth/HNG had decided to change the name of the combined companies to "Enteron." However, "Within days of the announcement, the soon to be Enteron was a laughing stock." Apparently, the dictionary definition of "Enteron" was "digestive tube." This was rather "unfortunate, given that Lay's company produced natural gas." So they decided to adjust the name to "Enron." (Quotes from Eichenwald 2005, 33-34)

More ominous than the embarrassing name, Enron had another problem right from its inception; a problem that was concealed for years until eventually it mushroomed into a monster and destroyed the entire company. The predicament was simply this: Enron began its life with too much debt. InterNorth's borrowing of hundreds of millions of dollars to acquire HNG for $2.4 billion, combined with other debt, meant that the newly formed Enron began its life *with over $4 billion of debt.*

While it was true that such debt would—for good reason—discourage future hostile takeovers, such large debt also presented large problems for the company itself. High debt means high interest expenses, which eat into profits. Also, the higher the debt relative to profits and to equity, the higher the risk that the debtor will default on payments. For this reason, lenders charge higher interest rates for future borrowing, exacerbating the problem of the high cost of capital. More troubling still, a company's high debt can cause analysts to lower their "buy" ratings on the company's stock. Perhaps most disturbing of all is that the debt has to be repaid eventually, and if it cannot be repaid the company will face bankruptcy. (Ironically, about twenty years later, at Lay's criminal trial in early 2006, his attorney would lament the fact that the banks had wanted their loans to be repaid, and argued that if the banks had not made this inconvenient request, Enron would still be in business.)

It is unlikely that Kenneth Lay, or "Kenny boy" (as then Texas Governor George W. Bush had named him) worried too much about the existence of debt—it was the appearance of debt that he did not like. Although Lay was master of all the pipelines and gas wells that Enron possessed, he did not become master of its debt. While Enron's management certainly manipulated the *reporting* of its debt, they never controlled the debt itself; indeed, eventually it mastered all of them.

Enron had yet another crisis early on. At the time of the merger, a large part of InterNorth had moved to Houston, but its small oil-trading division, which became known as Enron Oil, remained in New York and was largely allowed free rein by the Houston office. Louis Borget, who ran Enron Oil, liked it that way. However, a bank that was doing business with Borget became suspicious and contacted Enron. Kenneth Lay and a few other Enron employees paid a visit to Enron Oil and soon discovered that "the traders were keeping two sets of books, one for legitimate purposes . . . and another in which to record their ill-gotten gains" (Swartz and Watkins 2003, 31). It emerged that Borget had been making losses and concealing them by selling his losing oil futures at a "profit" to sham companies that he had set up in order to report false profits to inflate his bonus.

Everyone assumed that Borget would be fired, and everyone was surprised when Lay overlooked the fraud and kept Borget on. According to rumor, Lay explained his decision by saying that Borget would be kept in line. An accountant from Arthur Andersen, Enron's auditors, apparently commented later, "No one pounded the table and said these guys are crooks. They thought they had the golden goose, and the golden goose just stole a little money out of their petty cash" (quoted in McLean and Elkind 2004, 19). Lay's decision would come back to haunt him.

Borget was unrepentant and actually accelerated his oil futures trading. In October 1987, Lay was in Europe and received an emergency call from Enron president John M. "Mick" Seidl, who set up an urgent meeting with Lay in Newfoundland. At the meeting, Seidl told Lay that Enron was on the brink of collapse. Borget had committed them to delivering a staggering $1.5 billion of oil—oil that they did not have. If word got out that they were short this amount, other dealers would buy up the spot oil, driving up the price, and Enron would be bankrupted.

Lay put one of his traders, Mike Muckleroy, in charge of the salvage effort. Muckleroy fooled the markets by buying eight million barrels of spot oil and then offering each of the major dealers one million barrels of oil, saying that Enron had a surplus. This trick worked, and Enron was able to buy up spot oil and offload enough of Borget's contracts in the next sixty days for them to survive. Eventually, word got out of Enron's near miss, and Lay did what he would do again in 2002 on Enron's final collapse—he denied that he had ever known of the magnitude of the trading operation or its risks. Borget was later convicted of fraud, jailed for a year, and fined $6 million. Lay did not realize it then, but he was peering into a crystal ball and gazing at Enron's future.

No problems, however, were initially obvious to any outsiders. The golden goose appeared to be sleek and plump. Over the next few years, Enron was to offer dizzying amounts of stock options to its executives. In fact, Lay would eventually unload over $100 million of his Enron stock, before it became valueless.

Although Lay had moved from the public energy sector in the 1970s in anticipation of deregulation and the opportunity for the profits he was sure this would bring, he had not yet figured out a way for Enron to capitalize on deregulation, which had started but had not unfolded as neatly as he had hoped. In fact, while the previously regulated gas business had been steady and predictable, the process of semi-deregulation had produced some unintended consequences. With fixed purchase prices and fixed selling prices, the pipeline companies had entered into long-term contracts to purchase gas for years to come. When the purchase prices were deregulated, prices fell and companies were stuck with these "take-or-pay" contracts to purchase gas at prearranged fixed prices that were above-market. In addition, because of earlier price caps, a number of gas producers had closed down, and many industrial gas plants and utilities had experienced shortages of gas.

After deregulation, selling prices shot up during times of higher demand but plunged at other times, making it difficult for users to predict future purchase prices and to estimate whether or not an industrial gas plant or a gas utility would be profitable. Therefore, new utility companies and industrial plants increasingly used alternative energy sources—such as oil and coal—and avoided gas. Soon there was an oversupply of gas on the market, and Enron, like the other pipeline businesses, had a huge problem. Kenneth Lay—indeed the whole gas industry—needed someone who could figure out a way to make the deregulated gas industry profitable.

The golden goose was losing its luster, and Lay had to find someone to bring back the gloss.

Jeffrey Skilling: The Egghead Who Wanted to Fly

The man that Kenneth Lay turned to was a Harvard MBA—and intermittent risk taker—named Jeffrey Skilling, who worked at the prominent consulting firm of McKinsey & Company. Born in Pittsburgh in 1953, Skilling was the son of an engineer-turned-traveling salesman who lost his job, forcing the family to move to Chicago, where Jeffrey, with very little effort, did exceptionally well in high school. Interestingly, Skilling turned down Princeton University and selected Southern Methodist University, in Dallas, for his undergraduate degree. After getting married and working briefly in a bank, Skilling was accepted at Harvard Business School, where he graduated in the top 5 percent of his MBA class. He then joined the pricey and pretentious firm of McKinsey & Company, where the consultants thought of themselves "as secular versions of the Jesuits, gifted intellectuals uplifting the world of commerce with their vision" (quoted in Bryce 2002, 50).

As a consultant to InterNorth, which subsequently became part of Enron, Skilling began to realize that without stable, long-term gas prices, energy users—including industrial plants, utilities, and private customers—would not want to be dependent on gas. In addition, power producers were hesitant to explore and produce gas, and even willing potential producers could not raise financing because the banks required more reliable estimates of future prices in order to assess whether the producers would be profitable enough to repay their bank loans. The daily fluctuating "spot" prices of natural gas were just too volatile. Natural gas as a significant energy source would only make sense if one could get the wild instability out of the prices.

The industry was in desperate need of a business model that would provide the producers and users with the mechanism to reliably predict the prices as well as the demand and supply of gas. As a consultant to Enron, Jeffrey Skilling provided the answer, and he called it the "Gas Bank" (Swartz and Watkins 2003, 45).

○ Skilling's Gas Bank

The plan was for Enron itself to be the Gas Bank. Gas producers could contract to make "deposits" of gas with Enron for future years at previously agreed upon prices. In addition, gas users could contract in advance to make "withdrawals" (purchases) of gas from Enron, at specified prices for future years. Enron would make a percentage on the spread much the same way as a bank borrows from lenders at a certain interest rate and lends to borrowers at a higher interest rate. Gas producers, industrial gas users, and utilities would be able to estimate future prices and cash flows more reliably. Potential producers could obtain bank loans more easily for the exploration and production of new gas.

In 1987, on the advice of Jeffrey Skilling, Enron launched its Gas Bank. Industrial users and utilities quickly signed long-term contracts to buy gas at fixed prices. However, the plan faltered when gas producers were not as keen to lock themselves into long-term selling prices. Skilling became convinced that if *he* ran Enron's Gas Bank, he would be able to solve the problems and make it work. In 1990, Skilling left McKinsey & Company to join Enron as chairman and chief executive officer of a new division known as Enron Finance.

Skilling expanded his Gas Bank concept by announcing that Enron would get gas producers on board by paying them up front for their contracts to deliver gas in future periods; Enron was now financing gas-production companies. The producers would later have to deliver an assured supply of gas at fixed prices, and Skilling knew what price to set for the supplies of gas in order to make a profit on the spread, because Enron already had contracts to sell the gas at fixed prices in the future. The Gas Bank was certainly a brilliant concept.

Skilling, of course, had still bigger plans and he intended to transform the gas industry even further. He decided to chop up Enron's long-term supply contracts, as well as its long-term purchase contracts, into smaller ones and offer them all for sale. In other words, Skilling transformed the contracts into financial instruments to be sold on the free market, and he set up traders to buy and sell these financial instruments. The public could now buy from

Enron the right to purchase gas or to supply gas at fixed prices in the future. Jeffrey Skilling had invented a *futures market* in natural gas! Soon, companies on Wall Street followed Skilling's lead, and in 1990 the New York Mercantile Exchange began trading gas futures. Enron dominated the market and it "was the dominant company when it came to setting prices as well" (Swartz and Watkins 2003, 47).

○ Skilling and Mark-to Market Accounting

Once Skilling had established a trading floor and staffed it with traders selling financial instruments, he started to declare that his division—Enron Finance—was the real business of Enron. Financial service firms usually have a ready market price to refer to in order to establish the value of the financial instruments that they own and can readily sell. According to generally accepted accounting principles (GAAP), financial-service firms should normally carry the value of their financial instruments on their balance sheets at market price. If an instrument's market value increases while a *financial services* company owns it, the company revalues the asset on the balance sheet (i.e., marks it up to market value) and correspondingly records the increased amount as profit on its income statement, a practice known as "mark-to-market" accounting. Although Enron was not primarily a financial-services company, Skilling felt that he had an argument for his division to use mark-to-market accounting on the grounds that his division traded financial instruments (gas futures).

Obviously, there is a strong potential for abuse of mark-to-market accounting. It is one thing to have a market value for a futures contract to sell an asset in the not-too-distant future and recognize or record the increase in value of that contract. In fact, it is even possible to sell that contract today on the futures market and receive the market price in cash. It is quite another matter if you have a contract to sell gas for the next twenty-three years and there are no market prices to indicate what you will have to pay for the gas you intend to sell in twenty-three years' time. The longer the contract extends into the future, the less possible it is to estimate prices accurately. Because of this risk, the futures market does not usually enter into such long-term contracts.

Recognizing such future profit now—that is, revaluing the asset and booking the revaluation amount to current profit—involves highly unreliable estimates and is highly susceptible to abuse. Further, if the transaction involves actual work that has to be done in the future to realize a future profit, the profit can only be recognized once the work has been done. Mark-to-market accounting cannot be used in such situations. Bethany

McLean and Peter Elkind, in their book, *The Smartest Guys in the Room: The Amazing Rise and Scandalous Fall of Enron* (2004), pointed out: "This line of thinking suggests that General Motors should book all the future profits of a new model automobile at the moment the car is designed, long before a single vehicle rolls off the assembly line" (39, 40).

Since his arrival at Enron in 1990, Skilling had been intrigued with the idea of being able to currently record future profits using mark-to-market accounting. Then, in late 1990, Enron signed a twenty-three-year contract with the New York Power Authority "to deliver 33 million cubic feet of natural gas per day to power plants built or operated by the authority. . . . The total value of the contract was $1.3 billion." According to accepted accounting practice, Enron could only report one twenty-third of this revenue each year for the next twenty-three years. Using mark-to-market accounting, however, Enron would be able to report the entire twenty-three years of revenue in the current quarter. Skilling could not resist the temptation: "The huge—and immediate—revenues he could get from the NYPA deal convinced Skilling that mark-to-market accounting was the way to go." (Quotes from Bryce 2002, 65–66)

There was one small problem with Skilling's idea: there were no reliable market prices for gas futures anywhere close to twenty-three years in advance. He decided that Enron would pay consultants for estimates of potential price curves. Essentially, Enron could estimate any amount it wanted for the price it would have to pay for future gas deliveries. By abusing mark-to-market accounting, Enron would record highly unreliable future profits in the current period, and these profits would, in turn, drive up share prices.

In May 1991, Skilling persuaded Enron's audit committee to adopt mark-to-market accounting. With the help of lobbying from Arthur Andersen, the Securities and Exchange Commission (SEC) granted its permission to Enron in a letter, dated January 30, 1992, which stated that the SEC "will not object to the proposed change in the method of accounting by Enron Gas Services during the first quarter of its fiscal year ended December 31, 1992." This was the very first time that a company that was *not* a financial institution had received permission from the SEC to use mark-to-market accounting. Enron wrote back to the SEC and said that it planned to go ahead and use mark-to-market accounting *a year earlier* than the date approved by the SEC. To this day, it remains a mystery as to why the SEC did not object to that subsequent letter from Enron. Furthermore, "Enron started using mark to market in every part of the business, not just Enron Gas Services." On the day that the letter arrived from the SEC giving Skilling permission to use this new accounting policy, he bought champagne to celebrate with his division's staff. (Quotes from Bryce 2002, 67-68)

From this point onward, Enron began to focus more on recording accounting profit than on making cash—and so a huge problem was born. The magnitude of that loss of focus *cannot* be underestimated. Enron began to lose colossal amounts of cash on ill-advised projects while it reported "estimated" future profits as current-period profits and hid the mounting debt it incurred to cover the huge amounts of cash it squandered. In May 1991, when Skilling cracked open the champagne to celebrate his right to use mark-to-market accounting, he was focused on the ability to report massive amounts of expected future earnings as current-period profits, and the boost this would give to Enron's stock price as well as to his compensation.

Around this time, Enron Finance, Skilling's Enron division, merged with Enron Gas Marketing, and the segment was renamed Enron Capital and Trade Resources (ECT). Skilling became the CEO of this new division and he appointed Lou Pai, a brilliant trader with little respect for the hard-asset pipeline business, (and with a penchant for frequenting strip clubs), as head of the floor-and-trading operations.

From then on, Skilling wanted Enron to focus on its trading business as opposed to the hard-asset business of actually piping gas. Over the next few years, Enron's trading operations grew in many different directions, until eventually the trading division opened Enron Online, which bought and sold *over 800* different commodities. For the rest of Enron's business life, there would always be a tension within the company between those who wanted Enron to expand its "asset-lite" trading arm and those who wanted to consolidate its hard-asset pipeline business.

As head of ECT, Skilling was an Enron star and he was on the rise. He had remade himself as the coolest guy at Enron, and Enron was the coolest company in all of Texas. It was hard to believe this was the same man who had been described as "a wallflower in high school" and "a tortured soul" (McLean and Elkind 2004, 29). Kenneth Lay must have been proud of his protégé.

Andrew Fastow: The Banker Who Feathered His Nest

To fulfill his ultimate vision of Enron as a trading company, Skilling realized he had to find a financial expert who knew his way around the system and who could wheel and deal for Enron. Just a few months after moving to Enron, Skilling contacted a company of headhunters to locate someone for him, and they soon came up with the name of Andrew Fastow. At the time, Fastow was a young banker—with a degree from Tufts University and an

MBA from Northwestern University—living in Chicago with his wealthy wife, Lea Weingarten, who was originally from Houston. Fastow was working at Continental Bank, where he had become an expert in "securitization deals, or as they were known more commonly, structured finance." By the time he interviewed at Enron, Fastow was already adept at using special purpose entities (SPEs), which enabled a company to "monetize," or to "literally turn its assets into money and generate revenue." (Quotes from Swartz and Watkins 2003, 154-155)

Fastow was doing well, but he wanted to do better. He had never heard of Enron, however, and was rather skeptical when he traveled to Houston to meet Skilling. After all, he dwelled in the elevated world of finance, not "in pipelines—expensive, dirty pipelines" (Eichenwald 2005, 51). Skilling, however, with his unbridled enthusiasm and vision of Enron as a trading company, soon won over the younger man. Fastow was exactly the sort of Enron executive that Skilling had in mind: "Fastow's motto—'never say no to a deal'—came to mean pushing for any transaction, no matter how complex or how irrational" (Swartz and Watkins 2003, 156). As Enron grew larger and louder, so did Andrew Fastow.

Lay, Skilling, and Fastow

The three men who would steer Enron to eventual ruin were all in place by the beginning of 1990. Enron had all its ducks in a row, and the goose was getting fat.

Perhaps *this* is the real beginning of the Enron story, the story of a company that almost totally lost focus on generating real cash and making actual profits, but instead concentrated on playing around with its financial records. Armed with the power to report virtually any fictitious profit it wished and to hide almost immeasurable amounts of debt, Enron burned through billions of dollars on foolhardy projects on several continents. Some of these schemes included the infamous Dabhol Power Plant in India, the Azurix water debacle in England, the bungled Cuiába Power Plant in Brazil, the hugely incompetent Enron Broadband Services, and the massive Enron Online venture that went spinning out of control.

Enron would use the infamous system of "prepays" to facilitate overstatement of earnings and cash flow by essentially borrowing against future receipts for future deliveries of commodities and related-party transactions. It would also construct SPEs such as Chewco, LJM, and the Raptors, which would also use mark-to-market accounting and related-party transactions to overstate earnings and to hide the debt related to all the cash that had been recklessly lost.

For several years, three things kept Enron going—and growing—throughout its reckless and convoluted projects:

1. Enron constantly overstated its earnings and understated its debt with fictitious accounting via:
   i. mark-to-market accounting
   ii. contrived transactions with SPEs
2. Enron employed misleading transactions, using the infamous "prepays," which essentially took out loans on the strength of future contracts and recorded these loans as revenues.
3. Enron's energy trading—especially its gas trading and its trading on the manipulated California electricity market—generated profit and cash that staved off the inevitable crash from its huge losses and fictitiously reported profits.

Once the energy prices stabilized and energy trading profits waned, not even falsely reported profits and hidden debt could save Enron because eventually the debt had to be repaid. The game was up for Enron once the banks refused to keep extending credit to the company, either directly or indirectly through its SPEs.

In order to understand what went wrong with this behemoth company, and why it went so wrong, it is necessary to take a closer look at the following phases in the rise and fall of Enron:

- Enron's energy-trading business (Enron Capital and Trade)
- Enron's bizarre projects, and how the company managed to burn through billions of dollars
- Enron's exploitation of California's electricity problems
- Enron's outrageous accounting manipulations to hide its vast losses
- Finally, we will examine the signals of the alleged frauds. These signals were, in fact, scattered all over Enron's financial statements, but the business community did not bother to look too closely at the golden goose.

PART 2
FATTENING THE GOOSE: ENRON CAPITAL AND TRADE (ECT)

Jeffrey Skilling's brain wave to develop a futures market in natural gas, in 1990, was the beginning of Enron's venture into the trading business. In the 1990s, Enron Capital and Trade (ECT) developed quickly from a small trading department into a large and highly profitable division.

Given that Enron was involved in all aspects of the gas business, Enron's traders had extremely useful information to trade on. Enron had gas production supply contracts as well as pipelines and orders for gas from the big gas consumers, like utilities and industrial power plants. Enron's traders knew better than anyone how much gas was going to be needed, what supplies were available, and how much was going to be supplied. If Enron discovered that a gas producer was having production problems or that a big consumer needed more gas, the traders knew that they should invest in options contracts that gave them the right to buy gas in the future at today's price; in other words, they "went long on gas."

Bolstered by their success in trading gas, the traders became more inventive in writing derivative financial instruments and started regarding themselves as the Enron elite. To the eventual peril of the company, the trading arm expanded trading to a variety of businesses and commodities in areas that Enron knew absolutely nothing about. One particularly imaginative type of derivative that Enron began trading was its "weather derivative." The idea for this grew out of Enron's attention to fundamental weather information for its gas trading. Enron traders knew that if a cold front was advancing, it would cause gas prices to increase, so the company employed meteorologists to help them predict the weather and, in turn, to predict future gas prices. In fact, all the electric and gas utilities faced risks due to changing prices as a result of fluctuating weather conditions. Enron saw this as an opportunity and began trading weather derivatives with the utility companies: "The contracts worked like an insurance policy that utilities purchased from Enron. If temperatures deviated from normal temperature ranges during an agreed-upon time period, Enron would pay the customers to offset their losses" (Bryce 2002, 243).

Electricity trading worked well for Enron because several of the fundamentals behind the successful trading of gas futures also worked for trading electricity futures. In 1997, Enron moved into yet another branch of energy and began trading coal. Again, Enron's knowledge of gas and electricity trading provided the basics they needed for success in coal trading. At this point, however, because of the company's increasing conviction that the future of Enron lay in *trading* rather than *energy* per se, Enron began to drift outside of the energy business that it understood and into areas where it had little expertise. This would cause a great deal of friction within the company.

PART 3
PLUCKING THE GOOSE: HOW ENRON
LOST ITS GOLD

The Travels and Travails of Rebecca Mark

Every good fairy tale needs a princess, and the Enron princess was Rebecca Mark, another favorite of Kenneth Lay. Mark was a glamorous Harvard MBA graduate who had worked (and had an affair) with John Wing from the division that later became Enron Development. This division began huge power projects overseas, including the massive Teesside project in England. When Wing left Enron in 1991, Mark was made CEO of Enron Development; now she had Lay's attention—so much so that she became real competition to Skilling in his quest to be appointed the next CEO of Enron.

Mark apparently recognized that Enron had lost focus on actually making money and was more focused on recording profit in its income statement. Mark also appeared to have realized that Enron had access to massive amounts of borrowed cash, which it often lost on ill-advised projects while continuing to report earnings up front. As the new CEO of Enron Development, Mark set out to win power projects all over the world and extend Enron's international reach. In sharp contrast to Skilling's trading operation (which was "asset lite"), Mark's mandate was to build hard-asset projects such as pipelines, production fields, and other energy sources to supply power plants overseas. She developed these international projects with gusto. For example, by 1992, Enron had a part ownership in a pipeline in Argentina, and by "early 1994 Mark also had power plants in the Philippines, Guatemala and Guam." Next, Enron Development was "busy laying a pipeline in Columbia . . . . [and] constructing a plant in China." Soon Enron was working on a pipeline that was intended to go all the way from Bolivia to Brazil. (Quotes from McLean and Elkind 2004, 74).

However, there were a number of problems associated with this frenetic rate of growth. The first problem was that Rebecca Mark got an up-front bonus on the signing of many of these huge deals. Clearly, this policy encouraged large projects that might not be prudent. Second, " . . . Enron often ended up guaranteeing some or all of the debt." Third, hugely optimistic assumptions were made at the beginning of the projects, assuming that little or nothing would go wrong. Not surprisingly, problems and roadblocks usually did emerge. For example, a power project in the Dominican Republic caused soot to be blown onto a neighboring hotel, resulting in an extremely expensive lawsuit: "For Enron, the deal was a complete bust; through mid-2000 the company had collected a pathetic $3.5 million from its $95 million investment." Possibly the most infamous hard-asset losses for Enron—and the deals that Mark pushed hardest to accomplish—were the Dabhol Power Project in India and the Azurix water project in England. (Quotes from McLean and Elkind 2004, 77-78)

o **Rebecca Mark in India: The Dabhol Power Project**

In 1992, Rebecca Mark was trying to convince India's Maharashtra State Energy Board (MSEB) to authorize a twenty-year power contract with Enron for the province of Maharashtra. This would require Enron to build a massive energy plant estimated to cost just under $4 billion. The first phase of the plant would use a fuel known as "naphta," and the second phase would use liquefied natural gas (LNG), a rather expensive form of energy. The project was never really viable on at least two counts. First, coal was probably a better option than gas for India's electricity production. Second, the payment arrangements as set out in the contract were outrageously favorable to Enron but were not really feasible considering that in India the government often had to forgive many unpaid electricity bills.

The project seemed doomed when the World Bank refused to finance it and the MSEB wanted to end negotiations. However, Mark pushed ahead and managed to get partial financing from banks and additional financing from the U.S. federal government via the Overseas Private Investment Corporation (OPIC). Mark also lobbied over the head of the local MSEB in India, and in December 1993, the Indian government signed a contract for the first phase of the twenty-year project "that required it to pay Enron about $1.3 billion per year, or about $26 billion over the life of the contract." In fact, if the terms of the contract were fully realized, "India would pay Enron and its partners nearly nine times what Dabhol had cost." However, just after Enron began construction, India's Congress Party in Maharashtra lost power, and the new party stopped all work on the project, claiming that Enron was guilty of gross overcharging. (Quotes from Bryce 2002, 102-103)

Mark worked hard to renegotiate the contract and get the venture back on track, lowering the costs for the first phase and giving the MSEB a 15 percent share in the project. In spite of these amendments, the size of the financial obligation to MSEB was still outrageous—about $30 billion over twenty years—and would probably have bankrupted the province. The first phase began producing power in May 1999, two years behind schedule. Around this time, charges of bribery and corruption at the Dabhol plant began to circulate, exacerbated by an anonymous letter sent to Enron's head office. The letter also claimed that MSEB could not pay its bills. The company denied the bribery charges which were never proven, but the nameless writer certainly proved to be correct in one respect: MSEB refused to pay for the power from Dabhol, saying they could not afford it. In spite of all their attempts, there was nothing Enron executives could do to resuscitate the project. The plant remains empty and useless, a stark symbol of incompetence and greed: "Today, Dabhol, in which Enron invested some $900 million, sits silent, a gigantic, wasted marvel of modern technology" (McLean and Elkind 2004, 83).

○ Rebecca Mark in England: The Azurix Account

Mark's princess status began to diminish with the failure of many of her international power projects. Her decline from glory was aided by her nemesis, Jeffrey Skilling, who led the charge to have her removed from her position as CEO of Enron International (as the development division of Enron had been renamed). Rebecca Mark's Enron career was finally undone by her plan to start her own water utilities company—a sector in which she and Enron had absolutely no experience.

Toward the end of the 1990s, some countries had begun the slow process of privatizing their water utilities and wastewater facilities. Mark believed that this privatization would lead to deregulation, as had happened with the gas industry, and there would be a lot of money to be made in water. Two French companies, Vivendi and Suez Lyonnaise, were already operating water utilities for local governments around the world, and they were doing very well. So in 1998, Mark began her start-up water company called Azurix, which she financed with money from Enron via an Enron off-balance-sheet entity named "Marlin." It was extremely difficult to get a foothold in this industry, and Azurix was plagued with problems from beginning to end even though Mark was a hard worker and was always ready to fly around the world to try to drum up business.

The first Azurix project involved Wessex Water, a water utility company in England that was "one of the most profitable water utilities in the United Kingdom. It provided water or wastewater service to about 2.5 million people in southwestern England." In July 1998, Azurix purchased Wessex Water for $2.88 billion. However, by the end of the following year, seven weeks after Azurix had gone public, the company was shocked when Britain's water-regulation agency announced that water companies would have to drop prices. Wessex would have to cut its customer rates by 12 percent. A number of people in the water industry expressed the opinion that "Azurix should have known the move was coming." To make matters worse, the Wessex facilities had to be upgraded, and the cost for this was astronomical. By some accounts, Azurix lost more than a billion dollars in its first year of operation. (Quotes from Bryce 2002, 178, 187)

The next problem Mark had to face involved development costs. She had expected Wessex Water to be the silver bullet that would facilitate Azurix's entrée into the water world, after which it could easily buy out privatized utilities or win contracts to manage utilities for municipalities. However, this did not happen in spite of Mark's optimism and her large development teams that were "scouring the globe for water companies they could buy." The teams looked hard and spent hard, but didn't find much. One senior manager at Azurix claimed that "those teams were spending more that $60 million a month on hotels, consultants and airfare," and no one at Azurix or Enron pulled the plug on this wild spending. Instead, Mark was allowed to continue with her dream of making Azurix a public company. In June 1999, even though Azurix was in a state of disarray and not developing enough new business, its initial public offering (IPO) raised $695 million. It would come under scrutiny as it made public quarterly and annual filings of its financial statements and publicized revenue and earnings estimates followed by actual earnings releases. (Quotes from Bryce 2002, 176)

Azurix was still desperate for new business and it seemed as though the answer lay in Argentina. Buenos Aires was taking bids from private companies for a thirty-year contract to essentially rent and manage the Buenos Aires water utility and wastewater plants. While preparing to go public, Azurix had submitted an incredibly high bid of $439 million for the contact. The next highest bid was less than $200 million. In its haste to put the deal together, Azurix had ignored some significant information. For example, it had not realized that the actual office buildings were not included in the bid, and that the plant had not been well maintained. In fact, it soon became obvious that Azurix "had blown it" (Bryce 2002, 184). The fatal blow to the Buenos Aires project occurred when an algae outbreak contaminated the drinking water in early 2000 and Azurix had to purchase containers of water and deliver them to its customers at a huge additional expense.

Apart from the inefficiency and mismanagement that plagued Azurix, the company was also damaged by so many lavish expenses that Robert Bryce, in his book *Pipe Dreams*, commented: "Azurix didn't burn cash, it incinerated it" (176). Mark reportedly received a salary of $710,000 a year, had the use of a company aircraft, and spent company money extravagantly. For example, she ordered the construction of a $1 million special stairway to connect the ninth and tenth floors of the company offices. In addition, Azurix had so many highly paid executives that when the company had to shell out $7.6 million in severance pay, even Mark realized that spending had to be curbed.

However, not everyone believed that the failure of Azurix was entirely Mark's fault. From the outset, her company was saddled with debt when Enron financed it via the off-balance-sheet entity known as Marlin. In fact, "some of the $900 million of the money Fastow had raised [for Azurix] was paid right back to Enron." Even though Azurix burned through cash with its own ill-fated projects and mismanaged development costs, some claimed that Enron was not particularly supportive of Azurix, and that—in the battle to gain control of Enron—the "entire expensive episode had all been a grand conspiracy" to depose Rebecca Mark. (Quotes from McLean and Elkind 2004, 249-250).

Whether the plot existed or not, Jeffrey Skilling retained his position as future king of Enron, and at the end of 2000, Rebecca Mark was cut loose. In spite of her desperate plans to shore up the drowning company, the Enron board had lost confidence in her; even Kenneth Lay agreed that Azurix had been a tremendous waste of money, and that Mark had to resign.

The Enron board ended the Azurix hemorrhage when it paid over $300 million to buy back the shares—held by the public—at just over $8 a share when the shares were trading at around $3.50 per share. In early 2001, Enron's entire international division was sold. However, because Azurix had initially been funded by the off-balance-sheet entity, Marlin, Enron was still on the hook for Marlin's loans that had been used mainly on Azurix.

Before she left Enron, Mark sold over 100,000 Enron shares in "a move that brought her total stock-sale proceeds to $82.5 million. Counting her salary, and other compensation, Mark probably banked in the neighborhood of $100 million. That is truly staggering when you consider that her misguided deals in India, Argentina and elsewhere cost investors at least $2 billion" (Bryce 2002, 189). Although it did not seem so at the time, "Rebecca Mark was one of the lucky ones—she got out at the top" (McLean and Elkind 2004, 263). Indeed, Mark managed to hold on to that golden goose just long enough to snatch a golden egg.

Enron Energy Services

Meanwhile, buoyed by its rapid and spectacular success in gas trading, Enron purchased the Portland General Electric utility company in 1997, to establish itself in the electricity industry. As it transpired, Enron's experience and information base in the gas-trading business transferred quite well to the wholesale component of electricity trading. However, Enron also decided to launch into the retail electricity market and that same year formed Enron Energy Services (EES) to manage and provide electricity and gas directly to business organizations and households. Enron's expertise did not transfer well to the retail division of supplying and managing electricity services, and this venture became rather problematic and much more difficult than anticipated.

In attempting to sell its electricity, Enron had to aggressively seek business by promising various other companies and state organizations that it could provide their power supplies at rates that were cheaper than the rates they were currently paying. Unfortunately, Enron did not really plan ahead as to how they would fulfill all these promises of cheap power. In addition to selling power at bargain-basement prices, Enron had to start managing and maintaining electrical power plants—and it knew almost nothing about the electricity industry.

While most of Enron's wholesale traders expected that the cost of electric power would increase, Lou Pai, one of Skilling's chief traders, decided to take a huge gamble that prices would decrease. As it transpired, the price of electricity increased dramatically toward the end of 2000, and EES lost a fortune. (Behind the scenes, of course, many of the wholesale traders made big profits on California's manipulated electricity prices, but this will be covered in a later section.)

It was not too long before some of the problems in EES were noticed by other Enron employees. In February 2001, an accountant named Wanda Curry reported to Enron's chief accounting officer that she was investigating several discrepancies at EES. Some of these problems included the following:

- Many of the contracts were overvalued; Enron Energy "hadn't done much more than guess at energy loads its customers would require" (McLean and Elkind 2004, 300).
- EES had used "faulty price curves with their excessively optimistic assumptions" (McLean and Elkind 2004, 300). It is important to note that with mark-to-market accounting, these contracts were valued using these estimates for the balance sheet, and the expected future profit was recognized in current-period income statements.
- The contracts were not fully hedged, so that if price changes deviated from expectations, Enron would not have other contracts that would increase in value by compensating amounts.

- EES faced huge losses if the California energy crisis forced Enron's customers into bankruptcy, as occurred, for example, in the case of Pacific Gas.
- There were various speculative trading losses because EES had been trading on the bet that electricity prices would fall when, in fact, prices rose astronomically.

Overall, based on Curry's investigation, EES needed to recognize "a loss that would likely total more than $500 million" (McLean and Elkind 2004, 303). But mysteriously, a disclosure of these losses was nowhere to be found in Enron's financial statements.

Traders Gone Wild: The Tale of Enron Online

Moving into new trading markets usually meant that Enron had no comparative advantages, and there were often huge disadvantages to having absolutely no knowledge of the new industry. It also involved spending and losing vast sums of money to get started. For example, Enron purchased a couple of paper mills in order to begin a market for trading pulp and paper.

Then Enron attempted trading in metals and bought the British metals company, MG plc, "one of the biggest metals traders in the world, for $446 million" (Bryce 2002, 218). Greg Whalley, a talented trader in charge of Enron's wholesale trading operation, supervised the acquisition of MG plc. Enron was in such a rush to complete the purchase that most of it was accomplished in four days and "most of it done with heavy drinking in London bars" (McLean and Elkind 2004, 225). A Wall Street commodity trader is reported to have said that the metals company was worth only a fraction of what Enron had paid for it. Nobody seemed to care, however, because Enron was imbued with a sort of insane hysteria.

Around this time, an Enron team led by a British trader named Louise Kitchen had developed the technology to launch Enron's trading business on the Internet—and so Enron Online was born and went live in November 1999. From a purely technological point of view, the system was a marvel. Not only did Enron Online trade gas, electricity, weather derivatives, and metals futures, but within "a few weeks of its launch [. . .] Enron Online was the biggest e-commerce entity in the world. In all, the company was selling over 800 different products" (Bryce 2002, 217).

Now the trading arm of Enron really surged, and Enron became predominantly a trading company. The battle between hard assets and trading was finally settled. Through Enron Online, the Enron traders saw the prices that buyers and sellers were offering and with that advantage, they made a great deal of money in the products they really understood. However, unlike eBay, which offers a marketplace for other buyers and sellers, Enron Online actually purchased everything that it resold. This was significant "because Enron was in the middle of every transaction, [and] Enron would have to hold some of those commodities for days or even weeks. . . . That meant Enron had to have billions of dollars of cash at the ready." In fact, by the time they were trading over 800 products, the cash-flow problem became so bad that in the first half of 2000, "Enron borrowed over $3.4 billion to finance its operations. The company's cash flow from the operations was negative $547 million." The interest on the amount borrowed was staggering. By the middle of that year, "the Enron company was paying about $20 million per day in interest." (Quotes from Bryce 2002, 220-221)

While Enron made profits on many of the commodities, the company was losing money due to its interest expense, and due to trading commodities that the brokers did not understand. In addition, the trading volumes were so large that even in gas trading—where they had all the advantages—when the traders bet the wrong way, the losses were astounding. For example, when a cold arctic air front was moving toward Texas in early December 2000, many gas traders went "long" on gas, expecting the price to increase. However, the cold weather never arrived and gas prices fell, with the result that, on December 12, "The traders lost $550 million according to one report and $630 million according to another report" (McLean and Elkind 2004, 219).

The traders were young, egotistical, belligerent, and very partial to obscene language. They were rich beyond their wildest dreams, and totally unmanageable. But ultimately, they were gamblers and they "bet—on anything" (Swartz and Watkins 2003, 79). Eventually, the gambling—like the rest of Enron—spun totally out of control.

Web Weavers: The Story of Enron Broadband Services

In 1997, when Enron acquired the Portland General utility company to get into the utility business, an unintended consequence was that it also acquired FirstPoint, a small telecommunications Internet start-up company that was a tiny division of Portland General. As luck would have it, the stock prices of Internet companies and telecommunication companies began to rise dramatically. These companies had price-earnings ratios far higher than Enron's. In fact, in the late 1990s, these companies enjoyed soaring stock prices even when they had negative earnings! This was a situation ripe for exploitation.

Never one to miss an opportunity, Jeffrey Skilling turned to his newfound telecommunications division and came up with four big, bad ideas:

1. Skilling decided that Enron would join the broadband investment boom by expanding FirstPoint's investment in broadband capacity. This was at the time that Global Crossing, AT&T, and all the other big telecommunication companies were over-investing in broadband capacity, chanting the erroneous mantra: "Internet traffic is doubling every 100 days" (Malik 2003, 13). So Enron joined the rush to lay fiber-optic lines and to acquire small telecommunications companies with broadband capacity. Like everyone else, Enron would be caught with a huge overinvestment in broadband capacity that was in oversupply.

2. Skilling decided that Enron would trade broadband capacity, figuring that it would be much like trading gas futures—but he was sorely mistaken. Enron could move gas in its own pipelines, with its own connections, all the way from the power plant to the utility company. However, although Enron owned a great deal of fiber-optic lines, it did not have the connection facilities or the lines to transmit data all the way to its customers. This meant it could not guarantee the security of the transmitted information, and it would have to invest in connection facilities to move the data to its customers. Skilling therefore planned to build "two dozen pooling points across the globe. These pooling points would use sophisticated equipment [and]. . . . would act as hubs. Enron would buy and sell capacity on the Internet so that corporations and other carriers could get reliable network connections." However, there was a huge problem in that the technology necessary for Skilling's plan did not yet exist: "No one had built equipment that could provide instant bandwidth on demand." Furthermore, while Enron was spending a fortune on these highly dubious plans, it had yet to find any customers. The potential buyers of broadband capacity were the big telephone companies that did not like Enron much and believed that Enron's entry into their business was going to become a comedy of errors; they certainly had no incentive to trade with Enron. (Quotes from Malik 2003, 104)

3. FirstPoint was renamed Enron Broadband Services (EBS) and Skilling appointed his trusted friend, Ken Rice, as co-CEO (the other CEO was Joe Hirko of the original FirstPoint). Rice had been an exceptional salesman, landing enormous gas power plant

deals, but he had little experience in telecommunications and actually wanted to retire. To his credit, he first rejected the job, but Skilling talked him into accepting the position. As co–CEO with Hirko—and as Skilling's friend—Rice could do as he wished and had the final say, albeit no knowledge of the industry. Predictably, the co–CEO arrangement did not work, and Joe Hirko left the company in July 2000. Kevin Hannon, a trader who had risen to the top of Enron's trading operations, was appointed Ken Rice's deputy. With Rice and Hannon at the helm of EBS, Skilling believed that Enron would transform the telecom world. On the contrary, however, now neither the CEO nor his deputy had any deep broadband knowledge or experience, and the result was disastrous. Hannon "didn't know the most rudimentary information about the business," and Rice became strangely focused on the image of EBS, to the extent that he bought two costly Hellcat motorcycles for the company and decided that EBS would sponsor a Ferrari race car for the racing season. After a while, Rice stopped coming to work every day, and an EBS employee recalled that when he did attend meetings, he would "turn on his laptop and watch cartoons." Another employee commented that "Rice was simply a six-year-old in a forty-year-old's body. (Quotes from Bryce 2002, 194-198)

4. Enron was going to stream movies right into the television sets in all homes. Once again, this grandiose plan was not backed by the necessary technology and never even approached fruition.

All four of these ideas failed—some sooner, others later. But before the failures came the hype, and some of the people at Enron—as well as many of the Wall Street financial analysts—actually believed some of the fairy tales.

In January 2000, before the departure of co–CEO Joe Hirko, Skilling unveiled the grand plans for EBS at a meeting of financial analysts in Houston. He announced to the analysts that "Enron was going to apply the expertise it had learned in gas and power to the Internet infrastructure. It would trade capacity in new-tech pipelines." At that same meeting, when Scott McNealy, CEO of Sun Microsystems, announced that his company was going to partner with Enron on Internet development, the analysts went wild. They were so excited—and so naïve—that, according to *Fortune* magazine, McNealy's appearance "was like Jesus showing up at a tent revival. Analysts swooned; they cheered." On the day the analysts met, Enron's stock rose from $53.50 per share to $67.25. (Quotes from Bryce 2002, 191)

Unfortunately, the stock increase was based on fiction. The technology for most of the plans had not been perfected (or even developed); there were not nearly enough customers to support the ostentatious plans; and the price of bandwidth was soon to plunge. By the second quarter of 2000, Enron Broadband's revenues were way behind predictions. However, the accounting and financial problems were "solved" with the help of Andrew Fastow's SPE named LJM2. (In his later article in *Forbes Magazine*, Daniel Fisher (2002) explained to incredulous readers how Enron had "sold" a portion of its unused fiber to LJM2 at an inflated price, adding $100 million to Enron's revenue and about $67 million to its profit.)

Clearly, EBS would not let a little obstacle like the falling price of fiber capacity mess up its rosy picture of growth. Soon there would be a way to make real money with broadband. In fact, the Web weavers were already spinning another yarn: in April 2000, a few months after the formation of Enron Online, EBS had signed a twenty-year contract with Blockbuster. Under this agreement, Blockbuster would persuade the movie studios to give their partnership licensing rights to stream movies directly into private residences, using Enron's broadband network. The trouble was that Enron had not yet worked out the technical details to solve the "last mile problem—getting the content from Enron's network into people's homes" (McLean and Elkind 2004, 292). In addition, Blockbuster was having enormous difficulty convincing the studios to cooperate, because there was not much incentive in it for them. All these roadblocks did not stop Kenneth Lay from announcing, in July 2000, that Enron was about to enter the entertainment business.

However, without the technology in place, the Blockbuster project was a disaster. The most Enron ever achieved was a trial run of the service to only 1,000 test customers, and "many of those customers didn't even pay" (Bryce 2002, 82). The cities in the pilot program were especially chosen because they were areas where Enron had found small providers to solve the problem of moving the movie material from Enron into private homes, but ultimately, even the trial run was a dismal failure: "Broadband executives sat in meetings poring over reports of the pilots' comically pathetic results: the Care Bears Movie: Seven purchases—$8.40" (McLean and Elkind 2004, 293).

To deal with the losses on the Blockbuster debacle, Enron decided to spin a web of SPEs. A variety of these SPEs were used to confuse the situation in order to book a profit via a project known as *Braveheart*. Essentially, Enron persuaded the Canadian Imperial Bank of Commerce (CIBC) to finance a deal that appeared to be a sale of Enron's share in the twenty-year Blockbuster contracts. The contracts were first "sold" to a joint venture called nCube and an SPE called Thunderbird, which in turn was owned by the Enron entity called Whitewing. The joint venture then "sold" the rights to another SPE called Hawaii 125-0 at a price that had wildly optimistic off-target estimates of profits for Enron on the contracts. A few months after recording millions of dollars in profits on the Braveheart project, Enron cancelled its deal with Blockbuster, and "claimed $110.9 million in profits from the [Blockbuster] deal even though the company had never collected a dime in cash" (Bryce 2002, 282).

Finally, in mid-2001, the charade came to an end when EBS was gutted. On July 12, it was officially announced that EBS would be merged into Enron's wholesale division. The EBS farce had caused Enron to lose more than $1 billion.

In July 2005, several EBS executives were tried on various charges of fraud, insider trading, and money laundering. The jury deadlocked on some charges and found the defendants not guilty on the other charges. The judge "declared a mistrial on the dozens of counts on which the jury could not agree" (Flood 2005, July 21). Ben Campbell, the prosecutor at this trial, pointed out that "EBS' highly touted core software packages never worked properly and failed to generate much income" ("Enron Defendants Not Guilty for Charges" 2005). This point is actually not in dispute. What is in dispute, however, is whether or not the senior managers of EBS actually believed their own stories. At this particular trial, the defense argued that the EBS executives truly assumed that their network was viable, and evidently the jury was unable to ascertain otherwise.

Linda Chatman Thomsen, the SEC's deputy director of the Enforcement Division, commented that the Enron executives "played important roles in perpetuating the fairy tale that Enron was capable of spinning straw—or more appropriately, fiber—into gold" (SEC Release 2003-58, May 1, 2003). This was such a compelling tale that perhaps some of the officers actually working for the company were duped.

PART 4
STUFFING THE GOOSE: THE ELECTRICITY FIASCO IN CALIFORNIA

In order to comprehend the intricacies of the electricity saga in California, a little background information is necessary. In the late 1990s, the California Public Utilities Commission (CPUC) was in charge of revamping the rules for what was then referred to as California's electricity *deregulation*. This, however, was a misnomer, as California was really engaged in what amounted to a *semi*-deregulation of the prices that customers paid the utility companies for electricity, and the prices that the utilities paid the power companies. The CPUC initiated a 10 percent price cut for the end users and capped the amount paid by the utilities to the power companies at $750 per megawatt hour, but *left uncapped the amount paid for power purchased from outside California.*

California's much vaunted *deregulation* contained several other interesting rules:[2]

- The utilities were required to sell their power plants and buy their power on a daily (or even an hourly) basis from on-the-spot markets, yet sell the power at the fixed reduced rate.
- The utilities were required to fulfill their purchasing obligations on existing long-term contracts, while selling at reduced fixed rates to customers.
- No new long-term contracts were allowed.
- The state created two new agencies that were subject to additional rules:
  - The California Power Exchange (CAL PX): Power had to be bought and sold through CAL PX, which established hourly prices.
  - The Independent System Operator (ISO): When there were emergency energy shortages, power had to be purchased and sold though ISO auctions, subject to the $750 per megawatt cap on purchases of power from within California. ISO also administered California's electricity transmission lines.
- If at any time a transmission line's electricity flow exceeded its capacity, the ISO would pay a premium fee for removal of the congestion.

Undoubtedly, California's energy system was a formula for disaster—even without the pervasive abuse that engulfed it on so many fronts. There were just too many potential problems. What if the market price the utilities had to pay for the power went above the fixed price at which they were forced to sell the power? Obviously, if that situation continued for too long, the utilities would go bankrupt. If future power prices rose above the $750 cap for power purchased from California, would this be a disincentive for the construction of power plants in California? Clearly this would be the case.

---

[2] Information for these rules is from Swartz and Watkins 2003, 238; Eichenwald 2005, 342; McLean and Elkind 2004, 265, 266.

Conversely, the cap on customer rates would decrease customers' incentives to use less power at times when the utilities were paying more for power.

In addition to all this, there were traders and power companies eager to "game the system" and take advantage of the unintended consequences of this dysfunctional set of regulations. For Enron, "The easy money was just too tempting to pass up" (Eichenwald 2005, 342).

Ironically, California's bizarre regulations came into effect on April Fools' Day—April 1, 1998. While the system worked well at first, the power companies and traders soon began to see the potential loopholes. In fact, about a year after the new regulations came into effect, Timothy Belden, former head of Enron's Western energy trading desk, actually did an experiment to test weaknesses in California's power system. On May 24, 1999, Belden negotiated a deal to sell 2,900 megawatts of power to CAL PX, and "he identified a transmission route called Silverpeak as the means for getting the electricity to the state" (McLean and Elkind 2004, 268). Silverpeak was deliberately chosen because its lines could transmit only a small amount of electricity, with the result that, suddenly, California was facing an energy shortage and had to buy a large quantity of power at the last minute when prices increased dramatically. When the California authorities called Belden to find out whether the choice of Silverpeak had been an error, he was quite blatant that it had been done deliberately.

By May 2000, all the adverse forces had combined and California's power nightmare began in earnest. A long dry season reduced the supply of hydroelectricity and the start of a long hot summer increased the demand for electric power. The utility companies were caught in a bind: they were receiving the same, regulated rates from customers, but they were paying astronomical prices for power on the CAL PX auctions and the ISO emergency auctions because the utilities had been forced to sell their own power plants and had not been allowed to sign any long-term purchase contracts. In addition, there was some suspicion about just how much downtime the power plants really needed for maintenance.

Before May 2000, prices had hovered in the range of $25 to $40 per megawatt hour. On May 22, 2000, the ISO had to declare an emergency as prices "quickly hit the price cap of $750 per megawatt hour" (McLean and Elkind 2004, 272). Rolling blackouts began in June 2000, with schools, companies, and homes experiencing power cuts for two hours at a time during the day. By the time summer ended, California was experiencing an energy crisis. In August, the California utilities requested that the Federal Energy Regulatory Commission (FERC) conduct an investigation into trading abuses. However, this Commission was largely ineffective; it lacked subpoena power, and its lame efforts did not uncover the scams and schemes.

California's problems continued unabated through the winter, and in January 2001, California's Governor Gray Davis began calling for price caps over the whole western region to prevent California's power from being sent out of state to areas where there were no price caps. Enron, of course, argued vehemently against price caps on the grounds that it favored market prices— a most disingenuous argument because these electricity prices were certainly not purely market driven. There was no fully deregulated market to produce market prices. Instead, the prices were artificially inflated due to manipulations by unscrupulous individuals and a set of dysfunctional regulations.

The artificially high prices in this semi-deregulated market were making much more profit for Enron than market prices ever could. In fact, an article in the *Wall Street Journal*, in October 2002, reported that Enron's "overall electricity-trading profit soared to $1.8 billion during 2000 and 2001" (Smith and Wilke 2002). Back in California, the price of electricity was out of control: "Electricity that was selling $30 in late 1999 was going for $1500 a year later" (Bryce 2002, 243).

The jokers at Enron were laughing all the way to the bank. At a conference in Las Vegas, in mid-2001, Skilling quipped at California's expense: "What's the difference between California and the *Titanic*? At least when the *Titanic* went down . . . the lights were on" (Swartz and Watkins 2003, 267). Skilling chuckled over California's plight while schools and companies closed down during rolling blackouts, and Pacific Gas and Electric filed for bankruptcy.

Throughout this time, emboldened by the Silverpeak experiment, many of the other power companies and their traders used numerous ploys to manipulate power prices and congestion fees. These fees enabled the traders to earn more money by intentionally sending electricity on congested routes. Furthermore, the sellers could file inflated demand schedules to make an electricity line appear congested when it was not, and the ISO had no way of checking this information. The various bilking schemes became so pervasive that they had their own names. For example, making a line appear congested became known as *Load Shift* or *Death Star*. An article in the *San Francisco Chronicle* described this scheme as follows: "To pull off Load Shift, Enron submitted false schedules to the state's power grid that appeared to cause transmission line congestion, and forced grid officials to pay Enron to relieve the congestion." The same article described how Jeffrey Richter, an Enron trader, who later pleaded guilty to conspiracy to commit wire fraud and making false statements, also assisted in the development of Enron's *Get Shorty* scheme, which "involved Enron's selling power to the state at high prices in the day-ahead market and then buying it back the next day at much lower prices. In company memos, Enron officials admitted the company often did not have the power it was selling and then buying back." (Quotes from Berthelson and Martin 2003)

Another loophole pounced upon by unscrupulous suppliers and traders was based on the regulation cap that existed for the price of Californian power—but *not* for power from outside California. The traders simply directed the electricity supplies out of California and then redirected it back into the state. Presto! With a wave of a magic wand, the power was no longer from California. This dazzling scheme, which became known as *Ricochet,* allowed traders to charge "higher prices for out-of-state electricity" (Eichenwald and Richtel 2002).

After leading the charge to exploit the weaknesses in California's energy grid, Timothy Belden played the system for several years, but eventually he became too clever for his own good. In October 2002, the *Wall Street Journal* reported:

> Timothy Norris Belden, 35 years old, pleaded guilty to a single count of fraud. He told U.S. District Judge Martin Jenkins in San Francisco that he helped devise "schemes" to manipulate the California wholesale electricity market from when it was first deregulated in 1998 until Enron's collapse in 2001, "because I was trying to maximize profit for Enron." (Smith and Wilke 2002)

That same month, another article (in the *New York Times*) described how Belden admitted to "transmitting energy into a fictional world, complete with bogus transmission schedules, imaginary congestion in power lines and fraudulent sales of 'out of state' energy that, in fact, came from California itself." As a "reward" for creating this fine work of fiction, Enron actually paid Belden large bonuses, "totaling about $5 million . . . the seventh-highest amount of bonuses paid to any executive at the company that year." (Quotes from Eichenwald and Richtel 2002)

In July 2005, "Enron Corp agreed . . . to a $1.52 billion settlement of accusations that it gouged Californians during the 2000-01 energy crisis." However, it is probable that only a portion of this amount will actually be received, as the payments will be derived from one fund-pool shared by other bankruptcy creditors. This Enron settlement is "part of a quest for $9 billion in alleged overcharges from power suppliers during the energy crisis." Erik

Saltmarsh, who is the executive director of California's Electricity Oversight Board, is emphatic that Enron did not merely participate in California's energy upheaval, but Enron "was the cause of them." (Quotes from Peterson 2005)

Although California's electricity situation emerged from crisis mode in June 2001, concerns about the adequacy of its power supply persist, and the specter of Enron lives on. In August 2005, Joseph Kelliher, the chairman of the Federal Energy Regulating Commission, stated, "Five years after the crisis, we're still worried what the temperature will be in Southern California today" (quoted in Peterson 2005).

The enormous profit that Enron made on wholesale electricity futures, as well as its lucrative trading in natural gas, merely delayed its inevitable downfall from the huge losses it was incurring in the retail electricity business and on projects like Dabhol, Cuiába, Azurix, and Enron Broadband Services. As its plans and projects imploded one after the other, Enron fought to keep afloat the only way it knew how: by receiving cash up front in the infamous prepays, by reporting false earnings, and by keeping its huge debts off the balance sheet—in short, by fabricating financial fairy tales.

PART 5
HOW ENRON COOKED THE BOOKS: THE MAIN FICTITIOUS FINANCIAL REPORTING SCHEMES

Scheme #1: The Abuse of Mark-to-Market Accounting via Mariner Energy

When the SEC originally opened the door to mark-to-market accounting in 1991, Enron searched for every possible loophole to exploit this opportunity to overstate its earnings. Essentially, mark-to-market accounting allowed Enron to look at an asset—be it a merchant asset or a contract or publicly traded stocks—and revalue it to its "fair" value. This process involved increasing the asset's value on the balance sheet and increasing the profit on the income statement.

One of Enron's most spectacular abuses of mark-to-market accounting involved Enron's investment in a private oil and gas exploration company named Mariner Energy Inc. that Enron acquired in 1996. If Mariner had been a publicly traded company where shares could be sold at a moment's notice, there would have been valid, objective guidelines to use when revaluing Enron's shares in Mariner. Also, since publicly traded shares can be sold easily (if there is no sale restriction), it would have been fair to revalue Enron's shares in Mariner according to the objective market price and to recognize the corresponding profit (or loss) in the income statement. However, since Mariner Energy was a private company, it had no verifiable market price. Mariner specialized in highly speculative deep-water exploration, which made the value of its shares even more volatile. Nevertheless, the great clairvoyants of Enron knew exactly what the shares of this private company were worth. Not surprisingly, the Enron executives deemed the shares to be exceptionally valuable, and they became the shares that kept on sharing. In fact, one Enron vice president reportedly said that when Enron's earnings were tight, "People were asked to look and see if there's anything more we can squeeze out of Mariner" (quoted in McLean and Elkind 2004, 129).

The SEC, in a subsequent discussion of Enron's approach to the non-publicly traded businesses in its portfolio, alleged:

> Enron valued the businesses according to its own internal "models." Enron then manipulated these models in order to produce results necessary to meet internal budget targets. For example, under the direction of Causey [Enron's chief accounting officer] and others, company personnel fraudulently increased the value of one of the largest of Enron's merchant assets, Mariner Energy Inc., by $100 million in the fourth quarter of 2000. (LR 18851)

Enron had acquired Mariner Energy for $185 million and by "the second quarter of 2001, Enron had Mariner on its books for $367.4 million" (McLean and Elkind 2004, 129).

Scheme #2—The Abuse of Special Purpose Entities: An Overview

The Powers Report (2002) of the U.S. Congressional Special Investigative Committee on Enron stated that many of Enron's transactions involved "an accounting structure known as a 'special purpose entity'" (5). Such entities, usually partnerships, trusts, or joint ventures, are created as entities that are legally separate from a company in order to conduct "special" or specific kinds of business transactions that are not part of the company's normal operating activities. A special purpose entity (SPE) may borrow cash and incur debt in its own name, and under certain conditions, this debt need not be added to the company's debt on the company's group balance sheet. In accounting terms, the SPE's debt need not be "consolidated" with the company's debt and, of course, its assets are also not consolidated into the company's balance sheet.

The beauty for the sponsoring company is that, via equity accounting, the company's share of the SPE's earnings is accounted for in the company's income statement, and the company can record profits on its transactions with the SPE. Clearly, however, there needs to be an "arm's-length" of distance between the control of the SPE and the company. The Powers Report summarized these pre-Enron requirements as follows:[3]

A company that does business with an SPE may treat that SPE as if it were an independent, outside entity for accounting purposes if two conditions are met:

1. An owner independent of the company must make a substantive equity investment of at least 3% of the SPE's assets, and that 3% must remain at risk throughout the transaction.[4]

2. The independent owner must exercise control of the SPE.

In those circumstances the company may record gains and losses on transactions with the SPE and the assets and liabilities of the SPE are not included in the company's balance sheet even though the company and the SPE are closely related. (5)

The problem with Enron's SPEs arose because often the person who managed the SPE was not independent of Enron and often the minimum of 3 percent of equity capital that was purportedly provided by the independent outsider was, in fact, indirectly provided or guaranteed by Enron. Further, Enron often guaranteed the SPEs' debts. When these facts were revealed, it became clear that the SPEs' debts should have been consolidated with Enron's other debts, and this ultimately resulted in Enron being forced to restate its financial statements.

As mentioned earlier, although SPEs often take the form of partnerships, they can also be structured as corporations, trusts, or joint ventures. The charter of an SPE limits its activities, while its assets and debts are its own and "off balance sheet" (i.e., off the sponsor's balance sheet as long as the sponsor is not at risk for more than its invested capital). Enron used a multiplicity of these kinds of off-balance-sheet entities to generate false profits with contrived sales, and to keep debt off its balance sheet.

Although Enron began its SPE activity as a means to keep a joint venture's debt off its balance sheet, the SPE activity grew to include transactions with the SPEs that both hid debt and overstated Enron's profits. Eventually, Enron used vast, interlocking sets of SPEs to borrow huge amounts of

---

[3] For a discussion of the new post-Enron rules regarding SPEs and variable interest entities (VIEs), see the discussion in Chapter 9, "Reform: Is There a Magic Potion?" Also see the overview of the "Signals" section of this chapter.

[4] Post Enron, the 3 percent requirement has been raised to 10 percent.

money and to transfer the money to itself. These transfers were carried out via related-party sales of poorly performing Enron assets to the SPEs at inflated prices, thereby overstating Enron's earnings. Enron also used the SPEs to overstate earnings via mark-to-market accounting and to recognize profits on the increase in value of Enron's own shares.

Of course, financial institutions did not lend these huge sums of money to Enron without receiving guarantees, and eventually, when Enron was called upon to repay the debts of the SPEs, the company was bankrupted. By the time Enron collapsed, it had a confusing jumble of over 3,000 interrelated special purpose entities.

An examination of six of Enron's major SPE clusters will reveal how Enron deviously used these special purpose entities.

▪ Special Purpose Entity #1: JEDI

In 1993, Enron entered into an off-balance-sheet joint venture with the California Public Employees Retirement System (CALPERS). The joint venture was named JEDI, an acronym for Joint Energy Development Investments, a tongue-in-cheek reference to Andrew Fastow's admiration of the *Star Wars* film. Enron's $250 million was contributed in the form of issuing its own shares to JEDI, while CALPERS contributed its $250 million in cash. The purpose of JEDI was to invest in energy projects. As a legal entity, JEDI could, of course, borrow cash and the resulting debt incurred would be JEDI's debt—not Enron's. At the same time, Enron could account for 50 percent of JEDI's profits in its income statement. This particular accounting operation was completely legal; the debt really was JEDI's and not Enron's. There was no need to consolidate JEDI's assets and debts into Enron's balance sheet. It was equally true that 50 percent of JEDI's profits did belong to Enron and ultimately would be distributed to it or reinvested in JEDI for eventual distribution to Enron. By the same token, CALPERS had contributed its 50 percent share of JEDI's equity.

At this stage, Enron was not doing any related-party transactions with JEDI, which was doing its own successful transactions with outsiders. These investments did pretty well for Enron and CALPERS. By 1997, the CALPERS half of JEDI was valued at $383 million—an increase of $133 million in about four years. At that point, Enron wanted CALPERS to enter into a second, even larger, joint venture. CALPERS was willing to do this as long as it was bought out of its share of JEDI. Herein lay a problem: if Enron purchased CALPERS' share, it would own 100 percent of JEDI and would have to consolidate JEDI's assets and debts into its group balance sheet, and Fastow could not find any other party willing to buy CALPERS' half of JEDI.

While it is difficult to pinpoint exactly when Enron crossed the line from legal to fraudulent financial accounting, Fastow's next step must have been one of the first in that direction: Fastow constructed an SPE to buy CALPERS' half of JEDI. He named it Chewco, apparently after the *Star Wars* character, Chewbacca.

▪ Special Purpose Entity #2: Chewco

There were two major problems facing Fastow in financing Chewco as an SPE that could keep its assets and liabilities off Enron's balance sheet. First, it had to be controlled by someone independent of Enron. Second, it had to have a minimum of 3 percent of its equity capital contributed independently of Enron. Fastow selected Michael Kopper, an employee of his at Enron, to be the person who would "independently" run Chewco and purportedly contribute the required 3 percent of the equity capital—amounting to $11.4 million—to Chewco. The only problem was that Kopper, together with his domestic partner William Dodson, could come up with only $125,000. Undeterred, Fastow simply got Barclays Bank to provide the $11.4 million via ostensible "equity loans" (i.e., ownership capital that is at risk). Barclays stipulated that $6.6 million cash collateral had to be provided for repayment of the loan; Enron obligingly provided this cash collateral.[5]

The Powers Report later concluded:

> The existence of this cash collateral for the Barclays funding was fatal to Chewco's compliance with the 3% equity requirement. . . . As a result, Chewco should have been consolidated into Enron's consolidated financial statements from the outset, and because JEDI's non-consolidation depended upon Chewco's non-consolidation status, JEDI also should have been consolidated beginning in November 1997. (52)

In addition to the lame attempt to provide outside "equity" of $11.4 million to satisfy the 3-percent rule, the remainder of Chewco's financing came from another $240 million loan from Barclays Bank, which Enron guaranteed, as well as a $132 million advance from JEDI itself. From this financing, CALPERS was paid $383 million for its 50 percent share of JEDI.

---

[5] To complicate matters further, these loans were made via a contrived set of transactions with two other entities, named Big River and Little River. Big River was designated as Chewco's limited partner, and Little River was selected to be Chewco's sole member.

Michael Kopper was now in control of Chewco—a phantom entity. Although Kopper was not a senior officer of Enron, the fact that he was an Enron employee meant it was likely that Chewco would fail the off-balance-sheet SPE test on the grounds that Chewco was not controlled independently of Enron. This test would have been hypothetical since Chewco definitely failed the 3 percent outside equity test anyway. The situation was further complicated by the fact that Kopper later transferred his controlling interest to William Dodson but continued to "run" Chewco. In fact, Kopper received $1.6 million for managing Chewco.

According to the SEC's ensuing investigation, "Fastow secretly controlled Chewco and Kopper, and by virtue of that control, received a share of Chewco's profits as kickbacks from Kopper" (LR 17762). The fact that an Enron employee ran Chewco was not revealed to the board of directors and was a contravention of Enron's own policies and procedures guidelines. Moreover, Chewco's debt was guaranteed by Enron and as soon as it became likely that any debt guaranteed by Enron would have to be paid by Enron, such debt should have been accounted for on Enron's balance sheet.

Chewco and JEDI were significant in two major ways. First, as Bryce (2002) explained, "Skilling simply had to keep JEDI—and the $600 million in debt that came with it—off Enron's books" (139). Second, Enron used Chewco and JEDI to overstate its earnings with related party transactions—it boosted its profits by essentially doing transactions with itself—since JEDI and Chewco were really part of Enron. The Powers Report identified three sources of false earning streams, namely:

1. A guarantee fee
2. Management fees
3. Revenue recognized on Enron's own stock

In order to guarantee the repayment of the $240 million Barclays Bank loan to Chewco, JEDI "paid" Enron $17.4 million as a guarantee fee. Since neither JEDI nor Chewco were independent entities, this amount was a related-party transaction that, in effect, amounted to Enron paying itself. Further, Enron recognized the up-front amount of $10 million paid in 1997 as revenue for that period, instead of spreading the fee for the guarantee over the life of the guarantee. In addition, JEDI was required by Enron and Chewco to pay Chewco a management fee from 1998 to 2003. In 1998, using market-to-market accounting, Enron recognized the present value of the entire five-year period's management fees of $25.7 million in its income statement. So the phony fees earned by Enron via the management and financing of the bogus entities really amounted to Enron managing and financing itself. To bring this wily illusion full circle, we must not forget that Enron invested its original $250 million in JEDI in the form of Enron stock.

The Powers Report stated that in the first quarter of 2000, "Enron recorded $126 million in Enron stock appreciation during that quarter." In effect, Enron was actually recording the appreciation of its own stock on its income statement. To add to the cunning subterfuge, when the value of Enron stock owned by JEDI fell by approximately $94 million in 2001, "Enron did not record its share of this loss" (59). Exhibit 6-A provides a diagram from the Powers Report showing how Chewco and JEDI were financed.

Kopper and Dodson, who had originally come up with the paltry $125,000 portion of the $383 million financing for Chewco, also received strangely favorable treatment by Fastow during Enron's final repurchase of Chewco. The Powers Report stated: "As a result of the buyout, Kopper and Dodson received an enormous return on their $125,000 investment in Chewco. In total, they received approximately $7.5 million (net) cash during the term of the investment, plus an additional $3 million cash payment at closing" (64). Additionally, Kopper had also received $1.5 million in management fees for running Chewco for a few years. Clearly, Fastow had taken good care of his henchmen. Predictably, the SEC's Litigation Release No. 17692 alleged that Kopper "shared the $1.5 million management fee with Enron's CFO"—none other than Andrew Fastow. Furthermore, the same SEC Release claimed that Fastow also "received a share of Chewco's profits as kickbacks from Kopper."

▪ Special Purpose Entity #3: LJM1

Emboldened by the ease with which he had manipulated JEDI and Chewco to enhance Enron's balance sheet, Fastow concocted another SPE that he dubbed LJM, a name based on the initials of the first names of his wife, Lea, and children, Jeffrey and Matthew. This SPE was registered in the Cayman Islands in June 1999 as a Limited Partnership officially named LJM Cayman L.P., but was subsequently referred to as LJM1.

The Powers Report described how Fastow concealed and disguised the ownership of LJM1 with a series of interlocking partnerships: "LJM1 was formed in June 1999. Fastow became the sole and managing member of LJM Partners, LLC, which was the general partner of LJM Partners, L.P. This, in turn, was the general partner of LJM1" (69). Exhibit 6-B provides a diagram of the LJM1 structure.

Exhibit 6-A A Diagram of the Chewco Transaction*

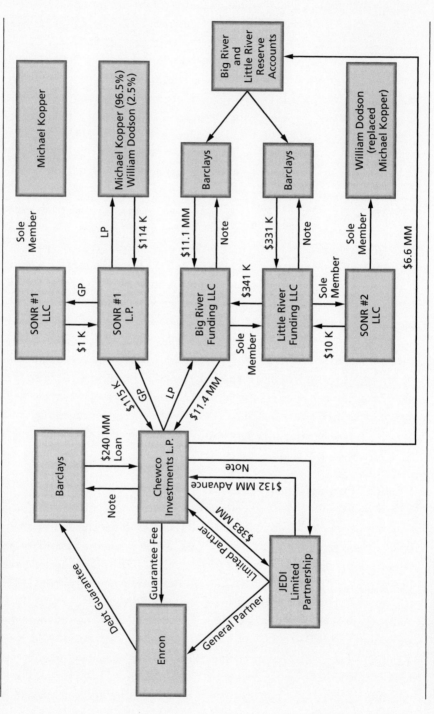

Exhibit 6-B A Diagram of the LJM1 structure*

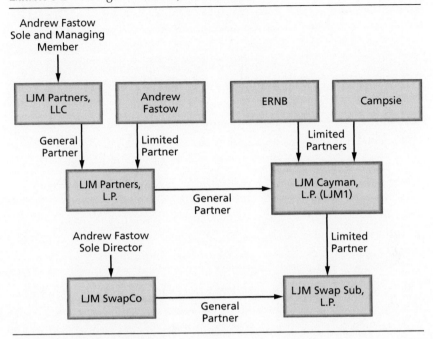

From: Powers Report: page 70.

By this time, Fastow had realized that he had free reign with the cash borrowed by an SPE, and the golden goose was his for the plucking. He persuaded Lay and Skilling to convince the board of directors to appoint *him* as general partner of LJM1. Fastow offered to invest $1 million of his own cash into LJM1, with a further $15 million to be controlled by limited partnerships, and Enron itself to invest 3.4 million shares of restricted stock, valued at about $246 million. Any worries the board may have had about a conflict of interests must have been put to rest when Fastow assured them that his participation as managing partner of LJM1 would not "adversely affect the interests of Enron" (Powers Report 2002, 69). At the Enron board meeting on June 28, 1999, the directors agreed to waive Enron's own ethics rule—which was supposed to prevent officers of the company from doing business with the company—and approved the formation of LJM1 to be controlled by Enron's own CFO, Andrew Fastow.

The Enron board's approval of an arrangement with such potential for disaster was astonishing. Fastow now had an ownership interest in LJM1, and he could get financing for the SPE via Enron's stock and Enron's guarantees of loans. Furthermore, he could buy and sell Enron's assets via LJM1. Did it not occur to any members of the board that the profits that Enron would record on sales to LJM1 would be absolutely meaningless? Did it not occur to them that Fastow had a large interest in getting Enron to guarantee numerous loans for LJM1 in order to acquire substantial amounts of cash for his own gain? Or that he could start buying and selling Enron's assets at prices more favorable to LJM1 than to Enron? It certainly must have occurred to Fastow. This was perhaps why he ensured that the trails of the ownership and financing of his SPEs were as complicated and convoluted as possible.

Essentially, via contrived sales with an SPE, Enron gave itself revenue that would simply be eliminated upon consolidation of the SPE's financial statements with Enron's financial statements. The trick, however, was that Enron had no intention of consolidating the SPE. Certainly Fastow must have known that an SPE had to be consolidated with the parent company if it was controlled by a senior officer of that company. He appeared to have forged ahead blatantly, without consolidating LJM1 into Enron's financial statements in direct contravention of GAAP.

The hidden problem at the heart of this accounting fantasy was that Enron secretly had to guarantee the SPE's debt in order for the SPE to get the loans. Eventually, Enron would have to recognize these secret debts when it was forced to pay them. This, however, did not seem to bother Fastow. His star was on the rise, together with that of his admired mentor, Jeffrey Skilling. (In fact, there are those who claim that Fastow named one of his sons for Skilling.) Fastow desperately wanted to impress Skilling, but he also wanted to feather his own nest.

Fastow's creation of illusory earnings via LJM1 far exceeded his comparatively modest manipulations with Chewco. His dress rehearsal with Chewco had given him practice in the exploitation of SPEs. It had shown him how easy it was to create artificial revenue in Enron's books—simply by charging an amount (for example, for a management fee or a contrived sale) to an SPE that he ultimately controlled. The SPE would then borrow money to pay Enron. With a deft sleight of hand, the ensuing debt was *the SPE's debt*—and not Enron's! How simple. How perfect. And how fictitious.

❖ LJM1 and Rhythms NetConnections

Enron first used LJM1 to create a false put option "hedge" for its investment in Rhythms NetConnections. The Rhythms transaction was actually the motivation for the formation of LJM1. Rhythms was an Internet service provider, and Enron had purchased 5.4 million shares of Rhythms NetConnections stock in March 1998, at $1.85 per share. In April 1999, the company went public and the stock jumped to $21 per share, and by May 1999, Enron's investment was worth almost $300 million. However, Enron was not allowed to trade its Rhythms stock before the end of 1999, and with the wild fluctuations of Internet companies, it was impossible to estimate what the stock would be worth by then. Precisely because of that uncertainty, GAAP rules do not allow a company to record the profit on such stock until it is marketable. Fastow, however, wanted to recognize the profit in Enron's books right then—in May. He had to find a way around the inconvenient GAAP rules.

At that point, Fastow decided that LJM1 would agree to "purchase" the Rhythms shares at a specific, profitable price on a future date. Accordingly, the actual amount of profit Enron would make on its Rhythms stock in the future would be "known" in May 1999. Since it was now guaranteed that Enron would make that minimum profit from selling the stocks to LJM1, Enron could use mark-to-market accounting to revalue the Rhythms stock and it could book at least that amount of profit. With his new mystic powers, Fastow ordered Enron to buy a "put option" from LJM1 in May 1999, which would give Enron the right to sell its Rhythms stock to LJM1 in June 2004 at $56 per share. This way, if the stock price fell by the end of 1999, Fastow reasoned that he did not have to devalue this investment because he had the "right" to sell it at $56 per share in *June 2004*. Enron then went ahead in 1999 and "recognized after-tax income of $95 million from the Rhythms transaction" (Powers Report 2002, 14).

The next piece of the puzzle was for Fastow to determine what LJM1 would use for cash to buy the Rhythms stock from Enron. Furthermore, he had to work out how LJM1 would handle the loss if the Rhythm's shares fell in price. Since LJM1 had received 3.4 million shares of Enron stock as part of its formation capital, the logic behind this hedge was that LJM1 would just sell its Enron stock to buy the Rhythms shares from Enron at $56 per share, irrespective of the market value of the shares. Did Fastow ever stop to consider what would happen if the Enron shares held by LJM1 fell so much in value that the sale of these shares was not enough to purchase the Rhythms shares at the option price? Fastow probably thought things would never get that bad, living as he was in his own fantasy.

Living in yet another parallel universe, Jeffrey Skilling—an ardent supporter of mark-to-market accounting—apparently supported Fastow's delusion. On the other hand, Vince Kaminski, Enron's chief research analyst (who had an MBA and a Ph.D in mathematical economics) was shocked to discover this hedge maneuver and exclaimed that the put option was "so stupid that only Andrew Fastow could have come up with it" (Bryce 2002, 160). Allegedly, because Kaminski objected to the formation of LJM so vehemently, Skilling transferred Kaminski and his group of analysts to other projects. Several years later, at the criminal trial of Lay and Skilling in 2006, Kaminski explained that using LJM had been like placing bets in a casino that was bankrupt: "'If you lose you lose, and if you win you lose' because the house can't pay your winnings" (Mulligan 2006). The put option hedge would fail if the value of both Rhythms' and Enron's shares fell at the same time. When the stock bubble burst, that is exactly what happened because the "hedge guarantee" that Enron would sell its Rhythms stock at $56 a share to LJM1 was not a guarantee at all. The so-called "profit" on the Rhythms stock had not really been earned in May 1999, and Enron could not legitimately recognize the profit in its income statement in 1999.

While Fastow liked to obscure the structure of his SPEs, he liked to complicate their transactions even more. He did not merely arrange for LJM1 to sell Enron the put option for Rhythms stock, he also created LJM Swap Sub L.P. and LJM SwapCo. for the transaction. He then used LJM1 to transfer $1.6 million of Enron shares and about $3.75 million in cash into LJM Swap Sub. The SPE known as LJM SwapCo was made general partner of LJM Swap Sub. It was actually LJM Swap Sub that issued the put option to Enron, giving Enron the right to sell 5.4 million of Rhythms shares to Swap Sub at $56 per share, in June 2004. Originally, Enron had issued 3.4 million restricted shares to LJM1. In exchange, Enron received the put option (from Swap Sub) valued at approximately $104 million, plus a note for $64 million. Bryce (2002) pointed out: "With the Swab Sub deal, Enron began buying and selling derivatives that were based on the value of *its own stock*. . . . Trading derivatives that are predicated on the equity value of your own company is like playing Russian roulette" (158).

Commenting on the convoluted, contrived set of SPEs involved in the exchange, the Powers Report concluded: "We do not know why Swap Sub was used, although a reasonable inference is that it was used to shield LJM1 from legal liability in any derivative transactions with Enron" (81). The complicated structure of the Rhythms transactions can be seen in Exhibit 6-C.

With these absurd procedures injected into Fastow's interlocking SPEs, it is no wonder that later, in attempting to unravel it all, Enron's postbankruptcy CEO, Steven Cooper, declared: "It looks like some deranged artist went to work one night" (quoted in McLean and Elkind 2004, 155). Further, regarding Swap Sub, the CEO of Arthur Andersen,

Exhibit 6-C A Diagram of the Rhythms Transaction*

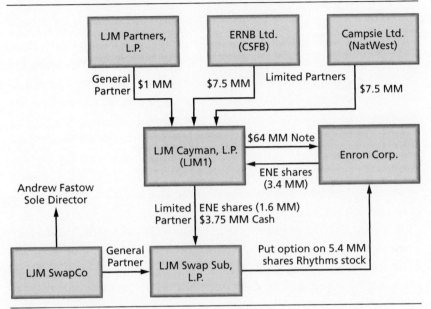

*From: Powers Report: page 81.

which was Enron's external audit firm, stated in Congressional testimony on December 12, 2001, "When we reviewed this transaction again in October 2001, we determined that our team's initial judgment that the 3 percent test was met was in error. We promptly told Enron to correct it" (Powers Report 2002, 84).

The Powers Report went on to explain:

On November 8, 2001, Enron announced that Swap Sub was not properly capitalized with outside equity and should have been consolidated. As a result, Enron said it would restate prior period financial statements to reflect the consolidation retroactive to 1999, which would have the effect of decreasing Enron's net income by $95 million in 1999 and $8 million in 2000. (84)

In the first quarter of 2000, Enron decided to sell its Rhythms shares and unwind the Rhythms put option. The period during which the Rhythms stock could not be sold by Enron had passed, the stock had fallen in value, and its price continued to be volatile. According to the Powers Report, Enron analysts had reviewed the financial viability of the structure of SPEs created for the Rhythms put option and "determined there was a 68%

probability that the structure would default and would not be able to meet its obligations on the Rhythms put" (87).

❖ LJM1 and the Cuiába Power Plant

Fastow amused himself with SPEs for several years before his maneuvers and deceptions caught up with him. One of his favorite fabrications had its origin in South America, where Enron owned 65 percent of a Brazilian company called Empressa Productura de Enerain Ltd. This company, also known as EPE, was building the Cuiába Power Plant in Brazil, and Cuiába was meant to connect to a natural gas pipeline that Enron was constructing, through tropical forests, from Bolivia to Brazil.

By mid-1999, the project had experienced several setbacks. It was far behind schedule and was experiencing opposition from environmentalists who were concerned that the project would harm the tropical forests and delicate ecosystem. Enron wanted to decrease its ownership of this problematic investment. Not surprisingly, there was no buyer foolish enough to buy into this messy situation. So what did Fastow do? He conjured up a buyer—his own LJM1—and sold a 13 percent stake in Cuiába/EPE to LJM1 for the sum of $11.3 million. (Essentially, Enron sold part of its own share of the Brazilian company back to itself, like a dog chasing its tail.) Fastow then concluded that with its reduced ownership in Cuiába/EPE, Enron no longer needed to consolidate Cuiába into its financial statements. Further, Fastow decided that Enron now had a market price for the Cuiába project based on the price of "selling" Cuiába back to Enron itself. In the third quarter of 1997—with circular logic—Enron figured if this 13 percent share that it had sold was worth $11.3 million then, using mark-to-market accounting, the remainder of its share must be worth an extra $34 million in the income statement. In fact, this allowed "Enron to—voila—realize an extra $34 million in mark-to-market accounting income in the third quarter of 1999" (Bryce 2002, 158). In the fourth quarter of 1999, Enron booked another $31 million using mark-to-market accounting on a further revaluation of this same plant.

Back in Brazil, Cuiába's problems worsened for the next few years, but in Texas, everything was just swell. Then Enron repurchased LJM1's stake of Cuiába in August 2001 for $14 million. Why on earth would anyone have wanted to buy the ailing project back when they had already "sold" it due to its difficulties? Obviously, the entire exercise had been for the purpose of generating some mark-to-market revaluation profits based on the ludicrous "market value" claim determined by the "outside" sale of 13 percent of

Cuiába/EPE to LJM1. The Powers Report stated that if Enron had agreed to make LJM1 whole (i.e., compensate it for any loss on its investment), "Enron would have been required to consolidate Cuiába/EPE, and could not have recognized the mark-to-market gains" (138). McLean and Elkind (2004) pointed out:

> . . . a June 1999 email from an Enron accountant named Kent Castleman described LJM as a "short-term warehouse" for the Cuiaba stake. Kopper later disclosed that the buy-back provision had even been included in drafts of the original Cuiaba sale documents. One thing was certain: the deal provided yet another windfall for LJM's investors. (203)

After the Cuiába deal, Fastow began a series of transactions using LJM1 (and later LJM2) to purportedly sell poorly performing assets or a share thereof to various SPEs, thereby recording profits on the sales. With this kind of finagling, it was no wonder that Enron-insider jokes began to circulate referring to Enron's mark-to-market accounting as "HFV" or "Hypothetical Future Value" accounting. Fastow also utilized mark-to-market accounting, from time to time, to revalue the remaining unsold part of the poorly-performing assets based on the contrived sales, and booked more profits on the revaluation of the assets. The strategy was essentially for Enron to use interlocking SPEs as a front to borrow cash from a financial institution, and then some of the money would be passed on to Enron via the contrived sale of Enron's poorly performing assets to that SPE. (In addition, Enron would generously guarantee the loan, so the banks felt that their money was secure!) Cash would actually have been loaned to Enron disguised as a sale, thus overstating Enron's profits and understating its debt.

There would be clandestine side agreements—with magic incantations, perhaps—to guarantee that the "sold" assets would be repurchased by Enron and that the cash received from the financial institutions would be repaid. Assets were parked in an SPE with the entire financing arrangement masquerading as a sale when, in fact, it was a loan. The false categorization of the loan as a sale overstated both earnings and cash flow in Enron's financial statements and understated its debt.

Riding high on his make-believe business acumen, Fastow also used LJM1 to make a brief investment in Osprey, which was part of the infamous Whitewing entity, one of Enron's wildest and most ambitious off-balance-sheet entities. Osprey will be discussed in more detail later in this chapter, as part of the analysis of Whitewing.

❖ The Liquidation of LJM1

To add insult to injury, Fastow hoodwinked a whole group of individuals in the final winding up of LJM1 and Swap Sub. The two limited partners that put up a joint amount of $15 million in the financing of LJM1 were Credit Suisse First Boston Bank and Greenwich NatWest Bank. Certain employees from the banks allegedly misled their own banks as to the amounts Enron would pay for the dismantling of the SPEs. Astoundingly, Fastow constructed yet another SPE, named Southampton, which he controlled and used together with other Enron employees and the banks' employees to buy out the interests of Credit Suisse and NatWest in the LJM1 set of partnerships. The SEC explained:

> In approximately February 2000, Fastow and others caused Enron to buy out the partnership interests of LJM1's limited partners, Credit Suisse First Boston and National Westminster Bank (NatWest). In connection with this transaction, Fastow and others told Enron that NatWest wanted $20 million for its interest in the partnership assets, but paid NatWest only $1 million of that sum and pocketed the rest. A purported charitable foundation in the name of Fastow's family received $4.5 million in proceeds of this fraud. (LR 17762)

Both Fastow's audacity and the level of his greed were staggering, and it did not end there. A few months later, in July 2000, Fastow received another $18 million from LJM1. In addition, his "management fees" from this SPE came to $2.6 million. According to McLean and Elkind (2004), "The Fastows' secret take just from this one partnership ultimately reached a staggering $25.1 million" (197).

With LJM1, Enron had overstated its earnings via its related-party transactions, had overstated the cash flow reported in its financial statements, and had falsely driven up its stock price. Furthermore, with LJM1, Fastow had caught even Skilling and Lay off guard in lining his own pockets with Enron's cash.

▪ Special Purpose Entity #4: LJM2 and the Raptors

The false profits generated by LJM1 for Enron by artificially "hedging" the Rhythms stock gain was preparation for Fastow's far more ambitious manipulations of earnings with his next SPE creation—LJM2. With LJM2, Fastow would not only dramatically expand his overstatement of Enron's earnings, but he would also fatten his own bank balance with Enron's cash, in various conflict-of-interest dealings between Enron and LJM2. Via a series of dizzyingly contrived and interlocking partnerships, LJM2 basically borrowed money—and used Enron's own stock—to purchase poorly performing assets from Enron in order to inflate Enron's earnings, hide its debt, and provide cash to keep Enron going.

Perhaps the most infamous of the LJM2 deals concerned the formation of four SPEs called the Raptors (numbered Raptor I through Raptor IV). The Raptors were devised by Fastow and approved by Enron's board of directors in May 2000. (These SPEs were named for the Raptor Golf Course where the scheme was devised, but ironically "raptor" is also the name of a type of dinosaurs believed to have been egg-thieves and predators. Like the dinosaurs, Enron was destined for extinction.) Ultimately, "Enron used the extremely complex Raptor structured finance vehicles to avoid reflecting losses in the value of some merchant investments in its income statement" (Powers Report 2002, 97).

By way of example, let us consider the convoluted transactions of Raptor I, which was started with the formation of an SPE officially called Talon LLC. (Of course, a "talon" is a "vicious claw"; another telling choice of name.) According to the Powers Report, LJM2 invested $30 million in cash in Talon, and Enron invested "stock and stock contracts with a fair market value of $537 million" as well as a $50 million promissory note and only $1,000 cash in Talon (100). The $30 million investment by LJM2 was meant to cover the 3-percent rule requiring an SPE to have at least 3 percent of its at-risk capital contributed by an *independent* entity, in order for Enron to avoid consolidating the SPE into its own financial statements.

Not surprisingly, there were numerous problems with this devious plan. First, LJM2's $30 million investment in Talon was not at risk, as the SEC later pointed out:

> Fastow allegedly entered into an undisclosed side deal in which Enron agreed that, prior to conducting any hedging activity with Raptor I, Enron would return LJM2's investment ($30 million) plus a guaranteed return ($11 million). As a result, Raptor I should have been consolidated into Enron's financial statements. (LR 18543)

Generally, Talon entered into hedges known as "total return swaps" on interests in Enron's merchant assets. The Powers Report described these return swaps as "derivatives under which Talon would receive the amount of any future gains on the value of those investments, but would also have to pay Enron the amount of any future losses" (108).

The main problem was that Talon was really another division of Enron, and Enron was just shifting its losing assets to another part of itself; after all, what sort of a business would purchase only investments that were on the verge of collapse? Another problem was that Talon's main asset was its Enron stock, and its fate was inexorably tied up with Enron's fate.

Soon, Enron began parking poorly performing assets in other Raptor structures to avoid recognizing losses on those poor investments. Then, of course, the inevitable happened. The assets that had been transferred to the Raptors fell in value, and Enron's stock plunged at the same time. This led to the possibility that Enron would have to devalue the Raptors by $500 million at the end of the first quarter of 2000 and recognize this enormous loss in its financial statements, since the Raptors could not meet their obligations. Still unwilling to face the reality of extinction, Enron contrived yet another structure to help the Raptors extend their artificial lives a little longer. However, the floundering investments moved to the Raptors continued to fall, and Enron's stock price continued to decline.

In the midst of all the shenanigans, Stuart Zisman, an attorney in Enron's legal department, sent an e-mail to his superiors on September 1, 2000, in which he wrote: "We have discovered that a majority of the investments being introduced into the Raptor Structure are bad ones. This is disconcerting . . . it might lead one to believe that the financial books at Enron are being 'cooked' in order to eliminate a drag on earnings" (Bryce 2002, 231).

Within close to a year, Zisman's suspicions were confirmed. The Powers Report subsequently presented a diagrammatic representation of the complicated set of interlocking structures that were used for the process wherein Enron basically transacted with itself in an endless hall of mirrors. Refer to Exhibit 6-D for a copy of this diagram.

The Powers Report examined the extent to which Enron used the Raptors to manipulate its reported earnings during the period from the third quarter of 2000 through the third quarter of 2001: "Transactions with the Raptors during that period allowed Enron to avoid reflecting on its income statements almost $1 *billion* in losses on its merchant investments." Without these manipulations, Enron's pretax earnings for that period would have been "$429 million, a decline of 72%." Now the writing was on the wall for all to see. (Quotes from Powers Report 2002, 99)

In the third quarter of 2001, "Enron finally terminated the vehicles. In doing so, it incurred the after-tax charge of $544 million ($710 million

Exhibit 6-D A Very Simplified Diagram of Raptor I*

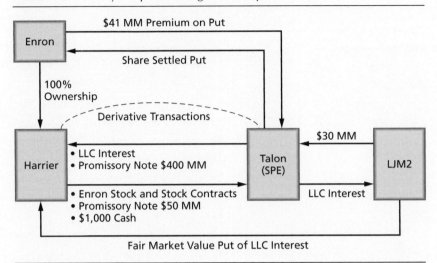

*From: Powers Report: page 101.

pre-tax) that Enron disclosed on October 16, 2001, in its initial third quar-ter release" (Powers Report 2002, 98). Of course, all the debt incurred by the SPEs—debt for which Enron was ultimately responsible—was kept off Enron's balance sheet until it became absolutely clear that the SPEs could not repay their debts. Enron was finally trapped and had no method or means of borrowing more money to keep hiding the situation.

As news of the chaos spread and Enron rapidly fell apart, the world was shocked to learn that the Raptors' connivances were just one part of the SPE labyrinth. Eventually, after investigating all of Enron's SPE transactions, as well as the prepays, the Bankruptcy Examiner concluded: "Enron's debt at December 31, 2000, would have been $22.1 billion rather than $10.2 billion as reported" (*Bankruptcy Report #2,* 2003, 47).

So ended the epoch of the Raptors.

• **Special Purpose Entities #5 and #6: Whitewing and Osprey**

Whitewing, yet another fabulous illusion devised by Fastow, was initially concocted with the apparent purpose of purchasing Enron assets. However, behind this fantasy, Whitewing was borrowing money to transfer to Enron in such a manner as to disguise the loan as the sale of Enron assets. These loans were made to a group of Enron's off-balance-sheet entities known as the Whitewing structure and filtered through this structure to Enron. The loans, which were disguised as sales, overstated Enron's sales, earnings, and cash flow from operations (CFFO). They also understated Enron's contingent liabilities in the notes to its financial statements. Further, as it became clear that Enron's contingent liability for Whitewing's debt would become an actual liability due to Whitewing's inability to repay its own debt, Enron's failure to record its liability for this debt understated Enron's own debt.

In addition, in the event that Whitewing lost money on the resale of the assets it had purchased from Enron (at inflated prices), Enron had guaranteed that it would compensate the Whitewing structure with the issue of Enron stock to make up the shortfall. This meant that the more Enron's share price fell, the more shares it would have to issue if Whitewing made losses on the assets it had purchased from Enron. Predictably, that is what ultimately happened.

As always, Fastow and his magic helpers made the actual flow of money rather difficult to follow through a dazzling maze of off-balance-sheet entities. To assist Whitewing, an off-balance-sheet share trust entity called Osprey Trust was created and it immediately borrowed over $3 billion. Amazingly, no one seemed inclined to ask why in the world any financial institution would lend money to a newly formed trust with no track record. Surely the answer would have been obvious: because Enron ultimately guaranteed the repayment of the debt. However, Enron's gatekeepers who reviewed the Whitewing structure and Enron's financial statements apparently did not ask that question.

After borrowing this money, Osprey invested $1.5 billion in the specially created partnership of Whitewing Associates. Enron also invested 250,000 shares of its preferred convertible stock in Whitewing, as well as $135.2 million of Enron notes. Whitewing then paid "$1.6 billion to purchase assets from Enron." Continuing with its tricks, "Enron recorded the proceeds of its sales of assets to the Whitewing Investment Entities as cash flow from operating activities." (Quotes from *Bankruptcy Report #2*, 2003, 75)

The Bankruptcy Examiner concluded that the Whitewing Associates should have been consolidated with Enron, and if this had been the case, the cash flow from operations on the sale of Enron's assets to Whitewing would have been eliminated. In the case of Osprey Trust, the Examiner acknowledged that it was debatable whether or not Osprey should have been consolidated. However, even without consolidation, the portion of Osprey's debt that was guaranteed by Enron should have been disclosed in the notes to Enron's financial statements as a contingent liability.

Adding to its impending financial implosion, Enron agreed to issue shares to cover losses made by Whitewing's resale of any assets that it had "bought" from Enron. In another dangerous maneuver, "The investors were assured that if Enron's shares fell below $48.55, Enron would distribute extra Enron stock to Whitewing's investors to cover any losses. In addition, the deal with the Osprey notes requested Enron to issue more stock if Enron stock fell below $47" (Bryce 2002, 290, 291). This is clearly death-spiral financing because if loans have to be repaid by the issue of shares, the more the stock price falls, the more shares have to be issued, which, in turn, drives the stock price down. This is similar to slicing a pizza into smaller and smaller slices; yes, there are more slices, but they are being reduced to mere slivers.

Originally, Enron had set up Whitewing and another major share trust entity, Marlin, in order to create "in the aggregate, $3.8 billion dollars in off-balance-sheet financing using support provided by Enron's preferred stock, related contractual obligations of Enron, and Enron notes." The Examiner concluded that "the Whitewing transaction functioned more like revolving financing with the aggregate amount of advances made by Whitewing entities to Enron over a two-year period exceeding $2.7 billion." (Quotes from *Bankruptcy Report #2,* 2003, 67)

As Enron's share price began its inevitable downward spiral, the Whitewing structure—like an albatross—circled back to accelerate Enron's demise. Bryce (2002) explained, "In return for loaning money to Whitewing, the investors got interest-bearing promissory notes from Osprey, a trust controlled by Whitewing, that were to be paid back in 2003" (290). The Bankruptcy Examiner calculated that the remaining assets in the Whitewing structure had "an estimated aggregate value between $700 million and $1 billion" (*Bankruptcy Report #2,* 2003, 67). By the end, Whitewing owed $2.43 billion in respect of the Osprey notes.

Scheme #3: The Prepay Transactions

Even with all the disguised financing from "sales" to the SPEs, Enron was still desperately short of cash. Much of the reported earnings were in the form of mark-to-market accounting, while many of the losing assets were hidden elsewhere, but not actually sold. Furthermore, the income from operations reported on Enron's income statement would be way below the CFFO reported in its statement of cash flows, unless something drastic was done to manipulate the CFFO.

Fastow, with his usual innovative flair, came up with an answer . . . or rather, he came up with a very temporary and rather short-sighted solution known as "prepays." In essence, with "prepays" Enron would enter into a contract with a party to deliver a commodity, like gas, in the future at a specified price. That in itself would not have produced any cash in a current period, nor should it have produced any profit until the gas was delivered. However, Enron would *sell* the contract to a financial institution for the amount of the total future cash selling price, less a discount, and Enron would get the cash upfront. Presto! The cash problem was "solved," or at least it appeared to be. However, Enron would have to agree to guarantee the repayment of all the cash received, plus interest, at some point in the future.

The beauty of the scheme for the current period was that Enron was able to report this loan transaction as a sale in its financial statements. It then raised similar amounts of current assets and current liabilities on the balance sheet under the headings of "Assets from Price Risk Management Activities," and "Liabilities from Price Risk Management Activities," with respect to these contracts. To confuse the deals even more, Enron would have a conduit entity agree to deliver the commodities in the future and to receive the prepaid cash. The cash would then be paid by the conduit entity to an Enron affiliate, usually Enron North America (ENA), which would agree to make the future repayments plus interest. For a diagram of a typical prepay transaction, refer to Exhibit 6-E. For a short while, this strategy produced cash and inflated the CFFO reported on Enron's cash-flow statement. It also overstated sales and income and kept the long-term debt—which was the true source of the temporary cash inflow—off Enron's balance sheet.

Exhibit 6-E Typical Prepay Transaction Structure*

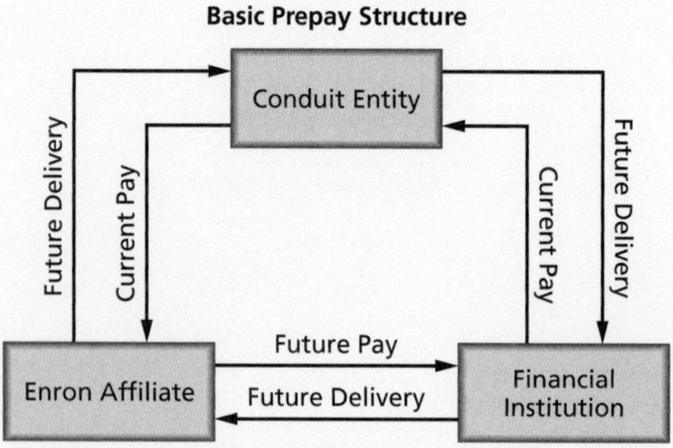

Basic Prepay Structure

*From: Powers Report: page 63.

While Enron had been doing prepays since the mid-1990s, it was clear that these deals "became bigger and more frequent under Skilling." Furthermore, one finance expert at Enron reportedly said that the prepays were "the financial equivalent of crack cocaine. If you want to destroy incentives to generate cash, this is what you do." (Quotes from Bryce 2002, 290)

To illustrate how the prepays worked, Bryce described one prepay with JP Morgan Chase where Enron entered into a contract to deliver $394 million of natural gas to a customer over the period 2001–2005. Enron sold the contract to the conduit, Mahonia—owned by JP Morgan Chase—for $330 million. Enron then agreed to buy the full $394 million of gas from another conduit, Stoneville Aegean, and pay for it in installments. Enron had just received $330 million cash and had to repay $394 million. As Bryce (2002) pointed out, "The accounting rules allowed the company to disguise what was really a loan . . . as a sale. And Enron got another valuable benefit: It was able to count the cash it got from Mahonia as cash flow from operations" (290). In a 1998 e-mail, a Chase banker wrote: "Enron loves these deals . . . as they are able to hide funded debt from their equity analysts" (quoted in McLean and Elkind 2004, 160).

Within a few years, Enron was, predictably, immersed in legal problems, and in January 2003, the Bankruptcy Examiner reached the following conclusions on the prepay transactions:

> Collectively, the Prepay Transaction may have been Enron's single largest source of cash during the four-year period prior to the petition date, providing Enron with $5 billion of cash. Yet, Enron's accounting, cash-flow reporting and disclosure of transactions were inappropriate. (*Bankruptcy Report #2,* 2003, 66)

Furthermore, the Bankruptcy Examiner concluded:

> . . . Enron should have accounted for the Prepay Transactions as debt rather than as price risk management activities, and . . . Enron should have reported the cash received as cash flows from financing activities instead of from operating activities. As a result, the Examiner has concluded that, pursuant to the Prepay Transaction, Enron:
>
> - Understated it's debt by approximately $5 billion in its June 30, 2001 balance sheet; and
> - Incorrectly reported the cash obtained through the Prepay Transactions as cash flows from operating activities. (*Bankruptcy Report #2* 2003, 59)

According to the Examiner's findings, Enron's cash flow from prepays in 1999 was $1.2 billion, which was greater than Enron's reported total cash flow from operations. In 2000, the Examiner showed that the prepays, if properly reported, would have increased Enron's debt from $10.2 billion to $14.24 billion. He concluded, "The prepay technique was a powerful tool employed by Enron to maintain its investment credit grade rating." In fact, the Examiner cited William Brown, who managed Enron's corporate finance group, as saying that "he understood the amount of any given prepay transaction was determined by the targeted cash flow Enron wanted to show the Rating Agencies." (Quotes from *Bankruptcy Report #2*, 2003, 62)

Part 6
Signals of the Enron Fraud:
Indications That Enron
was a Cooked Goose

Signals of Enron's Fictitious Reporting Schemes #1–#3

- Using off-balance-sheet entities or special purpose entities (SPEs) to understate debt and to overstate earnings by abuse of mark-to-market accounting, contrived transactions, and misclassification of prepays

Overview

Since SPEs are usually equity investments, i.e., investments in which the investor acquires an ownership interest in the investee, the information about SPEs is often included and hidden among the other equity investments on the investor's balance sheet.

Generally, equity investments in companies fall into one of three categories:

1. Holdings of less than 20 percent, where the investor has a passive interest in the investee. The investee's assets and liabilities are not consolidated into the investor's group balance sheet.
2. Holdings of between 20 percent and 50 percent, where the investor is deemed to have significant influence, but not control, unless information to the contrary exists. These investments are often classified as "investments in unconsolidated affiliates" on the balance sheet. The assets and liabilities of the affiliate are not consolidated into the investor's group balance sheet.
3. Holdings of more than 50 percent of the equity of the investee, where the investee is deemed to have a controlling interest. The investee's financial statements are consolidated into the investor's group financial statements.

The three categories become blurred, however, when investors or sponsors create special purpose entities.[6]

SPEs are also known as off-balance-sheet entities and are usually "created by a party (the transferor or the sponsor) by transferring assets to another party (the SPE) to carry out a specific purpose, activity or series of transactions. Such entities have no purpose other than the transactions for which they were created" (Soroosh and Ciesielski 2004). They are often partnerships, joint ventures, or trusts, and sometimes they are corporations.

Since such entities operate for a specific purpose, in pre-Enron accounting the Emerging Issue Task Force (EITF 90-15) allowed SPEs to be excluded from consolidation with the sponsor's group financial statements "as long as the equity interest of a third-party owner was at least 3% of the SPE's total capitalization; at the same time, the majority of equity voting rights cannot reside with the beneficiary" (Soroosh and Ciesielski 2004).

Many investors or sponsors began to bend the rules and create entities over which they had control, in which they had invested most of the equity capital (except for 3 percent), and for which they had further obligations for the entities' debt. They used the non-consolidation rule to avoid including such SPEs' debt in their balance sheets and to avoid eliminating profit on related-party transactions with these entities. These investments in off-balance-sheet entities were often lost or hidden in the investor's balance sheets as though they were typical "investments in unconsolidated affiliates" where the investor holds between 20 percent and 50 percent of the investee.

Today, accounting for SPEs is governed by the Financial Accounting Standards Board Interpretation FIN 46(R).[7] In essence, it requires investors to define an off-balance-sheet entity—in which they have liability for losses or debts beyond their invested capital—as a variable interest entity (VIE). VIEs must be consolidated into a company's group financial statements if the company is a primary beneficiary of the VIE. In addition, Final Rule 67 (FR 67)[8] issued in January 2003, now also requires disclosure in the MD&A section regarding certain details of off-balance-sheet arrangements. However, it is important to note that pre-Enron accounting rules also required many of Enron's unconsolidated SPEs to be consolidated into Enron's financial statements, but Enron failed to consolidate many of its now infamous SPEs. If some companies broke the old rules requiring certain off-balance-sheet entities to be

---

[6] For a discussion of the new post-Enron rules regarding SPEs and variable interest entities (VIEs), refer to Chapter 9, "Reform: Is There a Magic Potion?"

[7] For a discussion of FIN 46(R), refer to Chapter 9, "Reform: Is There a Magic Potion?"

[8] For a discussion of FR 67, refer to Chapter 9, "Reform: Is There a Magic Potion?"

consolidated, some will likely be tempted to break the new rules as well. Therefore, hints in financial statements and notes are instructive for telltale signs of problematic SPEs.

Enron's SPEs were hidden mainly among its investments in unconsolidated affiliates and other investments. Hints were left in references in the notes to the financial statements regarding unconsolidated affiliates, and also in the notes regarding related-party transactions, guarantees, and "sales" where some ownership rights in the "sold assets" were retained by the seller. There were also vague references, in notes to the financial statements, to investments in partnerships and trusts, and the financing of such entities with Enron's own stock.

Signal #1: When the amount of the assets and liabilities of unconsolidated affiliates or SPEs grows significantly, it is an indication that the company could be using off-balance-sheet entities to hide its debt or overstate its earnings.

In Enron's "Notes to the Consolidated Financial Statements" in its Annual Report, the note titled "Unconsolidated Equity Affiliates" showed that the magnitude of the assets and liabilities of the unconsolidated affiliates was alarming—their total liabilities grew from $8.3 billion in 1997 to $20.604 billion in 2000. Given that off-balance-sheet entities are often used to hide debt by removing it from a company's balance sheet, large amounts of debt held by unconsolidated affiliates must raise the concern that the company may be liable for the debts of the affiliated entities. There should have been concern as to why Enron was investing so much in unconsolidated entities.

Signal #2: References in the notes to the financial statements and particularly in notes regarding investments in unconsolidated affiliates, or references in the management discussion and analysis (MD&A) regarding off-balance-sheet entities that are vague as to one or more of the following:

- The nature of the transactions with the entity
- The reason for using the special entity
- The name of the entity
- The nature of the entity—whether it is a partnership, a trust, a joint venture, or an established corporation

When investments in unconsolidated affiliates or related-party transactions occur with specially constructed entities like partnerships, trusts, or joint ventures—as opposed to independently established companies—one should be on the alert that the company could be using SPEs to understate debt and boost earnings. It may also be blending the disclosure of these SPEs with regular investments in independently established companies. Therefore, users of financial statements must be on a higher alert for unconsolidated affiliates that are described in vague terms.

Unless a company operates in an industry where the use of SPEs is widespread, the financial statements and the MD&A should make very clear the nature of the SPE, as well as the reason for its use.

In an examination of the notes to Enron's financial statements, the following selection of alerts was revealed:

- In 1998, Enron's consolidated balance sheet already showed a $4.433 billion investment in unconsolidated affiliates. In the related notes, the relationships between Enron and some of these affiliates were described briefly, while others were not named or described at all. In fact, $1.199 billion of the $4.433 billion was simply described as "other." The note also stated, "From time to time, Enron has entered into various administrative service, management, construction, supply and operating agreements with its unconsolidated affiliates."
- In the 1998 Annual Report, the note titled "Merchant Assets" stated: "The investments made by Enron included public and private equity, debt, production payments and interests in *limited partnerships*." (Emphasis added.)
- In the 1999 annual financial statements, several of the LJM special purpose entities are mentioned in the notes under "Related Party Transactions," without using the term "special purpose entities." It becomes clear that Enron's own stock was invested in these partnerships by the statement that "LJM received $6.8 million shares of Enron common stock."
- Also in the 1999 notes to the financial statements, an alarming number of new affiliates was added to the list of "Unconsolidated Equity Affiliates," including the now infamous Whitewing structure that hid enormous debt and losses from Enron's financial statements. Vague descriptions were given of the Whitewing structure without a clear rationale for its existence in the first place. (The LJM structure of unconsolidated entities was not even listed in the unconsolidated affiliate's note, although it was mentioned under related-party transactions.)
- In 2000, the "Unconsolidated Affiliates" note listed an incomplete list of entities, and while some significant SPEs are omitted, the note did mention the sale of Enron's merchant assets to Whitewing. This piece

of information sheds some light on why the entity was created in the first place and why the vagueness. Enron was selling its own assets to this affiliated entity. Why would it do that? No rationale was given. (In the previous year, sales of merchant assets to Whitewing had not been mentioned in Enron's unconsolidated affiliates' note concerning Whitewing.)

By the time Enron's 2000 Annual Report was issued, investors should have been aware of Enron's investments in the partnerships and joint-venture entities of Whitewing, LJM, and JEDI, and should have realized that it was unclear as to why and how these entities were being used. This level of vagueness about off-balance-sheet entities should have been a strong alert that Enron may have been concealing something.

Signal #3: When unconsolidated affiliates—especially constructed entities such as partnerships—are used to generate a significant portion of the company's profit, it is a signal that the company may be using special purpose entities (SPEs) to manipulate its financial statements.

A company could be using the SPEs to move poorly performing assets off its financial statements to avoid dilution of reported earnings, or to generate gains. It is therefore important to search the notes to the financial statements for "gains" or profits earned outside of regular operations, especially where such gains appear to have been made in connection with unconsolidated affiliates of the company.

In Enron's case, an examination of the "Merchant Investments" notes and "Merchant Activities" notes in its annual reports revealed important information regarding the sales of Enron's merchant assets. Refer to Table 6.1 for Enron's pre-tax gains on sales of merchant assets, from 1997–2000.

Table 6.1*

Year	Enron's Pre-Tax Gains on Sales of Merchant Assets
1997	$136 M**
1998	$628 M
1999	$756 M
2000	$104 M

*Derived from Enron's Notes to the Consolidated Financial Statements
**M = million

Table 6.2*

Year	Enron's Pre-Tax Gains on Sales of Merchant Assets and Investments as a Percentage of Operating Income
1997	906%
1998	46%
1999	94%
2000	5%

*Derived from Enron's Notes to the Consolidated Financial Statements

Table 6.2 presents the calculation of Enron's "Pre-Tax Gains on Sales of Merchant Assets" as *a percentage of "Operating Income."*

It is mind boggling to discover that, in 1997, without these "gains" on sales of merchant assets, Enron's consolidated operating income of $15 million would have been an operating *loss* of $121 million. It is even more alarming since the "Merchant Investment" note in year 1998 shows that the majority of the merchant investments, totaling $1.859 billion, were held through unconsolidated affiliates, including partnerships. Therefore, without these transactions with unconsolidated entities, a significant portion of Enron's "profits" would not have existed.

Certainly, examining the income statement on the basis of normal, regular operating profit, one had to consider whether Enron stock had a value anywhere near the price at which it was trading. Ultimately, of course, it turned out that Enron was virtually worthless.

Signal #4: When the note to the financial statements on "Related Party Transactions" refers to transactions with unconsolidated specially constructed entities, such as partnerships or trusts, it is a signal that the company may be using the special purpose entities to hide debt or generate fictitious profits.

Enron's "Related-Party Transactions" note to the financial statements in its 1999 Annual Report stated: "A senior officer of Enron is the managing member of LJM's general partner." Furthermore, it explained that "LJM 2, which has the same general partner as LJM, acquired, directly or indirectly approximately $360 million of merchant assets from Enron, in which Enron recognized pretax gains of approximately $16 million." Although the phrase "special purpose entity" was not used in this note, the warning signs were unmistakable:

- An Enron officer was doing business with Enron for an Enron-constructed entity in a potential conflict of interest with Enron.
- Enron was selling its assets to itself.

The same note to the 1999 Annual Report also revealed that "Whitewing acquired $192 million of merchant assets from Enron. Enron recognized no gains or losses in connection with these transactions." Whitewing was another unconsolidated Enron entity, and here again, Enron was doing transactions with itself and moving assets to this structure. In such a case, one had to wonder whether the reason for this was to avoid recording large losses.

In the 2000 Annual Report, the "Related-Party Transactions" note referred to a "Related Party" that "acquired approximately $371 million of merchant assets and investments and other assets from Enron" in 2000. That same Annual Report revealed that Enron had expanded its investment in special purpose entities to an outrageous degree: "Enron . . . contributed to newly-formed entities (the Entities) assets valued at approximately $1.2 billion, including $150 million in Enron notes payable, [and] 3.7 million restricted shares of outstanding Enron stock."

Although Enron was not forthcoming about the fact that it was moving losing assets to these SPEs at values that hid the losses, the mere disclosure of the magnitude of the transactions—together with the involvement of Enron officials in the SPEs' transactions with Enron—should have alerted interested parties as follows:

- There was the opportunity for hiding losses in these transactions.
- There was no reliable market price for the sales of the assets.
- There was no objective way of calculating Enron's real profit.
- One had to blindly trust Enron and Enron's external auditor, Arthur Andersen, concerning the validity of the prices used for the related-party transactions.

Signal #5: Securitizations by nonfinancial institutions of current assets—whether accounts receivable or financial-instrument assets—indicate that a company may be experiencing cash-flow problems, and it needs to accelerate the realization (or liquidation) of an asset into cash faster than the asset would be liquidated in the ordinary course of business.

To test for an indication of a fictitious receivable, one should add the amount of the securitization (i.e., the cash received by selling a receivable that would normally be paid to the company later) back to the receivables (e.g., accounts receivable or, in Enron's case, "assets from price risk management activities") before calculating the ratio of the receivables-to-sales.

By the same logic, to test for an indication of overstated income that is not being realized in the form of CFFO, one should deduct the amount of the securitization from CFFO before calculating the ratio of operating income or net income to CFFO.

In Enron's annual financial statements for 2000, the note titled, "Price Risk Management Activities and Financial Instruments" contained a subsection identified as "Securitizations," which stated: "During 2000 gains from sales representing securitizations were $381 million and proceeds were $2,379 million ($545 million of the proceeds related to sales to Whitewing Associates L.P.)" This meant that close to half of Enron's CFFO came from securitizations of its current assets. Further, part of the securitization included a related-party transaction with an off-balance-sheet partnership entity (Whitewing).

It is time to sit up and become suspicious when:

- A company invests significant amounts in unconsolidated special purpose entities.
- That company engages in significant related-party transactions with these entities.
- The transactions include significant securitizations or sales of current assets to accelerate cash collections.

These are clear indications that a company may be sprucing up its reported financial statements, and that one cannot rely on the financial statements for analyzing the profit, the cash-flow generation, or the debt of that company.

(As a case in point, the securitizations signal for Xerox, as discussed in Chapter 3, indicated the importance of adjusting ratios to test the validity of accounts receivable and CFFO. This is done by adding back the securitized amount to accounts receivable and deducting the securitized amount from CFFO. With Xerox, the CFFO as adjusted for the securitization revealed that the amount by which CFFO lagged operating income was quite alarming.)

In Enron's case, the securitizations occurred together with references to related-party transactions, specially constructed entities, and sales where some ownership interests in the "sold" assets were retained by Enron. That combination of factors was more than a signal, it was a siren. It is important to search the 10-Ks and 10-Qs, and to pay attention to the notes to the financial statements, and look for the words "securitization," "factoring," or for the phrase "sales of accounts receivable," to pick up this acceleration of cash flow.

Signal #6: When a company has sales in which it retains any of the ownership interests in the asset sold, it is a signal that the company may actually be obtaining a loan and classifying it as a sale.

When such transactions involve off-balance-sheet entities, it is especially troubling. In Enron's 1998 Annual Report, the note titled "Merchant Activities" stated, "Some of these sales are completed in securitizations in which Enron retains certain interests through swaps associated with the underlying assets." We now know that many of these sales were, in fact, disguised loans in which the "certain interests" that Enron retained were the ownership interests, meaning that the "sales" were actually loans. Further, the profit or gains on these "sales" were included in operating income.

Signal #7: When a company guarantees the debt of its unconsolidated (off-balance-sheet) entities, it is a signal that these entities are being used to raise debt and hide the debt by keeping it off the company's own balance sheet and the group's consolidated balance sheet.[9]

In Enron's 1998 Annual Report, there is a note to the financial statements titled "Commitments." According to this note:

> Enron also guarantees the performance of certain of its unconsolidated affiliates in connection with letters of credit issued on behalf of those unconsolidated affiliates. At December 31, 1998, a total of $209 million of such guarantees were outstanding. . . . In addition, Enron is a guarantor on certain liabilities of unconsolidated affiliates and other companies totaling approximately $755 million.

The growth of Enron's guaranteed liabilities over the three-year period from 1998 to 2000 is quite staggering, as can been seen from Table 6.3.

Table 6.3 Guaranteed Liabilities Extracted from Notes in Enron's Annual Reports: 1998–2000

	December 1998	December 1999	December 2000
Guaranteed Liabilities for Letters of Credit on behalf of unconsolidated affiliates	$209 M*	$303 M	$264 M
Guaranteed Liabilities on behalf of certain liabilities of unconsolidated affiliates and other companies	$755 M	$1,501 M	$1,863 M

*M = million

---

[9] In post-Enron accounting, we are unlikely to find a disclosure of such a guarantee of an unconsolidated entity since such a guarantee would probably lead to the entity being classified as a VIE and to its consolidation by the entity's primary beneficiary in terms of FIN 46(R).

Although Enron did not fully disclose all the guarantees, or the fact that it was likely the entities would default and that Enron itself would be liable for the guaranteed amounts, these notes were unmistakable red flags due to the magnitude of Enron's unconsolidated affiliates and its related-party transactions with them.

The combination of these signals indicated that the off-balance-sheet activity was sufficiently significant as to render the published balance sheet wholly inadequate for analysis of the company. Indeed, we now know that the guarantees relating to special-purpose unconsolidated entities actually bankrupted Enron within one year of the issue of its 2000 Annual Report.

General Signals of Enron's Assorted Financial Problems:

- Overstatement of Earnings, Overstatement of Cash Flow from Operations (CFFO), and Problematic Debt Levels

Signal #1: When the accounts receivable amount increases as a percentage of revenue, it is a signal that the revenue recognized may be accelerated or fictitious.

This signal becomes an even greater alert if there is evidence (as disclosed in notes to the financial statements) that the company has created SPEs, and the company is also involved in related-party transactions. In Enron's case, unrealized revenues were split between accounts receivable and assets from price risk management activities (PRMA). The associated revenue from PRMA was specified in the note and included in the category "other revenue" in the income statement. Over time, Enron's accounts receivable and its PRMA grew as a percentage of revenues and "other revenues" respectively. From 1997-2000, Enron's trade receivables as a percentage of revenues (excluding "other revenues") grew from 7.23 percent to 11.12 percent. Refer to Table 6.4.

Table 6.4 Growth of Enron's Accounts Receivable as a Percentage of Revenue: 1997–2000

	1997	1998	1999	2000
Trade Receivables	$1.37 B*	$2.06 B	$3.03 B	$10.40 B
Revenues (Excluding Other Revenues)	$18.96 B	$27.84 B	$34.77 B	$93.56 B
Percentage of Revenue	7.23%	7.40%	8.71%	11.12%

*B = Billion

Signal #2: When cash flow from operations (CFFO) significantly lags operating income, it is a signal that the profit generated may be fictitious or that its recognition has been accelerated.

In Enron's case, the prepays and securitizations overstated the CFFO dramatically, so that this signal was blurred. Nevertheless, if one had deducted "securitizations" from the CFFO before comparing it to operating income, the ratio would not have presented quite so rosy a picture. One dramatic example of this can be found in 1997 where CFFO was stated as $211 million, but after adjusting for possible securitizations, it was reduced to *negative* $128 million. For 1999, the effect of the adjustment is even more dramatic. For an analysis of these numbers over the four-year period from 1997 to 2000, refer to Table 6.5.

With these adjustments, the CFFO lagged operating income in each year of the period from 1997 through 1999, and the CFFO as adjusted was, in fact, negative for two of those years. Of course, we now know that Enron was burning through cash at an amazing rate while it was pretending to have a healthy CFFO. By the year 2000, the prepays were disguising the cash-flow problem so heavily that the reported CFFO was positive, and greater than operating income, even after this adjustment. For example, in December 2000,

Table 6.5 Enron's Adjusted Cash Flow from Operations Compared to Its Operating Income: 1996–2000

	1997	1998	1999	2000
Cash Flow From Operations (CFFO)	$211 M	$1,640 M	$1,228 M	$4,779 M
Possible Securitizations**	($339 M)	($1,434 M)	($2,217 M)	($2,379 M)***
CFFO, Excluding Possible Securitizations	($128 M)	$206 M	($989 M)	$2,400 M
Operating Income	$15 M	$1,378 M	$802 M	$1,953 M

* M = Million

** For 1997 through 1999, this is the amount referred to in the Enron notes as, "sales of merchant assets and investments," and according to Enron's 1998 Annual Report, "Some of these sales are completed in securitizations." Not all of these sales were completed as securitizations, and there could have been other securitizations. Since the financial statements in those years did not specify the amount of the "securitizations" portion, it is safest to regard them all as securitizations since these sales were also the sales in which "Enron retains certain interests" (*Enron Annual Report* 1998). As such, these were sales that may, in fact, have been loans masquerading as sales.

*** In 2000, the securitizations amount was specified as $2,379 million, which was greater than the amount of the sales of merchant assets and investments.

the Mahonia project produced $330 million of illusory CFFO on one contract alone.

All the mechanisms discussed earlier regarding Enron's use of mark-to-market accounting, in conjunction with its false sales via SPEs, led to a gap not only between reported earnings and generated cash but also to lack of a strategic business focus on projects that generated real profits and real cash. A former Enron trader remarked: "No one ever talked to me about cash. It [cash] wasn't on our annual review or included in our targets. It had nothing to do with how we were measured for our bonus. It was nothing we were paid for, so who cares?" (McLean and Elkind 2004, 228).

Signal #3: When a company is late in publishing its balance sheet and statement of cash flows, it is a signal that it may be taking time to manipulate these statements because it has something to hide.

Enron generally issued only its income statement at the time of its earnings release conference call, and made the balance sheet and statement of cash flows available much later when it filed its financial statements with the SEC. The analyst and short seller Richard Grubman picked up this delay as a signal of problems at Enron. When Skilling held a conference call on March 22, 2001, in an attempt to allay investors' fears about the $5.06 drop in Enron's stock price the previous day, Grubman questioned Skilling about the delay and pointed out:

> "You're the only financial institution that cannot produce a balance sheet or cash-flow statement with their earnings."
>
> Skilling very eloquently responded, "Well, you're—you—well, uh thank you very much. We appreciate it."
>
> Grubman replied, "Appreciate it?"
>
> Whereupon Skilling snapped, "Asshole."
>
> (Conversation quoted in McLean and Elkind 2004, 326)

This exchange reveals that Skilling clearly appeared tense about the cash-flow situation and that Grubman had exposed a real problem. Furthermore, Skilling's angry response to Grubman alerted everyone on that conference call to this danger signal. From then on, analysts and business journalists adopted an increasingly skeptical attitude toward Enron's financial statements.

Signal #4: When the interest expense of a company is so large that it uses a significant portion of that company's income—or when interest increases

Table 6.6 Times-Interest-Earned Ratio:* 1998–2000

	1998	1999	2000
NI**	$703 M***	$893 M	$979 M
Interest Expense****	$ 550 M	$656 M	$838 M
Income Tax	$175 M	$104 M	$434 M
NI before Interest and Tax	$1,428 M	$1,653 M	$2,251 M
NI before I&T***** Interest	2.596	2.520	2.686

* Times Interest Earned is most often calculated as Net Income (NI) before interest and taxation expenses, divided by the interest expense.

** NI = Net Income

*** M = Million

**** This is interest expense only. Interest income has not been offset.

***** I & T = Interest and Tax

significantly as a percentage of income—it is an indication that the company may not be able to continue to pay its interest and, ultimately, may not be able to repay its debt.

In Table 6.6 an examination of Enron's times–interest–earned ratio over the period 1998 to 2000 clearly reveals that Enron had too much debt. Each period, this huge debt led to large interest expenses relative to Enron's income. This became a vicious circle because the company did not produce enough profit to repay its debt—and the debt kept growing.

In spite of the fact the Enron was hiding massive amounts of debt and interest via SPEs, the times–interest–earned ratio extracted from Enron's reported income statement was, nevertheless, a signal that the company may not have been able to sustain its debt with its operating plan. The ratio did not deteriorate over the period, but the interest remained too high as a percentage of income for the debt to be maintained and repaid. The times–interest–earned ratio remained between 2.5 and 2.6 over the period.

Apart from Enron's trading income, which was extremely volatile, nothing in Enron's financial statements indicated any recurring true operating income to handle this large debt. Enron's continued existence depended on its ability to borrow more and more money to repay earlier loans and finance its upcoming operations.

Signal #5: When the portion of a company's finance that is provided by lenders or outsiders (as opposed to being provided by owners) increases

Table 6.7 Debt-to-Equity Ratio: 1997–2000

	1998	1999	2000
Total Debt	$20,159 M*	$21,381 M	$51,619 M
Total Equity	$7,048 M	$ 9,570	$11,470 M
Debt: Equity Ratio	2,860	2.234	4.500

* M = Million

significantly, it is an indication that the company *may* be taking on too much debt.

It is therefore important to examine the company's debt-equity ratio. Of course, if a company takes on a large debt and uses that capital to earn profit at a rate of return that is much higher than the interest rate, it will be a very profitable company. However, when debt grows substantially and the times-interest-earned ratio does not improve, there is cause for concern that the company will be unable to maintain or repay its debt.

At Enron, the times-interest-earned ratio remained low while the debt-to-equity ratio increased, even though Enron understated its debt on its balance sheets. In the period from 1998 to 2000, there was a dramatic increase in the amount of Enron's capital that was financed by debt as opposed to equity, as can be seen in Table 6.7. Over that period, the debt-to-equity ratio increased from 2.85 to 4.51. Even with its debt understated this, together with the low times-interest-earned ratio, was a signal that Enron had a severe debt problem.

Signal #6: When a company uses "death-spiral financing," it is a signal that the company's future earnings per share could be diluted by the need to issue shares.

"Death-spiral financing" refers to an arrangement with another party that if certain circumstances occur, the company has to compensate that other party for a required amount in the form of the issue of the company's own stock. The number of shares issued depends on the market value of the stock at the date of the share issue. The most common form of "death-spiral financing" is a loan in which the terms specify that the amount must be repaid at a specified date by the issue of the borrower's shares. The problem, of course, is that the lower the stock price falls, the greater the number of shares that have to be issued, which, in turn, dilutes the earnings per share and reduces the stock price even further, requiring more shares to be issued . . . and so the spiral continues.

In Enron's case, as discussed earlier in the sections on Whitewing, LJM, and the Raptors, Enron used its SPEs to purchase its poor performing assets. These SPEs were partially funded by the issue of Enron's shares. In some cases, Enron had guaranteed to compensate the SPEs for any losses they may incur on the resale of Enron's assets, by issuing additional Enron stock to the entities. In other cases, since the entities depended on their Enron stock as a major asset, Enron had guaranteed that if the Enron stock price fell below certain specified amounts, Enron would issue more shares or cash to the entities to compensate them. Obviously, this resulted in a further decline in the Enron stock price.

Such death-spiral financing signals not only the risk inherent in the potential dilution of the value of the shares, but also the adoption of the high-risk strategy itself signals that the company is probably in a desperate position. This should warn the reader that the company may be tempted to hide debt, just as Enron used SPEs to keep what was effectively its own debt off its balance sheet.

Signal #7: When a company misrepresents the nature of its core business, or when a large portion of its profit is dependant on a type of business that is not its core business, it should be regarded as a signal that the company's ability to maintain its earnings is more risky than it wishes to disclose.

Profits that are made via trading depend on the volatility of prices and on betting successfully on the direction of the price changes. Because of the increased risks involved, investors usually demand a higher earnings-yield percentage for a trading company than a hard-asset operating company. Price earnings ratios are therefore usually lower for trading companies than operating companies.

Enron, while holding itself out as an operating or logistics company, became increasingly dependant on profits from trading, especially in its energy-trading sector, whose massive profits had, for a time, concealed Enron's fundamental problems. However, trading profits are extremely erratic, and Jim Chanos, a broker and short-seller, called Enron a "hedge fund sitting on a pipeline." Chanos also noted that "Enron was a speculative trading shop, which meant that, at an absolute minimum, its outsize price-to-earnings multiple made no sense." (Quotes from McLean and Elkind 2004, 321)

Skilling, of course, insisted that Enron was not a trading business. In fact, Enron's 2000 Annual Report stated: "We have metamorphosed from an asset-based pipeline and power generating company to a marketing and logistics company" (5). The problem was that when one excluded the gains from sales of its merchant assets and its trading profits, there was not enough traditional, recurring income for its "logistic" operations to sustain its stock price.

The company that had once been regarded as a golden goose was, in fact, a cooked goose!

Are They Living Happily Ever After?

≈ **Timothy Belden** (a former head of Enron's energy trading) pleaded guilty "to engaging in a conspiracy that illegally manipulated the California power market." He faces a maximum of five years in prison and a $250,000 fine. In addition, Belden "agreed to forfeit $2.1 million he maintained in two brokerage accounts at Charles Schwab" (Eichenwald and Richtel 2002). In February 2006, Belden appeared as a prosecution witness in the Lay and Skilling trial in Houston, Texas.

≈ **Richard Causey** (former Enron chief accountant) entered into a last-minute plea-bargain agreement toward the end of December 2005, just a few weeks before the start of the trial of Lay and Skilling. Causey "pleaded guilty to securities fraud and agreed to cooperate with prosecutors. He was the 16th ex-Enron executive to plead guilty" (Hays 2006).

≈ **Andrew Fastow,** former CFO of Enron, "pleaded guilty in January 2004 to two counts of conspiracy, admitting to orchestrate schemes to hide the company's debt and inflate profits while pocketing millions of dollars. He agreed to serve the maximum 10-year sentence, which will begin in July 2006, after he testifies against his former bosses" ("Status of High-Profile Corporate Scandals" 2005).

≈ **Lea Fastow,** Andrew's wife, has already completed a one-year sentence "on a misdemeanor tax charge for failing to report her husband's kickbacks" ("Status of High-Profile Corporate Scandals" 2005).

≈ **Kenneth Lay,** 64, went on trial (with Jeffrey Skilling) in Houston, Texas, in early 2006. On May 25, 2006, the jury found Lay guilty of three counts of securities fraud, one count of conspiracy and two counts of wire fraud. Further, on the same day, "after a separate three-day nonjury trial, US District Judge Sim Lake found Lay guilty of one count of bank fraud and three counts of making false statements to banks." In an interview after the trial, jurors revealed that "Lay's credibility was severely damaged by evidence that he quietly sold $70 million in Enron stock back to the company in 2001, while telling employees that the company was in fine shape and that the stock was a great buy." Lay is expected to appeal. (Quotes from Mulligan 2006)

≈ **Rebecca Mark** is reportedly living on a ranch in New Mexico with her husband and children. In early 2005, Mark "was one of 10 former Enron officers and directors who settled a lawsuit by shareholders—she contributed $5.2 million of the $13 million settlement" (Lavelle 2005).

≈ **Jeffrey Skilling,** 52, went on trial (with Kenneth Lay) in Houston, Texas in early 2006. On May 25, 2006, the jury "convicted Skilling of one count of conspiracy, 12 counts of [securities] fraud, five counts of making false statements and one count of insider trading. He was acquitted of nine other insider-trading counts" (Mullligan 2006). The jury "endorsed the prosecution's charges that Skilling oversaw a scheme to use off-the-books partnerships to manipulate Enron's finances" (Feeley and Brubaker Calkins 2006). Skilling is expected to appeal.

≈ **Enron,** once the biggest energy trading company in the world, was worth over $68 billion before it went bankrupt in December 2001. Its bankruptcy "wiped out thousands of jobs and at least $1 billion in retirement funds virtually overnight. Investors suing the company claim that accounting fraud . . . caused at least $25 billion in losses" (Feeley and Brubaker Calkins 2006). Enron-related litigation has so far resulted in settlements of $7.2 billion. The civil litigation continues.

References

"Annual Partnership Meeting," *LJM Investments*, October 26, 2000. http://smartmoney.com

Bankruptcy Report #1: First Interim Report of Neal Batson, Court-Appointed Examiner. 2002. U.S. Bankruptcy Court Southern District of New York. Chapter 11, Case No. 01–16034 (AJG), September 21.

Bankruptcy Report #2: First Interim Report of Neal Batson, Court-Appointed Examiner. 2003. U.S. Bankruptcy Court Southern District of New York. Chapter 11, Case No. 01–16034 (AJG), January 21.

Bankruptcy Report #3: First Interim Report of Neal Batson, Court-Appointed Examiner. 2003. U.S. Bankruptcy Court Southern District of New York. Chapter 11, Case No. 01–16034 (AJG), June 30.

Berthelsen, Christian, and Mark Martin. 2003. "Energy Trader Admits His Guilt," *San Francisco Chronicle,* February 5, A1. Available online via ProQuest database.

"Breakdown of Charges against Lay, Skilling," *Associated Press,* January 20, 2006. www.msnbc.msn.com

Brooks, Nancy Rivera. 2002. "Settlement Reveals Another Enron Strategy," *Los Angeles Times,* December 9, C1. Available online via ProQuest database.

Bryce, Robert. 2002. *Pipe Dreams: Greed, Ego, and the Death of Enron.* New York: Public Affairs.

Byrnes, Nanette, Mike McNamee, Diane Brady, Louis Lavelle, and
    Christopher Palmeri. 2002. "Accounting in Crisis," *Business Week,*
    January 28, Special Report, 44, 5p, 1c. Available online via EBSCOhost
    database.
Davis, Michael. 2002. "The Energy Trading Flop," *Houston Chronicle,*
    October 22. www.dukeemployees.com/deregulation2402.shtml
Douglass, Elizabeth. 2004. "Tapes Bolster Electricity Claims," *Los Angeles
    Times,* March 20, C1. Available online via ProQuest database.
Eichenwald, Kurt. 2005. *Conspiracy of Fools: A True Story.* New York:
    Broadway Books.
Eichenwald, K., and M. Richtel. 2002. "Energy Manipulation Conspiracy
    Guilty Plea," *New York Times,* October 22.
    www.dukeemployees.com/deregulation2402.shtml
Emshwiller, John R. 2006. "Executives on Trial: Enron Prosecutors, after
    Plea Bargain, Can Reduce Technical Jargon in Trial," *Wall Street Journal,*
    January 4. Available online via ProQuest database.
"Enron Defendants Not Guilty for Charges," *Economic Times Online,* July
    21, 2005. Bennett, Coleman and Co. http://economictimes.com
"Enron Timeline," *Houston Chronicle,* December 13, 2005. www.chron.com
"Fastow and His Wife Plead Guilty," *CNNMoney.com,* January 14, 2004.
    www.cnnmoney.com
Feeley, Jef, and Laurel Brubaker Calkins. 2006. "Enron's Skilling Convicted
    of Conspiracy; Lay Verdict Next." Bloomberg.com, May 25, 2006.
    www.bloomberg.com
Fisher, Daniel. 2002. "Shell Game," *Forbes Magazine,* January 7.
    www.forbes.com
Flood, Mary. 2005. "Not a Day for Court Fireworks," *Houston Chronicle,*
    April 28.
    www.chron.com/cs/CDA/ssistory.mpl/special/enron/3159346
Flood, Mary. 2005. "Broadband Trial: The Outcome," CBS *News,* July 21.
    www.cbsnews.com
Flood, Mary, and Tom Fowler. 2003. "The Fall of Enron," *Houston
    Chronicle,* February 5. Available online via ProQuest database.
Gruley, Bryan, and Rebecca Smith. 2002. "Anatomy of a Fall: Keys to
    Success Left Kenneth Lay Open to Disaster," *Wall Street Journal,*
    April 26. www.wsj.com
Harden, Blaine. 2005. "Utility Exposes Enron Green at Its Core,"
    Washington Post, March 1. www.washingtonpost.com
Hays, Kristen. 2006. "Enron Defense Argues Houston Too Hot to Be Fair:
    Lawyers Cite Anger Shown in Jury Pool Questionnaires," *Chicago
    Sun-Times,* January 5. Available online via ProQuest database.
Lavelle, Marianne. 2005. "Rebecca Mark-Jusbasche," *U.S News & World
    Report,* April 25.
    www.usnews.com/usnews/biztech/articles/050425/25eewhere.htm
Malik, Om. 2003. *Broadbandits: Inside the $750 Billion Telecom Heist.*
    Hoboken, New Jersey: John Wiley & Sons.

McLean, Bethany, and Peter Elkind. 2004. *The Smartest Guys in the Room: The Amazing Rise and Scandalous Fall of Enron.* New York: Portfolio.

Mulligan, Thomas S. 2006. "Enron Witness Tells of Transfer," *Los Angeles Times*, March 15.

Mulligan, Thomas S. 2006. "Enron's Top Executives Are Convicted of Fraud." *Los Angeles Times*, May 26, 2006.

Oppel, Richard A., Jr. 2003. "Panel Finds Manipulation by Energy Companies," *New York Times* (Late edition), March 27, A14. Available online via ProQuest database.

Peterson, Jonathon. 2005. "Enron Settles Claim of Price Gouging," *Los Angeles Times*, July 16, C1. Available online via ProQuest database.

Powers Report. *Report of Investigation by the Special Investigative Committee of the Board of Directors of Enron Corp.* William C. Powers, Jr., Chair, with Raymond S. Troubh and Herbert S. Winokur, Jr. February 1, 2002.

Roberts, Johnny, and Evan Thomas. 2002. "Enron's Dirty Laundry," *Newsweek*, March 11.

"SEC File Amended Complaint Charging Five Enron Executives with Fraud and Insider Trading Relating to Enron's Broadband Subsidiary," *U.S. Securities and Exchange Commission, 2003-58,* May 1, 2003. www.sec.gov/news/press/2003-58.htm

"SEC Charges Kenneth L. Lay, Enron's Former Chairman and Chief Executive Officer, with Fraud and Insider Trading," *U.S. Securities and Exchange Commission, 2004-94,* July 8, 2004. www.sec.gov/news/press/2004-94.htm

Smith, Doug, and Nancy Rivera Brooks. 2003. "Glendale Abetted Enron in Energy Ploys, Papers Imply," *Los Angeles Times,* March 29, A1. Available online via ProQuest database.

Smith, Randall. 2005. "CIBC to Pay $2.4 Billion over Enron," *Wall Street Journal,* August 3. www.wsj.com

Smith, Rebecca, and John R. Wilke. 2002. "Enron Trader Admits to Fraud in California Crisis," *Wall Street Journal* (Eastern edition), October 18, A3. Available online via ProQuest database.

Soroosh, Jalal, and Jack T. Ciesielski. 2004. "Accounting for Special Purpose Entities Revised: FASB Interpretation 46(R)," *The CPA Journal,* July Issue. www.cpajournal.com

SOX Report. *Report Pursuant to Section 704 of the Sarbanes-Oxley Act of 2002.* www.sec.gov/news/studies/sox704report.pdf

"Status of High-Profile Corporate Scandals," *Associated Press Financial Wire,* November 23, 2005. Available online via LexisNexis database.

Swartz, Mimi, with Sherron Watkins. 2003. *Power Failure: The Inside Story of the Collapse of Enron.* New York: Doubleday-Random House.

"UC Reaches $168-Million Settlement with Enron Directors in Securities Fraud Case," *University of California Office of the President: News Release,* January 7, 2005. www.universityofcalifornia.edu/news/2005/jan07.html

Wilke, John, and Robert Gavin. 2002. "Deregulation," *Wall Street Journal,* October 22. www.wsj.com

CHAPTER 7

TALL TALES

This chapter takes a look at the antics of:
- **Edison Schools**
- **Adelphia**
- **BellSouth**
- **Krispy Kreme Doughnuts**

THE EDISON LESSON

Edison Schools is presented here as an example of Inadequate
Disclosures in its Management Discussion and Analysis (MD&A).

Introduction

Taking advantage of problems in public schools throughout the United
States, Edison Schools, headquartered in New York City, was founded on the
premise that private-sector corporations could run public schools more
efficiently and effectively. Edison was listed on NASDAQ in November
1999. In its early years, Edison managed approximately 130 elementary and
secondary public schools in about twenty-two states. It had contracts with
public school districts and charter schools to implement its unique curricu-
lum and teaching methods, together with a longer school day, in the con-
tracting schools. The teachers in the Edison-run schools were the original
school-district teachers. Edison received approximately $6,500 per year for
each student enrolled at each school, and the teachers usually received compensation that reflected the extra teaching hours required in the Edison
schools.

The company was usually responsible for the costs of running the
schools, but the teachers themselves were often paid directly by the school

districts, and not by Edison. After an investigation into Edison's accounting methods, the SEC stated:

> The teacher salaries and non-instruction expenses paid directly by districts (collectively "District-Paid Expenses") comprise a substantial portion of the expense of operating Edison schools. These funds never reach Edison, but are expended by districts directly and then deducted from the district's remittances to Edison. (AAER 1555, 2002)

Publicly traded companies are required to include an MD&A section in their financial filings with the SEC, and this section "discusses the issuer's financial condition and results of operations to enhance investor understanding of financial statements." The MD&A is of particular interest and importance because it shows that the disclosure responsibility regarding financial statements goes beyond a mechanical application of GAAP rules and actually requires an accurate reflection of the company's financial condition and the results of its operations. The SOX Report stated: "Inadequate disclosure matters may involve situations where the issuer's financial statements are in conformity with GAAP, but fail in some material way to present an accurate picture of the issuer's financial condition." (Quotes from SOX Report 23)

Edison's Financial Reporting Scheme via Inadequate Disclosure

In the case of Edison Schools, Inc., the area of inadequate disclosure did not affect the amount of net income at all. The issue was whether Edison could report the gross amount of the fee per student as its revenues in its income statement, and then separately deduct the district-paid expenses, or whether it had to report the net payment from the district (i.e., fees minus expenses) as revenues. Although the net income is the same in both cases, the former method could give the impression of a much more active company.

It was Edison's practice to record the gross amount as revenues and include the district-paid expenses as its expenses in its income statement. This could present a misleading picture. For example, in the case of one district (District A) in 2001, no cash at all was paid to Edison because, according to the district, the total "Per Pupil Fees" amounted to $7.5 million and the amount of the district-paid expenses was $8 million in total. In its income statement, Edison "recorded the entire amount invoiced, $7.5 million, as gross revenue for FY 2001, also recording expenses of $8 million" (AAER 1555, 2002).

In another instance (District B), the SEC alleged that the district "has paid Edison only $400,000 in FY 2002, even though Edison has recorded over $17 million in revenues from District B for the first two quarters of FY 2002, along with over $18 million in expenses" (AAER 1555, 2002). In May 2002 the SEC issued a cease-and-desist order.[1]

Whether a company has zero revenue and zero expense, or positive revenue and an equally positive expense—leading to zero net income—can influence an investor's or lender's perception of the company's results and financial position.

In the case of Edison, the SEC alleged: "In its filings with the Commission, Edison has not disclosed the existence and amounts of these District-Paid Expenses. Instead, Edison has inaccurately stated in its Management Discussion and Analysis [MD&A] that it 'receives' all Per Pupil Funding" (AAER 1555, 2002).

It is important to note that the SEC acknowledged that at the time of Edison's accounting treatment of these items in 2001, it was not clear that the revenue in the income statement needed to be reported net of the district-paid expenses for those cases in which Edison was not the primary obligor. (A primary obligor has the ultimate responsibility to pay a vendor or provider of services.) The Emerging Issues Task Force clarified the situation regarding expenses for which a company is responsible but does not pay. Under the guidance of EITF 01-114, which became effective in 2002, the Commissioner stated:

> Under this recent accounting guidance, Edison must report revenue on a gross basis to include those District-Paid Expenses for which it is the "primary obligor" for the expense. Where Edison is not the primary obligor for the expenses, Edison must report revenue on a net basis to exclude such expenses. The choice between treatment of revenues on a gross or net basis does not affect net income. (AAER 1555, 2002)

The issue was that Edison's financial statements did not accurately and completely "describe the realities of Edison's operations" (AAER 1555, 2002). The SOX Report succinctly stated Edison's situation:

> The Commission did not find that Edison's revenue recognition practices contravene GAAP or that earnings were misstated. However, the Commission nonetheless found that Edison committed violations by failing to provide

---

[1] Edison consented to the order and to a settlement, without admitting or denying any of the findings contained in the order. As set out in AAER 1555, May 14, 2002.

accurate disclosure, thus showing that technical compliance with GAAP in the financial statements will not insulate an issuer from enforcement action. (24)

The Edison example involves the *choice* of an accounting treatment, and in this case, did not have specific signals. However, it is important for users of financial statements to be aware of different reporting methods, and to question why one method was chosen rather than another.

The Edison case is particularly interesting because it clearly reveals the basic purpose and ethical considerations at the core of financial reporting. A company is required to release fiscal reports in order to clearly and truthfully reveal its financial condition. It is therefore unacceptable for a company to merely abide by the letter of the law if this inadvertently allows for the dissemination of misleading information. In such a case, the spirit of the law must always be communicated.

Are They Living Happily Ever After?

≈ **Edison Schools** is still in operation, although a number of school districts have canceled their contracts with the company due to disappointing student performance (Martin 2005). According to the Edison Schools website, in the 2005—2006 school year Edison is serving over "330,000 [students] in 25 states."

≈ In early 2001, the Edison's shares were trading close to $40. Toward the end of 2002, the stock reached a low of 14 cents a share. Edison is no longer listed on the NASDAQ. The company was "taken private" in Fall 2003 ("Edison Schools Leaving Publicly Traded Stage" 2003).

THE ADELPHIA ACCOUNT[2]

Adelphia Communications Corporation is presented mainly as an example of:

- Failure to Disclose Related-Party Transactions and Improper Use of Related-Party Transactions
- Improper use of Non–GAAP Financial Measures

Established in 1952 in Coudersport, Pennsylvania, Adelphia grew into one of the largest cable television providers in the United States, operating in twenty-nine states and Puerto Rico. The company, founded by John J. Rigas, was also a provider of local telephone services.

In July 2002, the SEC alleged that the Adelphia case involved "one of the most extensive frauds ever to take place at a public company." In its complaint, the SEC maintained:

- From mid 1999 to the end of 2001, Adelphia excluded "billions of dollars in liabilities from its consolidated financial statements by hiding them in off-balance sheet affiliates."
- During this time, the company "falsified operations statistics and inflated Adelphia's earnings to meet Wall Street's expectations."
- Since 1998 or earlier, the company "concealed rampant self-dealing by the family that founded and controlled Adelphia, the Rigas family." (Quotes from BR-6413, 2002)

The Rigas family allegedly used company funds to purchase costly condominiums, plush holiday accommodation, luxury cars, and even to build a golf course. At his trial in mid-2004, John Rigas was accused of recklessly spending company money. According to examples given by the prosecutor, Rigas used Adelphia's funds to purchase two Christmas trees for $6,000 and to spend $26 million on 3,600 acres of land surrounding his house to ensure that the view would never be obstructed. A witness at the trial described how Adelphia had paid for a lavish family wedding, as well as for a personal trainer and masseur who worked full time for John Rigas and his sons.

The SEC named six senior Adelphia executives in its civil complaint; four of the six were members of the Rigas family (John Rigas and his three sons),

---

[2] Background information in this section is mainly from AAER 1599 (2002), "Adelphia Founder John Rigas Found Guilty" (2004), BR-6413 (2002), and Goldsmith (2005).

while the other two were James Brown and Michael Mulcahey, both vice presidents of the company.

Adelphia's Fictitious Financial Reporting Schemes

Scheme #1: Improper Use and Misleading Disclosure of Related-Party Transactions

Adelphia used related-party transactions to hide debt, boost earnings, and loot the company. Most of the offending transactions involved the use of off-balance-sheet partnerships. Highland Holdings, a Rigas family general partnership, and Highland 2000, a Rigas family limited partnership, were two of the "Rigas Entities" that were used for many of the related-party transactions between Adelphia and the Rigas clan. Dealings among Adelphia, the Rigas Entities, and the Rigas family itself became even more complicated and obscure by the commingling of funds between the various groups. Adelphia, its subsidiaries, and the Rigas Entities all deposited and withdrew cash from a joint cash management system called "Adelphia CMS" that was administered by Adelphia.

A brief examination of some of the major irregularities involving Adelphia's transactions with Rigas Entities or with members of the Rigas family will illustrate the need for concern wherever related-party transactions are revealed in a company's financial statements.

○ Issuing Adelphia Shares Directly to Rigas Entities

A number of direct placements of Adelphia shares were made to Rigas Entities. An examination of these transitions illustrates the dangers of transacting with entities owned or controlled by officers or directors of a company. The SEC claimed that, in October 2001 and January 2002, Adelphia made a direct placement to Highland 2000 of $423 million of Adelphia class "B" shares and notes payable. Adelphia simultaneously transferred $423 million of debt off its books and created false documentation for its auditors, claiming that Highland 2000 had paid cash for the securities.

The SEC's complaint alleged that the transaction was deceptive mainly because:

(i) $423,375,076 in debt was not paid down, but instead simply was shifted to Highland Video;

(ii) Highland 2000 never paid cash for the securities;

(iii) Adelphia remained jointly and severally liable for the debt; and

(iv) Highland Video's "assumption" of debt was a sham because it never
received any economic benefit from it and was not dealing at arm's length.
(BR-6413, 2002)

In addition, the Commissioner maintained that Adelphia engaged in a
number of similar transactions in which a Rigas entity received the securities
and as a result, while existing debt was taken off Adelphia's books, new debt
was taken on without the new debt being reported on the balance sheet.

○ Selling Adelphia's Excess Digital Converters to a Rigas Entity

Adelphia had purchased an excess inventory of digital converters and in
the last quarter of 2001, it sold $101 million of this inventory to Highland
Video. According to the SEC, Highland Video did not operate a cable
service and did not need the digital converters. Adelphia accounted for the
transaction by reducing its debt by $101 million and crediting inventory by
a corresponding amount.

○ Purchasing Land Rights from the Rigases

According to the Commission, Adelphia purchased certain rights, including timber rights, to 3,656 acres of land in Potter County, Pennsylvania,
owned by the Rigas family. The family paid under half a million dollars for
the land, and Adelphia purchased the timber rights to the land for over $26
million. A highly unusual clause is that the contract stated that the timber
rights would "revert back to the owner of the underlying land at either the
earlier of twenty years or if the percentage of Adelphia stock held by John
Rigas fell below 50% of all the outstanding company stock" (BR-6413,
2002). Adelphia's investors were not informed of this contract with the
Rigas family.

○ Self-Dealing Involving a Golf Course, Personal Margin Loans, and the Use of Luxury Condominiums

The SEC claimed that Adelphia used approximately $12.8 million of its
funds to construct a golf course on land owned mainly by the Rigases.
Again, this use of company funds for the personal benefit of the Rigas family was not disclosed to investors. In addition, the family had sole use of at
least four glamorous condominiums in the United States and Mexico, all
courtesy of Adelphia. The company also paid over $241 million in "personal
margin loans and other debt of the Rigas family" (BR-6413, 2002).

In the criminal trial of founder John J. Rigas and his son Timothy Rigas,
"Prosecutors alleged that the Rigas family siphoned $100 million from

Adelphia to pay for personal extravagances, hid $2.3 billion in debt and systematically deceived investors about Adelphia's subscriber growth and its bottom line." Prosecutors at the trial displayed "more than a dozen allegedly false SEC documents signed by various family members and receipts for personal expenses, large and small, including those for 100 pairs of slippers ordered by Timothy Rigas." In fact, the prosecutors accused the family of using Adelphia as a "private ATM." (Quotes from Masters and White 2004)

Scheme #2: Improper Use of Non-GAAP Information

Investors are not only interested in information disclosed in the financial statements but they also like to know that a company's customer base is growing and that the technical quality of the plant and products is high. Therefore, Adelphia did not restrict itself to misleading financial information, but misrepresented its performance in other areas as well. For example, in its 10-Ks for 2000 and 2001, the company was accused of misreporting and overstating the number of its cable subscribers. According to BR-6413, 2002, Adelphia added the following to its list of subscribers:

- 15,000 subscribers of an unconsolidated affiliate located in Brazil
- 28,000 cable subscribers of an unconsolidated Venezuelan affiliate
- Customers who received "Powerlink," Adelphia's Internet service
- 6,000 Adelphia's home security subscribers

To bump up the numbers even further, apparently Adelphia also added in some cable subscribers from other Rigas Entities, and even included some long distance telephone subscribers as basic cable subscribers.

Furthermore, the SEC maintained that when communicating with investors and financial analysts, Adelphia misrepresented the extent to which it had upgraded its cable plant. The upgrade was initiated to improve the cable plant in two important areas: first, to increase the plant's ability to transmit signals at greater speeds; and second, to enable the plant to transmit as well as receive signals from its customers. The phrase that Adelphia liked to use for this upgraded capacity was "two-way cable," but the SEC claimed that the extent of the two-way cable upgrade had been exaggerated. For example, the Commission revealed that in a 1999 presentation to potential investors in a stock offering, Adelphia had used an "overhead slide that contained a pie chart which represented that approximately 50% of Adelphia's cable plant [had been] 'rebuilt.' This claim was fraudulent because Adelphia's cable plant was only approximately 35% rebuilt at the time" (BR-6413, 2002).

Signals of Adelphia's Fictitious Reporting Scheme #1:

- Improper Use and Misleading Disclosure of Related-Party Transactions

Signal #1: Any disclosures in the notes to the financial statements that the company is doing transactions with any major shareholder, officer or director of the company, or any entity owned or controlled by these parties, should alert the reader to be very cautious. These transactions could be used to:

- Hide the company's debt
- Overstate the company's earnings
- Loot the company's assets in favor of the major shareholders, directors or officers

One should pay special attention to the related-party transactions note, but also study the entire financial statements in search of disclosures of any transactions between the company and its major shareholders, directors or company officers (or their families or affiliates). For example, the SEC pointed out that the footnotes in Adelphia's Annual Report for 2000 disclosed the following: "On January 21, 2000, Adelphia closed the previously announced direct placement of 5,901,522 shares of Adelphia Class B common stock with Highland 2000, L.P. a limited partnership owned by the Rigas family." The note then falsely stated that Adelphia had used a portion of this "to repay borrowings under revolving credit facilities." This was misleading because the debt had just been moved to the Rigas Entities. Even if the information in the notes is misleading, the limited disclosure often alerts the reader to the fact that related-party transactions are occurring, and such transactions are more likely to be manipulated than "arm's-length" transactions. (Quotes from BR-6413, 2002)

Signal #2: The commingling of a company's assets or liabilities with the personal assets or liabilities of its major shareholders, officers, or directors is a signal of poor internal control. This weakness could be exploited to loot a company's assets.

In Adelphia's Annual Report for 2000, a note referred to members of the Rigas family who were "co-borrowers with entities under credit facilities."

A disclosure that commingling occurs between a company's assets and liabilities and those of its directors, officers or shareholders, should be regarded as an alert that more related-party activity may be occurring than is being disclosed. The disclosure may be the tip of the iceberg because it could become very tempting for officers or shareholders to use the company as its own money machine.

Are They Living Happily Ever After?

≈ **James Brown,** former vice president for finance, "pleaded guilty to conspiracy, bank fraud, and wire fraud, [and] was the government's star witness at trial. Brown faces up to 45 years in prison but is hoping his cooperation will result in a lighter sentence" (Crawford and Dunbar 2004).

≈ **Michael Mulcahey,** former vice president, was found not guilty of conspiracy and securities fraud ("Status of High-Profile . . ." 2005).

≈ **John J. Rigas,** founder of Adelphia, was convicted of "conspiracy, bank fraud and securities fraud" ("Status of High-Profile . . ." 2005). In June 2005, he was sentenced to fifteen years in prison. He is out on bail, pending appeal. John Rigas has been diagnosed with bladder cancer (Bray 2006).

≈ **Timothy Rigas,** son of John Rigas, was "found guilty of conspiracy and 15 counts of securities fraud and two counts of bank fraud (Crawford and Dunbar 2004). He was sentenced to twenty years in prison. Timothy Rigas is out on bail, pending appeal ("Status of High-Profile . . ." 2005).

≈ **Michael Rigas,** son of John Rigas, entered a guilty plea in November 2005 to "a charge of making a false entry in a financial record" ("Status of High-Profile . . ." 2005). In March 2006, Michael Rigas was sentenced to twenty-four months of probation, which included ten months of confinement at home (Bray 2006). The judge in the case remarked that Michael Rigas "stands on an entirely different footing from the two members of his family that were convicted" (quoted in Bray 2006).

≈ **James Rigas,** son of John Rigas, was not criminally charged.

≈ **Adelphia** filed for bankruptcy in June 2002. In 2005, the company agreed to be sold to Time Warner, Inc., and Comcast Corp, but the proposed sale is "facing . . . obstacles." (Grant, 2006).

≈ **Deloitte and Touche LLP.** The SEC instituted public administrative proceedings against Adelphia's auditors and ordered them to pay a "$25 million civil penalty." The auditors agreed to a settlement "without admitting or denying the findings" (AAER 2237, 2005).

THE BELLSOUTH WARNING

> BellSouth is presented mainly as an example of Improper Accounting for Foreign Payments in Violation of the Foreign Corrupt Practices Act (FCPA)

BellSouth is a telecommunications corporation headquartered in Atlanta, Georgia. During the 1990s, the company significantly expanded its international operations via acquisitions of telephone companies in as many as eleven different Latin American countries, including Venezuela and Nicaragua. According to the SEC, it was in its business dealings with these two countries that BellSouth ran foul of the Foreign Corrupt Practices Act (FCPA) (AAER 1494, 2002).

The FCPA was passed in 1977 to combat improper dealings by U.S. companies operating in foreign countries, and the act is enforced by both the Department of Justice (DOJ) and the SEC. The FCPA is essentially comprised of two sections: the anti-bribery regulations and the accounting regulations. The consequences of violating any of the provisions of the act may be quite severe and may carry "potential criminal and civil penalties" (SEC v. BellSouth—Update 2002).

The bribery and accounting provisions frequently overlap because bribery payments are usually misclassified in the accounts, records, and financial statements. The accounting section of the FCPA clearly requires that publicly traded companies operating overseas must "make and keep books, records and accounts, which, in reasonable detail, accurately and fairly reflect their transaction[s] and disposition of assets, and devise and maintain a system of internal accounting controls. . . ." (AAER 1494, 2002). According to the SEC, BellSouth ran into problems with its acquisitions of both Telcel (in Venezuela) and Telefonia (in Nicaragua).[3]

BellSouth's Fictitious Financial Reporting Schemes

Scheme #1: The Use of Fabricated Invoices at Telcel

BellSouth entered the Venezuelan market in 1991 with its acquisition of a minority interest in Telcel, and in 1997 BellSouth increased its investment

---

[3] The SEC issued a cease-and-desist order against BellSouth in which the Commissioner found that "BellSouth violated the books and record provisions and internal accounting contract provisions" (AAER 1495, 2002). BellSouth consented to the entry of the order "without admitting or denying the Commissioner's findings." As set out in AAER 1495.

in Telcel to a majority holding. By 2002, Telcel had become the largest wireless supplier in Venezuela and was BellSouth's largest revenue earner in Latin America.

The SEC alleged that from 1997 to 2000, ". . . former Telcel senior management authorized payments totaling approximately $10.8 million to six offshore companies." Furthermore, the Commission stated that "Telcel recorded the disbursements in Telcel's books and records based on fictitious invoices." These fabricated invoices were for "services" rendered to Telcel, although no such services were ever verified and BellSouth was unable to furnish any information about these payments or about the location of the money. (Quotes from AAER 1494, 2002)

The strength of the FCPA legislation lies in the requirement that companies keep accurate books and records. Therefore, it is not necessary to first prove illegal intent regarding a payment; a suspicious payment in itself can result in an action. The failure to keep proper records is sufficient cause for an enforcement action.

Scheme #2: The Use of Inappropriate Payments and the Failure to Keep Accurate Records at Telefonia

In 1997, BellSouth had acquired 49 percent of the share of Telefonia in Nicaragua, as well as an option to acquire another 40 percent. However, there was a problem with the option because Nicaraguan law prohibited foreign companies from holding a majority of the stock in a telecommunications company.

In October 1998, Telefonia hired a lobbyist (at $6,500 per month) who was the wife of a Nicaraguan politician who happened to be the chairman of the telecommunications legislative-oversight committee. This committee had "jurisdiction over the foreign ownership restriction," and the chairman's wife worked primarily "on the repeal of the foreign ownership restriction" (AAER 1494, 2002). Although the lobbyist stopped working at Telefonia in May 1999, the movement to revoke the foreign ownership restriction was well under way, and the restriction was repealed in December 1999. By June 2000, BellSouth owned 89 percent of Telefonia. The lobbyist had received a total of $60,000, which included a severance payment.

According to the Commission, BellSouth was well aware that "its payments to the lobbyist could implicate the Foreign Corrupt Practices Act ('FCPA')." Furthermore, the SEC found that:

- Telefonia had "created false books and records" by describing the payments to the lobbyist as "consulting services."

- BellSouth had neglected "to devise and maintain a system of internal accounting controls at Telefonia, sufficient to detect and prevent FCPA violations." (Quotes from AAER 1494, 2002)

Signals of Improper Accounting in Violation of the FCPA

FCPA violations often consist of bribery where the amounts involved are not in themselves material, but the bribery itself can have serious consequences. This makes it difficult to pick up in the financial statements. Searches of news reports in the U.S. press and in the press of the foreign countries where a company operates should be done for stories on investigations of suspected bribery or corruption involving the company.

Are They Living Happily Ever After?

≈ **BellSouth** embarked on measures to "enhance its compliance program" (AAER 1495, 2002).

≈ **BellSouth** and SBC merged their wireless operations in 1999 to form Cingular Wireless, with BellSouth owning 40 percent of Cingular Wireless ("Dial a Deal" 2006; "BellSouth Profit up . . ." 2006). For the last quarter of 2005, BellSouth reported a "34 percent rise in quarterly profit as growth at its Cingular Wireless joint venture helped offset declines in its wireline business" ("BellSouth Profit up . . ." 2006).

≈ In March 2006, AT&T announced plans to purchase BellSouth. Some critics have pointed out that this merger would, in effect, be the "recreation of the old Ma Bell, which the government pushed to break up in 1984" (Searcey et al. 2006). The FCC will review the proposed purchase.

KRISPY KREME AND THE MISSING DOUGH[4]

> Krispy Kreme Doughnuts, Inc., is presented mainly as an example of Inappropriate Accounting for Roundtrip Transactions

Introduction

The original Krispy Kreme company was founded by Vernon Rudolph in North Carolina in 1937, and slowly developed a small string of franchises

---

[4] The background information for this section is mainly from Brooks (2004), Maremont and Brooks (2005), O'Sullivan (2005), "Scott Livengood, CEO, Krispy Kreme" (2004), "Summary of Independent Investigation" (2005).

with what has been described as "an almost legendary product and a loyal customer base" (O'Sullivan 2005). According to doughnut lore, a fresh Krispy Kreme is the ideal melt-in-your mouth doughnut, with just the right chewy texture of freshly fried, sugary dough, drizzled with the perfect glaze. And the customers can actually smell the sweet aroma and hear the hot sizzle of doughnuts being cooked to perfection; Krispy Kreme turned the doughnut business into the doughnut experience.

The company was sold to Beatrice Foods in the 1970s, a few years after the original owner died. Many Krispy Kreme devotees were upset by the sale, and several of the franchisees grouped together to repurchase the company in 1982. The business began to grow on the national level as customers all over America lined up to get their first taste of the mouthwatering confectionary.

The company's business model seemed like a dream come true: a product that needed no introduction, and a customer base waiting to sample the merchandise. Scott Livengood, the CEO of Krispy Kreme, took the company public with an initial public offering (IPO) in April 2000, and opened up a number of international franchises, with the first European outlet at the Harrods store in London. Livengood was reportedly such an avid fan of the doughnuts that he had a huge cake made up entirely of doughnuts when he got married in 2002. Krispy Kreme was constantly mentioned in the media, and even people who had never eaten a doughnut became familiar with the brand.

In the fiscal three-year span from February 2001 to February 2004, the number of stores grew from 58 company-owned stores and 86 franchises to 141 company-owned stores and 216 franchises. During this period, the company usually exceeded Wall Street's expectations, as annual revenue grew from $220 million to $665.6 million. Krispy Kreme's stock price "climbed most dramatically of all, from the IPO price of $5.25 per share to a high of $49.37 per share on August 18, 2003" ("Summary of Independent Investigation" 2005, 3).

Then things started to turn sour as Krispy Kreme was accused of having "sweetened results" in its attempts to keep Wall Street happy (Maremont and Brooks 2005). The corporation was beset with problems that ranged from store closures to rumors about problematic acquisitions and inaccurate accounting practices. In an attempt to shore up the struggling company, Livengood tried to blame Krispy Kreme's problems on the growing popularity of low carbohydrate diets, and the company even announced that it was developing a "sugar-free doughnut" (O'Sullivan 2005). However, by May 7, 2004, the stock price had dropped to $22.51 per share and kept sliding. The next month, one of several lawsuits was filed against Krispy Kreme, alleging that it had issued "materially false and misleading statements contained in press releases and filings with the Securities and Exchange Commission" (Chimicles & Tikellis LLP 2004). In October 2004, the SEC informed the company that it was under formal investigation. That same month, the board of directors set up a "special committee" to perform an independent investigation into the business practices of the company.

In the final "Summary of Independent Investigation" (2005), the special committee highlighted a number of problematic areas. In its examination of company management, the committee members stated: "It appears that Livengood was too focused on meeting and exceeding Wall Street expectations and gave too little attention to establishing the appropriate tone from the top" (6). The committee maintained that John Tate, the chief operating officer, was also largely responsible for "failure to set the appropriate managerial tone and environment . . ." (6).

Additionally, the investigation uncovered several accounting errors in Krispy Kreme's financial statements for 2004. Without these errors, the company would not have been able to meet its aggressive sales and earnings estimates quite as consistently as it did. It is important to note that the special committee did *not* conclude that the accounting errors were intentional, although it recognized that "government investigators . . . may uncover additional facts that will better illuminate the intent behind various individuals' actions and the underlying events" ("Summary of Independent Investigation" 2005, 2).

An Overview of Krispy Kreme's Operational Problems

Apart from the accounting errors, the company was beset by other problems, which included:

- Overly rapid growth with the addition of too many new franchised stores at the expense of existing franchises
- Same-store revenue (i.e., of existing franchises) was growing much more slowly than parent-company revenue which was boosted by the opening of new stores
- A lack of "controls, procedures and resources adequate for a business experiencing explosive growth" ("Summary of Independent Investigation" 2005, 5)
- There appear to have been too few independent outside directors to determine strategy and to control management

- Policies that were favorable to the parent company, but detrimental to its franchisees, such as expecting "franchisees to buy equipment and ingredients from headquarters at marked-up prices" (O'Sullivan 2005)
- Moving away from its core competency, such as adding new items to the menu and selling doughnuts that were not cooked on-site

Signals of Krispy Kreme's Operational Problem of Opening Too Many Franchises

Signal #1: An increase in the intangible asset of "franchise acquisition rights" could be an indication that too many franchises have been sold and that some are being repurchased because franchisees are "cannibalizing" each other as new stores are taking away business from existing stores (Chimicles & Tikellis LLP 2004).

Signal #2: Another signal of this problem is when growth in company sales is much greater than growth in existing-store sales. In the period from the second quarter of 2003 to the second quarter of 2004, Krispy Kreme reported an increase in company revenues of almost 15 percent, while same-store sales increased by less than 1 percent.

An Overview of Krispy Kreme's Fictitious Financial Reporting Schemes

An examination of Krispy Kreme's records revealed a number of accounting errors, including:

1. The recording of early shipments of equipment sales to franchisees, while the equipment remained unused until later periods
2. The misallocation of compensation expenses to the cost of the reacquisition of franchises by boosting the repurchase price of franchise rights
3. The failure to accrue the full amount of incentive compensation expense in accordance with the company's incentive plan
4. The recording of roundtrip transactions in which equipment sales were made to franchisees just prior to the reacquisition of the franchise, and the sales price of the equipment was added to the reacquisition cost of the franchise.

This fourth scheme of misreporting roundtrip transactions is the last of the top twenty schemes as listed in Table 1.1 of this book. It is mainly as an example of this method of fictitious financial reporting that Krispy Kreme is presented here.

The Krispy Kreme Scheme of Using Inappropriate Accounting for Roundtrip Transactions

The SOX Report defined roundtrip transactions as transactions that "involve simultaneous pre-arranged sales transactions, often of the same product, in order to create a false impression of business activity and revenue" (25). In the case of Krispy Kreme, the "Summary of Independent Investigation" (2005) stated that although the amounts involved were not very large, the "most egregious" accounting errors they uncovered were those involving roundtrip transactions with franchise acquisitions (8).

The vehicle that Krispy Kreme used to implement its roundtrip transaction stunt was the reacquisition of franchise rights. The special committee reported that in June 2003—just before the reacquisition of a Dallas franchise—Krispy Kreme sold approximately $700,000 of doughnut-making equipment to that same franchisee with an agreement "to increase the purchase price to cover the price of the equipment" ("Summary of Independent Investigation" 2005, 9). The net effect of this was that Krispy Kreme gave an extra $700,000 to the franchisee to reacquire the franchise, and the franchisee gave Krispy Kreme the $700,000 for the "sale" of the equipment. Krispy Kreme got its own equipment back after the reacquisition of the franchise. The cash and the equipment both went on a "roundtrip" to the franchisee and back to Krispy Kreme. Both sales and franchise acquisition rights (an intangible asset) were overstated in the process.

Signals of Krispy Kreme's Fictitious Reporting Scheme of:

• Misusing Roundtrip Transactions

Signal #1: As with any overstatement of sales, accounts receivable increasing as a percentage of sales as measured by, for example, days sales outstanding (DSO), is a signal of acceleration of fictitious sales.

Signal #2: The cash flow from operations (CFFO) may lag operating income until the "sale" is paid for from the ensuing complementary roundtrip transaction payment. In Krispy Kreme's case, the ensuing roundtrip payment was an inflated franchise reacquisition payment. With the various accounting errors at Krispy Kreme, CFFO lagged operating income, and there were times when CFFO was negative while operating income was positive.

Are They Living Happily Ever After?

≈ **Scott Livengood** was removed from his position as CEO in January 2005. Livengood was replaced by Stephen Cooper, the interim CEO of the defunct Enron. Livengood was offered a six-month position as an "interim consultant" (Nowell 2005). In March 2006, Daryl G. Brewster was named CEO of Krispy Kreme.

≈ **John Tate,** former COO of Krispy Kreme, left the company in August 2004 "to pursue another opportunity" (quoted in "Krispy Kreme COO Tate Leaving the Company" 2004).

≈ In June 2005, the special committee had decided that "six unnamed company officers should be fired" ("Six Krispy Kreme Execs Ousted" 2005). Shortly thereafter, five of the executives resigned and one retired.

≈ In the opening months of 2006, Krispy Kreme's stocks were trading in the $5.00–$7.00 per share range; quite a sharp drop from $49.37 per share in August 2003. The company has sold off a number of its franchises.

≈ As of May 2006, Krispy Kreme was reportedly still under investigation by the SEC.

References

AAER 1494. *U.S. Securities and Exchange Commission.* Accounting and Auditing Enforcement Release. January 15, 2002. www.sec.gov/litigation/admin/34-45279.htm

AAER 1495. *U.S. Securities and Exchange Commission.* Accounting and Auditing Enforcement Release No. 1495; Litigation Release No. 17310. January 15, 2002. www.sec.gov/litigation/litreleases/lr17310.htm

AAER 1555. *U.S. Securities and Exchange Commission* Accounting and Auditing Enforcement Release. May 14, 2002. www.sec.gov/litigation/admin/34-45925.htm

AAER 1599. *U.S. Securities and Exchange Commission.* Accounting and Auditing Enforcement Release No. 1599; Litigation Release No. 17627. July 24, 2002. www.sec.gov

AAER 1664. *U.S. Securities and Exchange Commission.* Accounting and Auditing Enforcement Release No. 1664; Litigation Release No. 17837. November 14, 2002. www.sec.gov

AAER 2237. *U.S. Securities and Exchange Commission.* Accounting and Auditing Enforcement Release No. 2237. April 26, 2005. www.sec.gov

"Adelphia Founder John Rigas Found Guilty," *Associated Press,* July 8, 2004. www.msnbc.com

"BellSouth Profit up on Wireless Growth," *Reuters,* January 25, 2006. www.news.com/BellSouth

BR–6413. *Securities and Exchange Commission.* Complaint against Adelphia Communications Corp., John Rigas, Timothy Rigas, Michael Rigas, James Rigas, James Brown, and Michael Mulcahey. Release No. 17627. July 24, 2002. www.sec.gov

Bray, Chad. 2005. "Moving the Market: Adelphia Ex-Officer Admits to Filing False Report," *The Wall Street Journal,* November 25. Available online via ProQuest database.

Bray, Chad. 2006. "Ex-Adelphia Executive Michael Rigas Avoids Jail Time for Role in Fraud," *The Wall Street Journal,* March 3. www.wsj.com

Brooks, Rick. 2004. "SEC Commences a Formal Probe of Krispy Kreme," *Wall Street Journal,* October 11. Available online via ProQuest database.

Chimicles & Tikellis LLP. 2004. "Class Action Lawsuit against Krispy Kreme Doughnuts Inc." June 22. www.chimicles.com

Crawford, Krysten, and Winnie Dunbar. 2004. "John Rigas Guilty of Conspiracy: Adelphia Founder, Son, Found Guilty on Some Charges that they Looted Cable Company," CNN/Money, July 8. http://money.cnn.com/2004/07/08/news/midcaps/adelphia_verdict/

"Dial a Deal," *Wall Street Journal,* March 5, 2006. www.wsj.com

Edison Schools website. www.edisonschools.com

"Edison Schools Leaving Publicly Traded Stage," *TheStreet.com,* July 14, 2003. www.thestreet.com

Goldsmith, Jill. 2005. "Perk Parade Hits a Slump: 'Will Adelphia Indulgences Jerk Benefits for Hollywood?'" *Variety.com,* March 28. www.variety.com

Grant, Peter. 2006. "Adelphia's Sale Plan Suffers a Blow." *Wall Street Journal,* April 19, 2006.

"Krispy Kreme COO Tate Leaving the Company," *The Business Journal,* August 16, 2004. www.bizjournals.com

"Krispy Kreme Names CEO: Shares Jump," *Los Angeles Times.* March 8, 2006.

Maremont, Mark, and Rick Brooks. 2005. "Report Shows How Krispy Kreme Sweetened Results; Panel Says Doughnut Maker Used 'Egregious' Practices, Blames Ex-CEO, Directors," *The Wall Street Journal,* August 11. Available online via ProQuest database.

Martin, Dan. 2005. "Edison Schools are Only Average," *The Honolulu Star-Bulletin,* October 10. www.starbulletin.com

Masters, Brooke A., and Ben White. 2004. "Adelphia Founder, Son Convicted of Fraud," *Washington Post,* July 9. www.washingtonpost.com

Nowell, Paul. 2005. "Krispy Kreme Ousts CEO in Turnaround Bid," *The Washington Post,* January 19. www.washingtonpost.com

O'Sullivan, Kate. 2005 "Kreamed! The Rise and Fall of Krispy Kreme is a Cautionary Tale of Ambition, Greed, and Inexperience," *CFO Magazine,* June 1. www.cfo.com

"Scott Livengood, CEO, Krispy Kreme," June 22, 2004. www.cnn.com

Searcey, Dionne, et al. 2006. "AT&T Nears $65 Billion Deal to Buy BellSouth," *The Wall Street Journal*, March 5. www.wsj.com

"SEC Charges Adelphia and Rigas Family with Massive Financial Fraud." SEC Press Release. July 24, 2002. www.sec.gov

SEC v. BellSouth-Update. *Foley FCPA Enforcement*: SEC and DOJ Enforcement Actions and Opinions. March 16, 2002. www.fcpaenforcement.com

"Six Krispy Kreme Execs Ousted," *Associated Press*, June 21, 2005. www.msnbc.com

SOX Report. *Report Pursuant to Section 704 of the Sarbanes-Oxley Act of 2002*. www.sec.gov/news/studies/sox704report.pdf

Snider, Shane. 2002. "SEC Settles Action with BellSouth," Triangle Business Journal, January 15. www.bizjournals.com/triangle/stories/20002/01/14/daily21.html

"Status of High-Profile Corporate Scandals," *Associated Press*, November 23, 2005. Available online via LexisNexis database.

"Summary of Independent Investigation" by the Special Committee of the Board of Directors of Krispy Kreme Doughnuts, Inc. Published on the Securities and Exchange Commission website. August 10, 2005. www.sec.gov

Woodward, Tali. 2002. "Edison's Failing Grade," *CorpWatch*. June 20. www.corpwatch.org

CHAPTER 8

THE PENSION-FUND FANTASY

. . . pension accounting is beyond magic.
It is alchemy.

Bradley Belt, Executive Director, PBGC

PART 1: THE DISAPPEARING PENSION

"They lived happily ever after" is the standard fairy-tale ending, which implies that the characters will have no financial concerns as they grow old gracefully. Those of us who do not manage to snag a filthy rich princess or prince will turn to our nest eggs—the pension funds that have promised to sustain us in our golden years. The guaranteed or "defined benefit" pension was developed to provide for specific formula-driven monthly or annual payments to employees upon retirement. (On the other hand, the 401(k) plans do not guarantee specific payments and are dependent upon the employees' contributions that are sometimes matched by the employers. Employees own their own retirement assets and bear the related risks.) For many years, the traditional, defined-benefit pension was regarded as the gold standard—the reward for loyalty and service to a company—guaranteeing financial security to company retirees. In 1980, almost "one-third of American workers were covered by defined benefit plans" (Testimony of Bradley D. Belt 2005). By 1999, less than 10 percent of U.S. workers were covered by these plans. And the tale gets worse.

In October 2005, a disturbing *Time* magazine cover story, titled "The Broken Promise," by Donald L. Barlett and James Steele, sounded the alarm for a potential economic pandemic of pension-fund failures. The article pointed out that, over the last few decades, Congress established bankruptcy regulations and pension rules that have played a pivotal role in eroding the guarantee that retiring employees will receive their pension funds and health benefits. The bankruptcy rules allow corporations to declare bankruptcy and then dump their pension obligations—to present and future retirees—on the federal Pension Benefit Guaranty Corporation (PBGC). However, the

PBGC will only cover pension payments up to a maximum amount: "For single employer plans ended in 2006, workers who retire at age 65 can receive up to . . . $47,659 a year" (PBGC Fact Sheet 2006). Therefore a retiree receiving, for example, a $90,000 pension payment per year could find it cut by almost half if his or her past employer declares bankruptcy and the pension responsibility is turned over to the PBGC. For example, Robin Gillinger, a United Airlines flight attendant with fourteen years of service, "has another 14 years to go before she can take early retirement. Under the old pension plan she would have received a monthly check of $2,184. Because of givebacks, that's down to $776. . . . And there is a distinct possibility it could be less than that" (Barlett and Steele 2005, 44).

The problems do not end with companies that declare bankruptcy. Even employees who have not yet retired and are still paying into defined-benefit pension plans are now finding that the rules allow companies to decrease employees' future retirement payments—virtually at will. Companies can simply freeze current employees' contributions and benefits. This has created an extremely stressful situation: "Recent announcements that General Motors, International Business Machines and Verizon communications are 'freezing' pension plans strike fear into the hearts of many workers counting on regular pension income when they retire. And for good reason" (Francis 2006).

Of course, Congress alone is not to blame for the defects of pension funds. The center of gravity of the demographic age distribution has always been with the baby boomers, who are now beginning to retire in larger numbers than previously and are living longer than retirees of the past. This is creating larger pension obligations, together with proportionately fewer younger workers contributing to the plans. Watson Wyatt, a human resources consultant for Worldwide, estimated that of the 614 *Fortune 1000* companies offering traditional pension plans, "About half have assets that would cover 80 percent or less of what the plans are supposed to pay" (quoted in Isadore 2005).

In addition, accounting rules allow much subjectivity in the estimation of the rate of return on assets and on the rate used for discounting future payment obligations to their present value. Many companies have miscalculated the cost of funding their retirement plans. After taking over a company's pension obligations, the PBGC often discovers that the unfunded liability of the pension plan is greater than the amount stated in the notes to the company's financial statements. For example, General Motors (GM) has estimated its pension deficit to be $10 billion; however, "The PBGC estimates it at $31 billion" (Barlett and Steele 2005, 44).

In another instance, UAL Corp. (the parent company of United Airlines) stated in an SEC filing in March 2005 that its pension shortfall for 2004 was

$6 billion. However, the PBGC estimated this shortfall to be almost $10 bil-lion. According to a *Newsweek* article, "UAL was accounting for its plans as if it were going to run them for decades, even though the company had been in Chapter 11 protection for two years and was in the process of dumping the plans onto the PBGC. The agency did its pension math differently be-cause it was terminating the plans." Joan Medina, spokesperson for United Airlines, defended the $6 billion figure: "The way we accounted for the pension shortfall is dictated by generally accepted accounting principles." Clearly, the gap between the two figures is problematic and illustrates how difficult it sometimes is "to translate SEC filings into economic reality." (Quotes from Sloan 2005)

So many pension plans are declaring bankruptcy and dumping their obligations onto the PBGC that there is a real worry that the PBGC itself will soon become bankrupt. If this occurs and a federal bailout becomes necessary, such a bailout could be quite controversial because it would entail the use of tax money and, in effect, people *without* pension plans would be subsidizing those with pension plans.[1] At the same time, abandoning loyal retirees who worked for companies for years, lulled by promises of defined-benefit pension plans, is not a fair solution either.

Meanwhile, the defined-benefit pension plan is steadily becoming a thing of the past in corporate America. Statistics show that, in the last twenty years, the number of company-sponsored pension plans insured by the PBGC dropped from 112,000 to 29,652. In addition, while the number of compa-nies offering defined-benefit pension plans is decreasing, the claims paid out by the PBGC increased sharply at the turn of the millennium. In fact, 70 per-cent of its payments occurred in the five-year period from 2000–2004. In this period, "Claims from failed single-employer pension plans totaled $14.3 billion in 2000–2004." (Quotes and statistics from PBGC Public Affairs News Release, May 27, 2005)

It is interesting to examine the growth in claims over the last twenty years:

> Historically, the pension insurance program has absorbed large losses during economic downturns, but the most recent surge dwarfs anything in the agency's history. The 2000-2004 total is 18 times larger than the $783 million in claims booked in 1995—1999. During the period of 1990—1994 claims totaled $2.8 billion, [almost] . . . twice the $1.7 billion incurred during 1985—1989. (PBGC Public Affairs News Release, May 27, 2005)

---

[1] Presently, the PBGC is not financed by general taxes but "largely by insurance premiums paid by companies that sponsor pension plans and investment returns" (from PBGC Public Affairs News Release, June 7, 2005).

Furthermore, in a report to the Senate Finance Committee in June 2005, Bradley Belt—the executive director of the PBGC—testified that, for 2004, "Companies with underfunded pension plans reported a record shortfall of $353.7 billion in their latest filings with the Pension Benefit Guaranty Corporation." In spite of the fact that large companies with "more than $50 million in unfunded pension liabilities" are required to file reports with the PBGC, due to anomalies in laws and accounting guidelines, a company like United Airlines "was able to go for years without making any cash contribution to the plans, without paying additional premiums to the PBGC, and without sending underfunding notices to plan participants." (Quotes from PBGC Public Affairs News Release, June 7, 2005)

A November 2005 article by Marilyn Adams in *USA Today* provided the following table listing a selection of major companies with pension plans that were underfunded from 25 percent to well over 6,000 percent:

Table 8.1 Underfunded Companies*

Companies with pension plans that are expected to be underfunded by at least 25% of their market capitalization as of October 14, [2005]:[2]

	2005 Estimated Underfunded (Amount in billions)	Estimated Market Cap. (in billions)	Percent Underfunded
Delta Air Lines	$5.8	$0.1	6,791%
Delphi	$4.6	$0.3	1,712%
Goodyear Tire & Rubber	$3.1	$2.5	125%
Visteon	$1.0	$1.0	96%
Ford Motor	$13.5	$16.0	85%
General Motors	$12.3	$15.8	78%
Unisys	$1.2	$2.0	58%
Navistar International	$1.0	$1.9	51%
Dana	$0.4	$1.0	47%
Maytag	$0.6	$1.3	43%
Hercules	$0.4	$1.3	28%
Raytheon	$4.1	$16.5	25%
Lockheed Martin	$6.7	$27.0	25%

*Source: David Zion, Credit Suisse First Boston. Printed with permission.

---

[2] With stock market gains in early 2006, these underfunded amounts have changed and will continue to vary with stock market conditions.

PART 2: THE ALCHEMY OF PENSION ACCOUNTING

While the SOX Report does not list pension accounting as one of the frequent methods of fictitious financial reporting—probably because accounting rules allow for so much imaginative interpretation—it is an area that is rife with fairy tales. In fact, pension accounting experts such as David Zion and Bill Carcache like to refer to the "magic of pension accounting." In a speech to the National Association for Business Economics, Bradley Belt pointed out that while most companies, in fact, adhere to pension accounting rules, these rules are so complex and confusing that an examination of pension accounting was like following "Alice down the White Rabbit's hole into a looking-glass world."[3] Belt went on to explain:

> . . . the pension alchemy we see practiced every day is permitted, even encouraged, by financial accounting standards, ERISA funding rules, and actuarial convention. But it is disconnected from the economic reality in which you must operate, it obfuscates what every worker, retiree, investor, and creditor has a right to see. (Belt 2006)

According to generally accepted accounting principles (GAAP), each year, if the amount funded by an employer to its pension trust is less than the annual pension expense, a pension liability accrual is made in the income statement for the difference. Further, if the accumulated benefit obligation exceeds the fair value of pension-plan assets, an additional liability is accrued in respect of the difference. However, while the accumulated benefit obligation at any particular date is the present value of future benefits attributed to employee service rendered to that date, it does not take into account assumptions regarding future compensation levels of the employees. The projected benefit obligation does take expected future compensation levels into account, and the projected obligation is therefore usually greater than the accumulated benefit obligation. Current GAAP does not require companies to accrue a liability on the balance sheet for the excess of the projected benefit obligation over the fair value of the fund assets. That difference is known as the amount by which the pension plan is underfunded, and under current GAAP, it only has to be disclosed in the notes or footnotes to the financial statements. Further, under current legislation, companies do not have to transfer assets to the pension plan itself for the full amount of the shortfall

---

[3] Shortly after his "Through the Looking Glass" speech, Belt announced that he would be leaving the PBGC at the end of May, 2006.

between the fair value of the assets and the projected benefit obligations. Hence, many pension funds are spectacularly underfunded.

The company simply has to disclose in footnotes the extent to which the pension plan itself has a shortfall. Also, if the company overstates its estimate of the rate of return on the assets, or understates the future obligation, both the liability on the company's balance sheet and the footnote disclosure of the unfunded portion of the plan is understated. In addition, the manipulation of the rates used in the estimates can be used to overstate the company's earnings.

Belt lamented that under current pension-fund accounting rules, "companies can book to income not the *actual* return on those pension assets but the *expected* return." He went on to point out that, for certain companies, "the pension plan has been a primary source of . . . *phantom* profits." (Quotes from Belt 2006)

The Financial Economist Roundtable (FER) pointed out that the Pension Fund Equity Act "permits companies to increase the discount rates used for valuing their pension liabilities, thereby allowing them to understate the amount for which they are actually liable." In addition, pension funds may be invested in illiquid assets for which the market values often "cannot be readily determined or effectively determined." (Quotes from "Statement on Corporate Pension Fund Accounting" 2004)

Reform is underway on two fronts. First, legislation is in process in Congress to require companies to accelerate payments into pension funds to close the deficits. Second, the accounting rules are being changed to require the underfunded amounts to be disclosed on the balance sheet instead of just in the notes. (Refer to Chapter 9 of this book for further discussion.)

Signals of Problems with Pension-Fund Obligations

According to David Zion and Zachary Shannon, there are two major indications of problems with pension funds. These indications are the first two signals.

Signal #1: When a company has a very large "proportion of unfunded pension obligations compared to market capitalization," it is a signal that this unfunded obligation could cause serious problems in the future (Zion and Shannon, cited in Brush 2004). This problem is more widespread than one would expect, and applies to a wide range of companies, as can be seen from Table 8.1.

Investors and employees should obtain the size of the unfunded portion of a company's pension plans from the notes to the financial statements and calculate the percentage that amount represents as a percentage of the company's market-capitalization value. Underfunding also puts pressure on the company to use estimates that understate the pension liabilities and overstate earnings. Employees should consider whether the anticipated pension-plan benefits will likely decrease before they retire.

Signal #2: When a company derives "the biggest chunk of [its] net income (excluding unusual items) from *assumed* returns on their pension investments," it is a signal that the company's reported earnings may be too optimistic (Zion and Shannon, cited in Brush 2004). The assumed rates of return on assets may be too subjective to accept them at face value.

Signal #3: If companies use an assumed rate of return on pension assets that is higher than other companies in their industry, or if the assumed rate increases more than that of other companies in the same period, it is a sign that the company could be using an unrealistically high assumed rate of return to overstate its earnings. For a more precise test, one should compare a company's assumed rate of return on its pension assets with the rate of other companies with similar asset allocation strategies.

Signal #4: If a company discounts its pension obligations at a higher rate than other companies in its industry, it is a sign that the company could be understating its pension obligations. Also, if the disparity between the company's pension obligation discount rate and prevailing interest rates increases, it is a signal that the company may be understating its pension liabilities.

References

Adams, Marilyn. 2005. "'Broken' Pension Systems in 'Crying Need' of a Fix," *USA Today*, November 14. Updated November 15, 2005. www.usatoday.com/money/perfi/retirement/ 2005-11-14-pensions-usat_x.htm

Barlett, Donald L., and James Steele. 2005. "The Broken Promise," *Time*, October 31, 32–47.

Belt, Bradley D. 2006. "Through the Looking Glass: Adventures in Pension Land." Remarks before the National Association for Business Economics. March 13. www.pbgc.gov/media/news-archive/ExecutiveSpeech/sp15669.html

Brush, Michael. 2004. "40 Companies Sitting on Pension Time Bombs," *MSN Money*, August 25.
www.moneycentral.msn.com/content/P87329.asp

Francis, Theo. 2006. "Watch Out for Painful Pension Math," *The Wall Street Journal Online*, February 19. www.online.wsj.com

Isadore, Chris. 2005. "Pension Problems 101: How Private Employers' Plans Took a Hit, and the Changes Being Proposed; Is Your Money at Risk?" *CNN/Money*, May 17.
www.money.cnn.com/2005/05/17/retirement/pension_problems

Katz, David M. 2006. "Q&A: Pensions on the Brink," *CFO.com,* April 4.
www.cfo.com

PBGC Fact Sheet. 2006. www.pbgc.gov/media/key-resources-for-the-press/content/page13540.html

PBGC Public Affairs News Release, 202-326-4343. 2005. "Seventy Percent of PBGCs Losses Incurred in 2000-2004." May 27.
www.pbgc.gov/media/news-archive/2005/pr05-40.html.

PBGC Public Affairs News Release, 202-326-4343. 2005. "Companies Report a Record $353.7 Billion Pension Shortfall in Latest Filings with PBGC." June 7.
www.pbgc.gov/media/news-archive/2005/pr05-48.html

PBGC Public Affairs News Release, 202-326-4343. 2006. "PBGC Executive Director Bradley D. Belt Announces Departure." March 23.
www.pbgc.gov/media/news-archive/2006/pr06-32.html

PBGC White Paper. 2005. "The Impact of Pension Reform Proposals on Claims against the Pension Insurance Program, Losses to Participants, and Contributions." October 26.

Pizzani, Lori. 2003. "A Primer: Turmoil in Pension Plan Funding," *CFA Institute,* February. www.cfainstitute.org/pressroom/fjnews/fjFeb03.html

Sloan, Allan. 2005. "Translating the SEC's Pension Fund Filings," *Newsweek* on *MSNBC.com,* June 5.
www.msnbc.msn.com/id/7887784/site/newsweek

SOX Report. *Report Pursuant to Section 704 of the Sarbanes-Oxley Act of 2002.* www.sec.gov/news/studies/sox704report.pdf

"Statement on Corporate Pension Fund Accounting." Financial Economists Roundtable, December 22, 2004.
www.luc.edu/orgs/finroundtable

Testimony of Bradley D. Belt, Executive Director, Pension Benefit Guaranty Corporation, Before the Subcommittee on Select Revenue Measure, Committee on Ways and Means, United States House of Representatives, March 8, 2005.

Zion, David, and Bill Carcache. 2005. "The Magic of Pension Accounting, Part III," Credit Suisse First Boston, February 7.

CHAPTER 9

REFORM: IS THERE A MAGIC POTION?[1]

The result in the Enron trial is a victory for all
Americans, whose jobs and economic security
depend on the integrity of our capital markets.

SEC Chairman Christopher Cox[2]

PART 1: INTRODUCTION

In authentic fairy tales the villains are usually vanquished and banished by
dashing young princes or fabulous fairy godmothers. Business fairy tales,
however, offer no such heroes or happy endings. The endings, in fact, are
usually rather dreary and depressing, involving SEC investigations, insolvent
companies, dejected employees, and disgruntled investors. In order to prevent this dismal scenario from constantly repeating, change is essential, and
to achieve genuine change, the financial community must emphasize ethical
business practices and reform in the marketplace, without sacrificing the
free-market energy and dynamic competition that are trademarks of the
U.S. economy.

In December 2001, after Enron's collapse caused huge losses to investors
and employees, the public's attention became riveted on the fraudulent financial reporting that had falsely enhanced Enron's published financial position.
Congress began hearings on the financial reporting environment but was hesitant to pass legislation in this regard. However, in July 2002, the billion-dollar
WorldCom, riddled with accounting fraud, declared bankruptcy. This galvanized Congress into action, and at the end of July, the Sarbanes-Oxley (SOX)
Act of 2002 was passed. This act—sponsored by Senator Paul Sarbanes
(D-Md.) and Congressman Michael Oxley (R-Ohio)—was intended to
restore what Senator Sarbanes called the "fundamental integrity" of U.S.
markets. Initially, some ardent supporters of the legislation regarded it as a

---

[1] Information on Sarbanes-Oxley in this chapter mainly from *Executive Summary of the Sarbanes-Oxley Act of
2002*, Sarbanes-Oxley Act of 2002, and U.S. House of Representatives Hearing (2005b)

[2] From: SEC News Release 2006-81. May 25, 2006. www.sec.gov

type of magic potion, a cure-all for the problems plaguing the corporate world. While it was drawn up and passed quite rapidly, it took several years, countless squabbles, and many millions of dollars for the various facets of the Sarbanes-Oxley Act to be implemented.

The expensive, complex, and often vague requirements of the contentious and much-maligned Section 404 of SOX have driven several critics to argue that the hefty compliance costs actually impede corporations. In response to this complaint, Congressman Barney Frank (D-Ma.) commented: "Well, not compared to the money they pay the top people" (U.S. House Committee 2005b, 3). Frank mentioned that in 1980 the ratio of pay of a CEO to the average worker was 42:1; and by 2003 that ratio had soared to 500:1. The question of corporate compensation—only partially addressed by the SOX Act—is another difficult issue with no easy answers in a free market economy.

The Sarbanes-Oxley Act also has its quirky side with some unexpected consequences.[3] For example, Section 301 of SOX mandates the establishment of hotlines for anonymous whistle-blowers. These hotlines must, for obvious reasons, be run by a third party, resulting in a sharp increase in the hotline industry. Additionally, Section 301 is causing problems for some U.S. companies with European subsidiaries, because some countries in Europe discourage whistle-blowing, while other countries have labor laws against anonymous whistle-blowing.

Some less controversial aspects of the SOX Act such as the "Fair Funds" provision (Section 308a), have been generally well received. This particular provision was set up to "use civil penalties collected in enforcement cases and add them to disgorgement funds for the benefit of victims of securities law violations." Over $5 billion has already been earmarked "for anticipated distribution to harmed investors." (Quotes from U.S. House Committee 2005b, 45-49)

In spite of the glitches that are still being worked out, the reform movement is a rational response to a problem that endangers the fundamental stability of our capital markets. In addition to the SEC's efforts to fulfill the requirements of the SOX Act, a number of other organizations have been working to clean up the corporate environment:[4]

- The Financial Accounting Standards Board (FASB) has issued or updated several accounting standards.

---

[3] Information in this paragraph is from *HR Euronews* (2005), *National Hotline Services*, and Bond and Campbell (2005).

[4] Information in this section is mainly from Glassman (2005).

- The Public Company Accounting Oversight Board (PCAOB) has developed an extensive inspection program.
- The New York Stock Exchange (NYSE) and NASDAQ have added new requirements for their member companies.
- The Corporate Fraud Task Force (CFTF) was launched and housed in the Department of Justice.
- The Department of Justice has made corporate fraud a priority for 2006. There are also increased penalties for corporate fraud and other corporate crimes.
- Business schools from coast to coast are establishing courses in business ethics and corporate governance issues.
- An ongoing project has been launched to integrate U.S. generally accepted accounting principles (GAAP) with international financial reporting standards (IFRS).
- Numerous professional organizations throughout the country are addressing various issues, setting guidelines and standards for their members.

Of course, too many controls and limitations will have an extremely constricting effect, resulting in a negative impact on the U.S. economy. In fact, some critics maintain that SOX may have already gone too far in its attempts to clean up the U.S. business landscape: "But the question is not whether better controls lead to less risk—how could they not?—but whether that reduction in risk is worth the price" ("The Trial of Sarbanes-Oxley" 2006). The trick now is to find the right blend of a vibrant, free-market economy and the checks and balances needed to ensure that corporate gatekeepers are carrying out their tasks. Some of the main areas of corporate governance reform since the SOX Act of 2002 include the following:

- Internal Control Requirements (SOX Section 404)
- Responsibilities of Corporate Management (SOX Section 302)
- Loans to Executives
- Auditor Independence and Oversight
- Director Independence and Responsibility
- Independence of Analysts
- Corporate Crime Enforcement
- New Accounting Rules
  - Accounting for Stock Options
  - Accounting for Special Purpose Entities

The question now is whether the recent reforms have been reasonable and balanced or whether they have, in fact, created problems of their own. In other words, is the magic potion effective, or it is having unpleasant side effects?

PART 2: CORPORATE GOVERNANCE REFORM SINCE 2002

Internal Control Requirements (Section 404)

While internal control is certainly not new, Sarbanes-Oxley emphasizes it to such an extent that one of the most hotly contested parts of the SOX legislation has been Section 404, on the grounds that compliance is extremely expensive and time consuming. A contentious debate has erupted as to whether the benefits of Section 404's internal-control compliance outweigh the costs.

Section 404 requires management to take responsibility for the company's internal control, and each annual report of the company must include a report in which management states its responsibility for and its assessment of the company's internal-control system. Section 404 requires that internal-control reports should:

1. State the responsibility of management for establishing and maintaining an adequate internal control structure and procedures for financial reporting; and
2. Contain an annual assessment of the effectiveness of the company's internal control structure and procedures.

In addition, Section 404 requires that the company's external auditors must also attest to and report on management's assessment of its internal control.

○ The Cost of Compliance

Proponents of SOX believe that the question is not whether we *can* afford the SOX requirements, but whether we can afford *not* to have them. They point out that we must not forget the reason for the passage of SOX legislation in the first place. After the series of spectacular financial reporting and audit failures, confidence needed to be restored in the integrity of corporate financial statements. The colossal losses suffered by investors, retirees, and employees had to be stopped or at least dramatically slowed. Without this restoration of confidence, more companies would go bankrupt, more jobs would be lost, and more capital would be diverted from the U.S. economy.

Some supporters of Sarbanes-Oxley viewed it as cause for alarm that companies have been finding it so hard to comply with "new" regulations, because many of these regulations are not that new. One high-ranking regulator was quoted as saying: "The fact that companies are having difficulty complying, after controls have been in federal law for 25 years, doesn't speak well for the quality of their controls" (quoted in Henry et al. 2005).

On the other hand, there are those who argue that the cost of implementing the SOX internal-control requirements has caused some companies to avoid going public, and has even caused some smaller public companies to "delist" and go private. There are those who say that some smaller companies could ultimately be driven out of business. Opponents of SOX have pointed out that, as it becomes more difficult to do business in the United States, more U.S. companies are listing their shares overseas. In addition, *The Economist* recently noted that foreign companies listing on U.S. stock exchanges "have become a rarity" ("In Search of Better SOX" 2006).

In the first year of implementation, companies spent a great deal of money on internal control compliance. For larger companies, "the average direct cost of Section 404 was $8.5m; for smaller public companies . . . the average cost was around $1.2m." On a more optimistic note, as time passes, the cost of compliance seems to be dropping, and second years costs "are expected to fall by around 40%." (Quotes from "The Trial of Sarbanes-Oxley" 2006)

While Byrnes (2005) pointed out that the "cost of a typical audit has already jumped by up to 60% since the law's passage," SEC Commissioner Cynthia Glassman (2005) maintained that too many companies have been focusing on minutia, and "controls for controls' sake." On May 17, 2006, the SEC announced that it will "issue guidance" to assist public companies—especially smaller ones—in the implementation of Section 404 (SEC News Release).

≈ Is the Magic Potion Effective?

Potion 404 is having expensive side effects and many complain that its cost is prohibitive. Attempts are underway to make the medicine easier to swallow.

Corporate Management and Certification of Annual Reports (Section 302)

Section 302 requires that the chief executive officers (CEOs) and the chief financial officers (CFOs) of public companies assume the responsibility for certifying specific areas of "each annual or quarterly report filed or submitted" to the Securities and Exchange Commission. The *Executive Summary of the Sarbanes-Oxley Act* presented guidelines for CEOs and CFOs who are required to certify the following:

- The report does not contain untrue statements or material omissions
- The financial statements fairly present, in all material respects the financial conditions and results of operations
- Such officers are responsible for internal controls designed to ensure that they receive material information regarding the issuer and consolidated subsidiaries
- The internal controls have been reviewed for their effectiveness within 90 days prior to the report
- Any significant changes to the internal controls.

Section 302 also states that company officers who fail to certify financial reports may be held criminally liable. In addition, SOX allows for up to twenty years of imprisonment for officers who knowingly certify a statement that does not comply with the SOX legislation.

≈ Is the Magic Potion Effective?

Potion 302 is generally palatable although there are some continuing reports of side effects.

Loans to Executives

Some of the most outrageous corporate looting in the last decade has taken place via a two-step loan process. First, clubby boards of directors authorized huge loans to company officers. Second, the board sometimes conveniently authorized the "forgiveness" of the loans. This process of granting outrageous company loans was particularly rampant in the case of WorldCom; for example, in 2001 the WorldCom Compensation Committee authorized loans to Ebbers for $150 million!

SOX now prohibits company loans to company officers and directors.

≈ Is the Magic Potion Effective?

The potion seems to be working.

Independence and Oversight of External Auditors

○ Establishment of the PCAOB:

The Sarbanes-Oxley Act established a Public Company Accounting Oversight Board (PCAOB) for the oversight of the audit of public companies. The act requires public accounting firms to register with the PCAOB and it requires the board to establish or modify, as required, standards for auditing, reporting, ethics, and quality control. It also requires the PCAOB to inspect and investigate registered accounting firms and to enforce compliance with the established standards.

Furthermore, the act requires annual inspections of larger public accounting firms that provide audit reports for more than 100 publicly traded or listed issuers of financial statements. Accounting firms that provide audit reports for 100 or less public companies must be inspected at least once every three years. Additionally, SOX adds "teeth" to the oversight of audit firms by empowering the board to impose disciplinary penalties for misconduct.

(The New York Stock Exchange and the NASDAQ have also strengthened corporate governance and filing requirements.)

o Provisions to Ensure Independence of External Auditors

▪ Consulting Services

Performing consulting services for the very firms that the "independent" public accounting firms audited was probably perceived by the public as the greatest threat to auditor independence. As mentioned in Chapter 1 of this book, Arthur Levitt, the former SEC chairman, fought a losing battle to prohibit this practice during his tenure as chair. The SOX Act of 2002 finally prohibited public accounting firms from performing specified non-audit services for the firms that they audit. Some of these prohibited services include:

* Financial information system services
* Bookkeeping services
* Appraisal services
* Investment advice

The audit committee of the company may approve certain non-audit services that are not specifically prohibited, such as tax preparation.

▪ Senior Auditors Switching Jobs

If a senior executive of a company was previously employed by the company's auditor and worked on the company's audit, the audit firm is prohibited from auditing that company for a period of one year. (It is worth noting that Enron was notorious for hiring ex-Arthur Anderson employees who had worked on Enron audits.)

- **Rotation of Lead Auditors**

SOX mandates auditor rotation by prohibiting an audit partner from being the lead or reviewing auditor of the same company for more than five consecutive years.

- **Reporting to the Audit Committee**

In an attempt to decrease the likelihood of auditors being pressured by management into adopting manipulative accounting treatments, SOX requires the reporting of the following to the board's audit committee for its review:

- Critical accounting policies and practices used by the organization, including methods, assumptions, and judgments;
- Alternative accounting treatments that were discussed with management, as well as their possible effects. (This provision could prevent the situation that arose at Enron, where Arthur Andersen's technical oversight partner, Carl Bass, objected to some of Enron's accounting treatments and was removed from involvement with the audit at Enron's request.)

≈ Is the Magic Potion Effective?

So far the potion seems to be working. Hopefully, the disease is being cured and it is not mutating.

Independence and Responsibilities of Company Directors

Pursuant to SOX, the Securities and Exchange Commission adopted a number of rules requiring greater independence and accountability for directors of public companies. Consequently, the New York Stock Exchange and NASDAQ also made some changes to the regulations regarding directors. While there are slight differences for companies trading on the NYSE or on NASDAQ, the latest major requirements regarding boards of directors listed on both exchanges can be identified as follows:

○ Provisions to Ensure Independence of Directors

The majority of the directors on a company's board must be independent. Three of the more important factors determining that a director is not independent are:

- The director is an employee of the company or the director has a family member who is an executive officer of the company.
- The director receives more than $100,000 (NYSE) or $60,000 (NASDAQ) from the listed company, other than director fees, committee fees, or pension compensation for prior service.

- One of the director's close family members receives more than $100,000 (NYSE) or $60,000 (NASDAQ) in compensation other than director's fees, a pension, or certain other deferred compensation for prior service.

○ Three-Year Look-Back Period

A three-year look-back period is required for each of the prohibitions previously discussed. This means that a director is not regarded as independent for three years after any of these conditions lapse.

○ Final Responsibility

The financial responsibility rests with each board of directors to determine which directors are independent, when taking all material relationships into account. While Sarbanes-Oxley provides several other specific disqualifications from being considered independent, it is important to note that no exhaustive list of exclusion factors is given.

○ Meetings of Independent Directors

In addition to meetings of all the directors, meetings of only independent directors are required and no other directors may be present at these meetings.

○ Audit Committees

Audit committees consisting of a minimum of three independent directors are required. In addition, the SEC requires disclosure as to whether at least one financial expert is serving on the audit committee—or the reason why there is no financial expert on that committee. Responsibilities of the Audit Committee include:

- The appointment, compensation, and oversight of the company's external audit firm
- Reviewing all major accounting principles and issues underlying the company's financial statements, including alternative treatments and their ramifications
- Reviewing reports on the company's internal control system
- Receiving and dealing with complaints according to procedures set up by the company
- Receiving and dealing with reported disagreements between the auditors and company management

≈ Is the Magic Potion Effective?

The potion seems to be fairly successful. Recently, company shareholders have indicated that they would like the authority to prescribe certain doses of the potion. (For further discussion, refer to Part 3 of this chapter: Emerging Reform Issues.)

Independence of Analysts

○ Provisions to Ensure Independence from Employers

Several of the accounting scandals involved investment-banking analysts who publicly gave certain company stocks "buy" ratings but left email trails revealing that they believed those stocks were actually poor investments. To deal with this issue, SOX added provisions mandating independence of analysts from their investment-banking employers.

The new rules include:

- Provisions against supervision of analysts by superiors who also perform investment-banking work
- Provisions against employers who retaliate when analysts submit negative reports on their clients or potential clients
- Provisions against investment bankers who seek to preapprove analysts' reports

○ Disclosures to Avoid Conflicts of Interest

The *Executive Summary of the Sarbanes-Oxley Act of 2002* noted that SOX requires specific conflict of interest disclosures when analysts submit reports or make public statements. These disclosures include:

- Whether the analyst holds securities in the public company that is the subject of the appearance or report
- Whether any compensation was received by the analyst, or broker or dealer, from the company that was the subject of the appearance or report
- Whether a public company that is the subject of an appearance or report is, or during the prior one year period was, a client of the broker or dealer
- Whether the analyst received compensation with respect to a research report, based upon banking revenues of the registered broker or dealer. (6)

≈ Is the Magic Potion Effective?

The potion seems to be reducing outbreaks of the condition. There is no fear of an epidemic.

Corporate Crime Enforcement

More generally, the SOX legislation also increases penalties for other corporate crimes beyond the certification of false financial statements. For example:

- It provides for fines, or up to twenty-five years of imprisonment, for any person who willfully defrauds shareholders of publicly traded companies.
- It increases the penalties for mail fraud and wire fraud from five years to twenty years of imprisonment.
- It extends the imprisonment period to up to twenty years for tampering with a record or otherwise impeding an official investigation.
- Violations of the Securities Exchange Act of 1934 are extended and may now result in a maximum of twenty-five years in prison and fines of up to $25 million.
- The legislation authorizes the SEC to freeze payments to persons under investigation and to prohibit certain violators from serving as officers or directors of publicly traded companies.

Table 9.1 presents the number of prosecutions in the five-year period, from 2000 to 2004. There is a significant increase in prosecutions after 2002.

≈ Is the Magic Potion Effective?

The potion seems to be providing strong medicine for some ailments, but is ineffective for others. The search for a cure continues.

Table 9.1 Number of Prosecutions for Securities and Corporate Fraud from 2000—2004

Year	Number of Securities Fraud/ Corporate Fraud Prosecutions	Number of Defendants
2000	204	404
2001	202	414
2002	260	443
2003	319 (141 corporate fraud and 178 securities fraud)	612 (313 corporate fraud and 299 securities fraud)
2004	280 (152 corporate fraud and 130 securities fraud)	527 (279 corporate fraud and 248 securities fraud)

New Accounting Regulations

○ Accounting for Stock Options as a Compensation Expense in the Income Statement

During his tenure as SEC chairman, Arthur Levitt (2002) looked with anxiety at the dramatic increase in the portion of executive compensation that was comprised of stock-option grants. He worried that the incentive to overstate earnings in order to boost stock prices could lead to fictitious financial reporting. However, he and many others fought a losing battle for the adoption of accounting rules to report the value of stock options granted to company employees as an expense in the income statement. Levitt felt that the resulting impact on earnings would likely temper the growing use of stock options as executive compensation. This would also show shareholders the size of this form of compensation more clearly than mere footnote disclosure of the estimated value of the options granted.

During Levitt's term, the corporate executives and the accounting profession lobbied and fought hard enough to stop the expensing of stock-option compensation in the income statement. However, after the furor of the corporate accounting debacles, work on amending accounting rules for stock options began in earnest. On December 16, 2004, the Financial Accounting Standards Board (FASB) issued its new standard requiring that the compensation associated with share-based payments should be expensed in the income statement.

While this standard, FAS 123(R), does not specify one model for valuing the cost to the company of the options granted, it is important that it is *not* the benefit to the employee that is the compensation expense to be valued, but rather the cost of the grant *to the company* at the time of the grant. In a Memorandum on March 18, 2005, the Office of Economic Analysis stated:

> The standard expressly allows for the use of models that comply with the basic principles of modern financial economics, which include:
>
>> The modified Black-Scholes-Merton model, which estimates the value of employee stock options using a closed form equation.
>>
>> The lattice, binomial and Monte Carlo approaches, which estimate the value of employee stock options using standard numerical methods. (Spatt et al. 2005, 3)

Whatever model is used, it must take into account the expected volatility of the stock, the exercise price, the current price or market value of the stock, the term, the expected dividends, and the interest rate. The value of the options granted is calculated at the date of the grant, and that amount is expensed in the income statement as a compensation cost over the time of the vesting period.

Based on the recent decrease in the granting of stock options to company executives, it does appear that the new rules requiring the expensing of options have decreased the popularity of this form of executive compensation. According to a survey of companies that voluntarily adopted the new rules early, 68 percent of respondents said that in the future they intended to place more emphasis on some form of long-term compensation other than stock options (survey reported in Kunkel and Lau 2005).

Opponents of expensing options criticize the new rules on a number of grounds. Those against the new standard "argue that its implementation will hurt the competitiveness of American industry, especially the technology companies that rely on stock options to attract and retain key employees." Opponents also insist that footnote disclosure and the disclosure of the diluted earnings per share due to options are sufficient. Standard & Poor's estimated that the "accounting rules would reduce reported 2004 earnings among the S&P 500 by 7.4%." Apparently, the impact on technology companies will be even more significant, with the result that "trade groups such as the American Electronics Association have vigorously opposed the new rules." (Quotes from Kunkel and Lau 2005)

Proponents of the rules maintain that the company gives up a benefit when options are granted, and they remain convinced that—for the sake of fair and accurate reporting—such compensation should be recognized as an expense on the face of the income statement.

○ **New Accounting Rules for Special Purpose Entities (SPEs)**

After Enron was undone by all the debt hidden in its special purpose entities, the accounting profession began to accelerate its progress toward establishing rules for off-balance sheet entities.

In January 2003, the Financial Accounting Standards Board issued Financial Interpretation 46 (FIN 46) and updated it in December 2003 with the issue of FIN 46(R). These rules increased the 3 percent requirement of outside equity to a 10 percent minimum before a company can avoid the consolidation of off-balance sheet entities. Further, FIN 46(R) provides that if a sponsor company has an interest in an off-balance sheet entity that fits the definition of a "variable interest," then the SPE becomes a variable interest entity (VIE) that has to be consolidated into the sponsor's group financial statements, if the sponsor is a primary beneficiary of the entity. Most importantly, this means that if an off-balance sheet entity is likely to require further capital from its sponsor to fulfill its obligations, the entity is a VIE.

FIN 46(R) defines the criteria that determine whether an entity is a VIE. (For these criteria refer to Exhibit 9-A at the end of this chapter.)

○ **Disclosure of Off-Balance Sheet Entities in the Management Discussion & Analysis (MD&A)**

On January 26, 2003, pursuant to Section 401(a) of the Sarbanes-Oxley Act, the SEC issued Final Rule 67 (FR-67) titled "Disclosure in Management's Discussion and Analysis about Off-Balance Sheet Arrangements and Aggregate Contractual Relations." The rule requires a listed company "to provide an explanation of its off-balance sheet arrangements in a separately captioned subsection of the MD&A section of a registrant's disclosure documents" (FR-67). The rule takes a principles-based approach to disclosure, and also provides four specific items that require disclosure. (For further details on FR-67, refer to Exhibit 9-B.)

≈ **Is the Magic Potion Effective?**

The potion appears to be relieving symptoms for some ailments and does not seem to have serious side effects, as some had previously feared. For other ailments, however, the dosage needs adjustment.

PART 3: EMERGING REFORM ISSUES

Amid several emerging issues, three are particularly controversial: shareholder activism and the election of directors; executive compensation; and pension-fund reform.

❖ **Shareholder Activism and Election of Directors**

One of the most hotly debated areas is that of the election of directors through shareholder proposals. Currently, it is very difficult and costly for the shareholder to nominate directors. The shareholder has to "hand out a separate proxy paper, containing only its candidate and secure more votes than the official slate of board candidates on the proxy distributed by the board" ("Battling for Corporate America" 2006, 70). This campaign has to be paid for by the shareholder, whereas the company pays for the campaigns of the candidates that the board publishes. For this reason, shareholder campaigns for directors are rare and ultimately fail.

Consequently, to "give shareholders a stronger voice, the SEC has proposed a proxy-access initiative that would allow shareholders to nominate members to the board of directors." This proposal would allow shareholders to nominate board members if one of two triggering events occurred: "35% of the voters fail to support a company's nominee to the board, or 50% of voters approve a shareholder proposal to allow a shareholder-nominated candidate on the company proxy." The proposed revisions were made available for comment in October 2003, and the SEC received an astounding 13,000 comments in response to the proposal. It is interesting that "the SEC has taken no action on this proposed revision." The increased number of shareholder resolutions in 2005 and 2006 may be a response to that inaction. (Quotes from Schooley, Renner, and Allen 2005)

Presently, shareholders cannot dictate management actions: "Most of the shareholder resolutions on the proxy are 'precatory' that is, advisory only. Boards have a record of ignoring such advice" ("Battling for Corporate America" 2006, 70). In addition, boards have discretion in deciding what resolutions are allowed to be put on the proxy. Much of recent shareholder activism has been focused on resolutions that would alter company by-laws to introduce majority voting in general; that is, make majority shareholder votes binding on boards and management. Majority voting power could then be used for an array of other issues, including the election of directors and the setting of executive compensation.

Opponents of fairer nominations of directors by shareholders, and of binding majority voting in general, also present strong arguments. *The Economist* cites a number of opponents to shareholder power, such as Stephen Bainbridge, Leo Strine, and John Bogle. Bainbridge, from the UCLA School of Law, asserts that greater shareholder power would interfere with management's need for "space and discretion" to make "business decisions with speed and efficiency that modern commerce demands. . . ." Also, Bainbridge maintains that shareholders may favor their own political motives over the company's interests. Strine, a Delaware judge, argues that the pension funds and mutual funds may not act in the interests of longer term shareholders. Bogle, the founder of Vanguard, believes that many of the shareholding institutions are torn by conflicting interests and are "failing in their fiduciary duty." Clearly, this is an extremely contentious issue, and the intense debates will continue. (Quotes from "Battling for Corporate America" 2006, 71)

❖ **Executive Compensation and Shareholder Activism**

As part of the growing trend of shareholder activism, many now want to go further and require shareholder approval for executive compensation packages. In "Battling for Corporate America" (2006), *The Economist* noted that in the first few months of 2006, shareholder proxy resolutions seeking to tie executive pay to performance were almost as popular as resolutions related to the election of directors.

A new bill, titled "The Protection against Executive Compensation Abuse Act," was introduced to the committee process in the House of Representatives on November 10, 2005.[5] The bill would impose four requirements on publicly traded companies:

> Provide all details about how much executives earn in cash, incentives and perks each year and submit the packages for shareholder approval . . .
>
> Disclose the full market value of company-paid perks, such as executives' personal use of a company jet . . .
>
> Publicly report the specific criteria by which executives earn incentive pay . . .
>
> Tell shareholders "in a clear and simple form" how much the executive officers stand to make on a proposed takeover or acquisition that requires shareholder consent. (Kristoff 2005)

Without a doubt, the bill will be hotly debated on both sides of the floor, and by corporate lobbyists as well as groups of galvanized investors. Whether or not the bill passes, it will certainly intensify the spotlight on executive compensation.

While the proposals on submitting executive compensation for shareholder approval will face very stiff opposition, full disclosure of executive compensation, including projected retirement payments and severance provisions, has already been proposed by SEC Chairman Christopher Cox, and those rules are expected to take effect in 2007. Some companies, for example Bank of America, have already begun full disclosure of executive compensation, including estimated values of stock options. When considering executive compensation, many boards of directors are now using "tally sheets," which keep a track of all forms of executive compensation taking into account "everything from salary and perquisites to equity grants, deferred compensation severance and supplemental pensions" (Lublin 2006). Clearly, shareholders, legislators, and the SEC are paying greater attention to the issue and disclosure of overall executive compensation.

---

[5] The bill was referred to the House subcommittee on January 5, 2006. For additional information on the progress of the bill, visit: http://thomas.loc.gov

❖ Pension-Fund Reform[6]

Thousands of employees throughout the United States are reeling at the news that their pension funds are grossly underfunded, while the CEOs of some of the underfunded companies have ensured that their own retirements will be quite luxurious: "For example, while IBM's worker pension plan is $7.38 billion underfunded, IBM's CEO has a $4.1 million annual pension." This is clearly a case of employees feeling "all the pain." (Quotes from U.S. House Committee 2005a)

On November 16, 2005, the Senate approved legislation aimed at saving private pension plans that are underfunded by a shortfall "currently estimated at $450 billion" (Abrams 2005). The provisions of this legislation attracting the most attention are as follows:

- Requirements that "would give companies seven years to pay off their unfunded liabilities"
- Provisions that extend the time for the airline industry beyond seven years to deal with their unfunded pension liabilities
- Requirements regarding the interest rate used to calculate future pension obligations
- Provisions that would "encourage companies to put more money into their pension plans when times are good"
- An increase in the PBGC insurance premium from $19 to $30 per year per participant in a pension plan

(Quotes from "Senate Passes Bill . . ." 2005)

In December 2005, the House of Representatives passed its own bill, the Pension Protection Act (HR 2830). The two bills will be "merged into a single measure" by the recently formed House-Senate Pension Reform Conference. John Kline (R-Mn.), one of the conference members, stated: "For the first time in a generation, we're poised to update flawed pension funding rules that have placed at risk the retirement security of far too many Americans." (Quotes from U.S. House Committee 2006)

Although both the House and the Senate have clearly indicated that there is a necessity for such reform, there are still those who argue against it on the grounds that stiffer requirements regarding corporate pension plans could cause more companies to abandon their deferred benefit-pension plans. There are also those who oppose the special caveat for the airline industry

---

[6] For more information on pension funds, refer to Chapter 8.

that gives them more than seven years to get their pension plans fully funded.

In November 2005, the Financial Accounting Standards Board (FASB) voted to overhaul pension fund accounting in two stages. During the first stage "companies would be required for the first time to show on their balance sheets the amounts by which their pension plans are underfunded." It is expected that the new rules for the first stage will be completed during 2006. The second stage "will consider all elements of the current pension fund accounting system" and this stage is expected to take a few years before completion. (Quotes from Weil 2005)

Conclusion

It is obvious that there is no instant, one-dose magic potion to restore our post-Enron corporate environment to complete health. While legislation and enforcement can certainly help to develop more reliable and consistent reporting, kowtowing to every minuscule rule and regulation can lead to different types of problems. The SEC has made it clear that a "mechanical and even overly cautious" application of legislation is not the solution. The business community must exercise "reasoned, good faith . . . [and] professional judgment." (Quotes from SEC News Release 2005-74, 2005)

The responsibility for reform rests not only with government organizations and the business community, but with private individuals as well. Anyone who relies on a company for employment, retirement or investment should be actively engaged in scrutinizing not only the quality of that company's management, but its financial statements as well. In order to do so, it is essential to recognize the signals of fictitious financial reporting. (For a summary of twenty-five of the most important signals indicating potentially fictitious reporting in financial statements, refer to Table 9.2 following.)

Ultimately, the purpose of accounting reform is to ensure that public corporations refrain from telling fairy tales in their financial statements, because these tales ultimately disrupt the stability of the U.S. economy. As the quantity of business fairy tales diminish, we can look forward to an increase in the quality of our corporations, and to an upsurge in the number of happy endings.

Table 9.2 The Top Twenty-Five Signals Indicating Possible Fictitious Reporting in Financial Statements

The Top Twenty-Five Signals	The Schemes that a Company May be Concealing
1. Suspicious track records of top executives, particularly when their previous companies reported swift earnings turnarounds that suddenly evaporated	May be indicative of any method of overstatement of earnings, or overstatement of cash flow from operations (CFFO), or understatement of debt
2. Receivables that increase significantly as a percentage of revenues, as measured, for example, by days sales outstanding (DSO)	Possible overstatement of revenue via accelerated revenue, or fictitious revenue, or improper valuation of revenue
3. CFFO that significantly lags operating income	Overstatement of revenue or understatement of expenses
4. Unusual securitizations or factoring of receivables. (In this case, when testing signals 2 and 3 above, remember to adjust receivables by adding back securitization amounts and to adjust CFFO by deducting securitization amounts)	The need for the securitization itself could be an indication of cash-flow problems. The company could be hiding the CFFO shortfall compared to operating income, and also hiding a build up in receivables by accelerating a portion of their liquidation into cash
5. Inventory that increases substantially as a percentage of cost of goods sold as measured, for example, by the inventory-turnover ratio	Possible overstatement of inventory, or obsolescence of inventory, or understatement of cost of goods sold
6. Significant fluctuations in gross margin as a percentage of sales	Overstatement of ending inventory or of revenues; understatement of purchases or cost of goods manufactured
7. The creation of large reserves via one-time charges, such as restructuring charges, followed by the drawing down of reserves	Possible overstatement of reserves to boost later periods' earnings by the release of the excess "cookie-jar' reserves back into income
8. Large amounts allocated to goodwill on the acquisition of other companies, accompanied by the creation of large reserves on acquisition	Improper use of acquisitions for the overstatement of acquisition reserves, and a corresponding overstatement of goodwill; the possible release of excess cookie-jar reserves into income in future periods, in order to overstate post-acquisition earnings

(continued)

Table 9.2 (*Continued*)

The Top Twenty-Five Signals	The Schemes that a Company May be Concealing
9. Large amounts allocated to goodwill on the acquisition of companies that do not have a supernormal return on assets, and the acquisition is not followed by supernormal returns on assets	Overstatement of goodwill on acquisitions for the purpose of overstating acquisition reserves in order to release the cookie-jar reserves into earnings later on
10. Adjustments that increase goodwill in a later period with respect to an earlier acquisition	Overstatement of acquisition reserves for the purpose of overstating later periods' earnings via the later release of the cookie-jar reserves into earnings
11. A significant decrease in the ratio of sales to assets (asset-turnover ratio), or a decrease in the ratio of sales to any particular asset such as, for example, property, plant and equipment (PPE)	This could indicate improper capitalization of expenses; for example, the classification of expenses as PPE. The fictitious asset cannot be used as part of the real infrastructure to produce sales
12. When an expense that has a fixed-cost component remains a constant percentage of sales revenue, as revenue decreases	Improper capitalization of an expense as an asset. For example, WorldCom's line-cost expense was misclassified as PPE
13. Expenses, or a category of expenses, that decline significantly as a percentage of sales	This could signal understatement of expenses via omitting to record the expenses, or by deferring the expenses, or by improper capitalization of the expenses
14. Current liabilities that decline significantly as a percentage of current assets and sales	Understatement of expenses via "lack of accrual"
15. Deferred costs or prepaid expenses that increase significantly as a percentage of total assets, or as a percentage of sales	Understatement of expenses via deferral of expenses
16. When the development of a product or a program is accompanied by the recording of a significant, intangible asset—such as development costs or start-up costs—and the company hits scheduling problems that are reported in press articles or on the notes to the financial statements, but the intangible asset is not written off	Failure to record asset impairments

(*continued*)

Table 9.2 (*Continued*)

The Top Twenty-Five Signals	The Schemes that a Company May be Concealing
17. The reserve for bad debts decreases as a percentage of accounts receivable	Understatement of bad debts expense
18. When a company has multiple-element contracts and there is a proportional increase in a revenue stream that is more quickly recognized and a decrease in a revenue stream that is recognized more slowly	Acceleration of revenue via improper use of multiple-element contracts through misclassification of revenue streams
19. Deferred revenue decreases as a percentage of total revenue	Aggressive recognition of revenue that will be earned only in future periods
20. A significant decrease in allowances for returns as a percentage of sales	Allowance for returns may be understated
21. Large increases in investments in unconsolidated affiliates or increases in the assets and liabilities of unconsolidated affiliates especially partnerships, trusts, joint ventures and company sponsored corporations as opposed to established independent corporations. This signal becomes stronger if the nature of the entities or of their transactions are vaguely described	Overstatement of Earnings and CFFO, and/or understatement of debt via contrived transactions with special purpose entities (SPEs)
22. The above signal becomes especially strong if there are related–party transactions with any of the off-balance-sheet entities; it becomes even stronger if a significant portion of the company's profit comes from transactions with these entities. Be particularly wary if there are contingent liabilities in respect of these entities.	Overstatement of Earnings and CFFO, and/or understatement of debt via contrived transactions with special purpose entities (SPEs)

(continued)

Table 9.2 (*Continued*)

The Top Twenty-Five Signals	The Schemes that a Company May be Concealing
23. Aggressive revenue recognition accounting policies such as, for example, bill and hold sales, or guaranteed or right of return sales (especially when accompanied by increases in discounts as a percentage of sales). Also be wary of percentage of completion method where unbilled sales increase as a percentage of total sales	Overstatement of sales via channel stuffing or acceleration of revenue recognition or fictitious revenue recognition
24. Aggressive accounting policies in terms of capitalization of expenses compared to previous periods or compared to other companies in the same industry, for items such as capitalized interest costs, software costs, development costs or direct response advertising costs	Improper capitalization of expenses to overstate earnings
25. When the company consistently meets sales or earnings estimates every quarter	Possible overstatement of earnings via any method of overstatement of revenues or understatement of expenses

---

**Exhibit 9-A: Definition of a Variable Interest Entity (VIE)
According to FIN 46(R)***

Interpretation 46(R) defines a VIE as an entity that meets one of the following characteristics:

- ° The total equity investment at risk is not sufficient to permit the entity to finance its activities without additional subordinated financial support provided by any parties, including equity holders.
- ° The equity investors lack one or more of the following essential characteristics of a controlling financial interest:
    - The direct or indirect ability through voting rights or similar rights to make decisions about the entity's activities that have a significant effect on the success of the entity.
    - The obligation to absorb the expected losses of the entity.
    - The right to receive the expected residual returns of the entity.

Exhibit 9-B: Partial Disclosure Requirements for Management's Discussion and Analysis: Off-Balance Sheet Arrangements and Aggregate Contractual Obligation**

- ° The principle throughout the amendments is that the registrant should disclose information to the extent that it is necessary to an understanding of a registrant's material off-balance sheet financial condition, revenues or expenses, results of operations, liquidity, capital expenditures or capital resources.
- ° The amendments contain the following four specific items to bolster the principles-based approach. These items require disclosure of the following information to the extent necessary for an understanding of a registrant's off-balance sheet arrangements and their effects:
    - The nature and business purpose of the registrant's off-balance sheet arrangements;
    - The importance of the off-balance sheet arrangements to the registrant for liquidity, capital resources, market risk or credit risk support or other benefits;
    - The financial impact of the arrangements on the registrant (e.g., revenues, expenses, cash flows or securities issued) and the registrant's exposure to risk as a result of the arrangements (e.g., retained interests or contingent liabilities); and
    - Known events, demands, commitments, trends or uncertainties that affect the availability or benefits to the registrant of material off-balance sheet arrangements.

---

* From Soroosh, Jalal, & Jack T. Ciesielski. "Accounting for Special Purpose Entities Revised: FASB Interpretation 46(R)." © *The CPA Journal*, July 2004.

** From: U.S. Securities and Exchange Commission. FR-67; *Final Rule: Disclosure in Management's Discussion and Analysis about Off-Balance Sheet Arrangements and Aggregate Contractual Obligation*, Release Nos. 33-8182; 34-47264, January 8, 2003, page 8. www.sec.gov/rules/final/33-8182.htm

References

Abrams, Jim. 2005. "Senate Approves Pension Overhaul Plan," WashingtonPost.com, November 17.

Atkins, Paul S. 2006. "Remarks before the U.S. Chamber Institute for Legal Reform." Washington, D.C., February 16. www.sec.gov/news/speech/spch021606psa.htm

"Battling for Corporate America." *The Economist*, March 11-17, 2006.

Bond, Robert, and Greg Campbell. 2005. "Sarbanes Oxley Ethical Hotlines: CNIL Publish Draft Guidelines," *Faegre & Benson*, November 7. www.faegre.com/articles/

Byrnes, Nanette. 2005. "Professional Services: Cleaning Up By Cleaning Up," *Business Week Online*, January 10. www.businessweek.com

Cox, Christopher. 2005. "Speech by SEC Chairman: Remarks before the Securities Industry Association," U.S. Securities and Exchange Commission, Boca Raton, Florida, November 11.

Deloitte & Touche, Ernst & Young, KPMG, and PricewaterhouseCoopers, comps. 2005. "Key Newsmaker Quotes." In *Letter to Stakeholders*, GE Annual Report, February 11.

Executive Summary of the Sarbanes-Oxley Act of 2002. P.L. 107—204.

Glassman, Cynthia A. 2005. "Remarks before the Conference on Listed Companies and Legislators in Dialogue Danish Ministry of Economic and Business Affairs." Speech in Copenhagen, Denmark. November 17. www.sec.gov/news/speech/spch111705cag.htm

Greenspan, Alan. 2005. "Commencement Address." Speech at Wharton School of Business, University of Pennsylvania, Philadelphia, May 15.

Henry, David, and Amy Borrus, with Louis Lavelle, Diane Brady, Michael Arndt, and Joseph Weber. 2005. "Death, Taxes & Sarbanes Oxley?" *Business Week*, January 17.

Hymowitz, Carol, and Joann S. Lublin. 2003. "Corporate Reform: The First Year; Boardrooms under Renovation," *The Wall Street Journal*, July 22.

Johnson, Carrie. 2005. "Corporate Legislation Works, Sponsors Say: Sarbanes, Oxley Urge Congress to Wait before Changing Law's Provisions," *Washington Post*, March 11. www.washingtonpost.com

"In Search of Better SOX." *The Economist*, April 22-28, 2006.

Kristoff, Kathy M. 2005. "Bill Targets Executive Compensation," *Los Angeles Times*, November 10.

Kunkel, Gregory, and Richard T. Lau. 2005. "Compensation Plans and the New Stock Option Accounting Rules," *The CPA Journal*, January.

Lublin, Joann S. 2006. "Adding It All Up," *The Wall Street Journal*, April 10, R1.

Levitt, Arthur. 2002. *Take on the Street*. New York: Patheon Books.

May, Jeff. 2003. "Reforms Haven't Erased All Funny Business," *Seattle Times*, July 27.

National Hotline Services. "Sarbanes–Oxley Act of 2002: Employee Complaint Procedures." www.hotlines.com/sarbanes_oxley.htm

Office of Economic Analysis. 2005. "Memorandum," March 18.

"Ownership Matters." *The Economist*, March 11–17, 2006.

Sarbanes, Paul S. 2002. PACE Lecture at Salisbury University, October 22. www.salisbury.edu

Savage, Joseph, and Christine Sgarlata Chung. 2005. "Trends in Corporate Fraud Enforcement: A Calm During the Storm?" *Law Journal Newsletters: Business Crimes Bulletin* 13, no. 2, October.

Schooley, Diane K., Celia Renner, and Mary Allen. 2005. "Corporate Governance Reform: Electing Directors through Shareholder Proposals," *The CPA Journal*, October. www.nysscpa.org/cpajournal/2005/1005/essentials/p62.htm

SEC News Release 2005-74. May 16, 2005. www.sec.gov

SEC News Release 2006-75. May 17, 2006. www.sec.gov

"Senate Passes Bill to Shore Up Private Pensions," *USA Today,* November 16, 2005. www.usatoday.com/news/washington/2005-11-16-money-senate-pensions_x.htm

Soroosh, Jalal, and Jack T. Ciesielski. 2004. "Accounting for Special Purpose Entities Revised: FASB Interpretation 46(R)," *The CPA Journal,* July. www.cpajournal.com

SOX Online: The Vendor-Neutral Sarbanes Oxley Site. www.sox-online.com

Spatt, Chester S., Cindy R. Alexander, David A. Dubofsky, M. Nimalendran, George Oldfield. 2005. "Economic Perspective on Employee Option Expensing: Valuation and Implementation of FAS 123(R)," Office of Economic Analysis Memorandum, March 18.

"The Trial of Sarbanes-Oxley." *The Economist,* April 22–28, 2006.

U.S. Congress. House. Committee on Education and the Workplace. 2005a. Report. "Runaway Executive Pay...While Families Work Harder for Less." Report prepared by Rep. George Miller (D-CA). December. http://edworkforce.house.gov

U.S. Congress. House. Committee on Financial Services. 2005b. *The Impact of the Sarbanes-Oxley Act: Hearing before the Committee on Financial Services.* 109th Cong., 1st sess., Serial No. 109-21, April 21.

U.S. Congress. House. Committee on Education and the Workforce. 2006. News Release. "Workforce Committee Sends Four to House-Senate Pension Reform Conferences." March 8. http://edworkforce.house.gov

U.S. Congress. House. 2002. *Sarbanes-Oxley Act of 2002.* HR 3763. 107th Cong., 2nd sess., January 23. http://firstgovsearch.gov

Weil, Jonathan. 2005. "FASB Votes to Revise Pension Rules." *The Wall Street Journal,* November 11.

"Whistle While You Work? The Legality of Whistleblowing Hotlines." Eversheds, *HR Euronews* 4, September 2005. www.eversheds.com

THE TRUE PHILOSOPHER'S STONE: MAKING ETHICAL DECISIONS IN THE BUSINESS WORLD

Everything that can be counted does not necessarily count; everything that counts cannot necessarily be counted.

Albert Einstein

Overview

Surprisingly, in post-Enron times, accounting has emerged as the latest trendy subject among college freshmen; in fact, accounting is now the "new 'sexy' college major." The reason for its upsurge in popularity is, apparently, directly related to the accounting frauds of recent years: "Academics say the numerous corporate accounting scandals over the last few years have piqued the interest of today's students."[1]

Together with an increased interest in accounting, for whatever reason, there is also a renewed focus on the importance of ethics in the business world in general, and in the accounting field in particular. However, too many texts on ethics and accounting concentrate on external rules, regulations and laws, without any authentic comprehension of the essential nature of ethics and morality. In order to understand why ethics must be a vital component of any large corporation or small business, it is necessary to take a brief look at some of the fundamental approaches to the philosophy of ethics.

Theories of Ethics

We can distinguish three major ethical theories or schools of thought as to what is most important in the pursuit of morality—namely, *consequentialism, deontological theory*, and *virtue ethics*. To the consequentialist, the most important issue in morality is to choose the right action, and this choice is determined by examining the consequences of that action. On the other

---

[1] Quotes from *"The Surprising No. 1 College Major"* (2004).

hand, to the deontologist, the most important issue in morality is to do the right thing because it is right or, as it is often stated, "Do your duty for duty's sake." Under this view, if it is right to be honest, then avoiding lying and telling the absolute truth is always right, irrespective of the consequences. There is a moral imperative to be honest, no matter what the situation. Coming from a third perspective, the virtue ethicist holds that the most important aspect of morality is having the right character, or set of traits or "dispositions" as they are often called. In a nutshell, according to the virtue ethicist, possessing the right set of virtues is central to morality, because what makes an action right is that it is the action that a virtuous person would take. In other words, the integrity of an action flows from the virtuous character performing such an action, and that character is comprised of the virtuous traits.

Let us now examine these three theories more closely, and then discuss how they have relevance to the modern business world in general, and to accounting issues in particular.

Consequentialism

While the term *consequentialism* refers to all the approaches to the study of morality that evaluate conduct or actions in terms of the consequences that they produce, it is possible to distinguish between different forms of consequentialism. Some schools of thought focus on actions in terms of the proportion of benefits to costs; while others evaluate actions in terms of their benefits to the nation (nationalism), or their effects on a specific utility such as knowledge (epistemism), or benefits for oneself only (egoism). The leading and best-known form of consequentialism is identified as *utilitarianism*. Conceived by Jeremy Bentham (1748–1832), utilitarianism holds that the right action ethically is the action that maximizes the "good." Bentham thought that there was only one "good," namely pleasure, and one "evil," namely pain. Bentham's protégé, John Stuart Mill (1806–1873), defined happiness as the presence of pleasure and the absence of pain, and believed that actions have *utility* when they maximize happiness. According to Mill, actions are *right* in proportion to the happiness they tend to promote, and the morally best action of those open to us is the action that maximizes happiness, or (in his sense) has utility. Mill, who became the leading utilitarian scholar, specified that the net pleasure to be maximized when performing the right action referred to the pleasure of all who would be affected by the action, and not just one's own pleasure.

As consequentialist philosophy has developed over the years, different philosophers have specified different definitions of the "good," or what ought to be maximized, but the unifying thread is that they all judge actions according to the sum of the net "good" that they cause among all those affected by the actions. To the strict utilitarian, it is the total of the pleasure for all parties in the aggregate that determines whether the action is right, irrespective of how that pleasure or utility or "good" is allocated among the parties involved.

Recent terminology uses the term *consequentialism* to refer to all the utilitarian approaches, whether they refer to Mill's strict definition of the "good" to be maximized or to more flexible definitions. Philosopher Stephen Cohen (2004) succinctly described the essence of modern consequentialism: "It is the effects, or consequences, that are morally significant, not intentions or rules or commitments." Of all forms of moral analysis, *utilitarianism* is probably the most widespread, and many argue that it is the most intuitive approach to judging what action is right and what action is wrong.

However, consequentialists are vulnerable to the argument that one cannot predict all the consequences that will follow, in perpetuity, from one's actions. Further, even if we could predict all the consequences, consequentialists are criticized on the basis that the different "goods" are not homogeneous, and there is not a common denominator by which to measure and aggregate the benefits or harmful effects of actions, in order to determine which actions to follow or which to avoid.

Deontology

The word "deontology" is derived from the Greek *deon,* which means *duty.* The *deontologist* does not look to the future or to the effect of actions in order to judge an action as right or wrong. Here, moral action is chosen not because of its consequences, but because it is the right thing to do. Essentially, deontologists assert that one must do the right thing because it is one's duty to do so. The leading deontologist was Immanuel Kant (1724–1804). According to Kant, if you perform an action—for example, if you tell the truth mainly because of the positive consequences of telling the truth—the act does not have moral worth because you were not doing it simply out of your duty always to tell the truth. The same action is moral only if performed because it is right, but it is not of moral value if it is performed only because of its consequences. Kant went even further by saying that if you perceive telling the truth as a duty, you must *always* tell the truth for that reason in itself. Moreover, you must tell the truth even if telling the truth will cause a negative consequence. A common example given of this proposition is a situation where you may know the location of a person who is hiding from an ax murderer. According to Kant's deontological view of ethics, if that murderer asks you if you know the whereabouts of the person in hiding, you are duty bound not to lie. Kant's view holds that if you perceive telling the truth as a duty, then it is an unassailable duty, and telling a lie is *always* wrong, irrespective of the consequences.

Kant's standard test was that one ought to act as though a personal maxim were a universal moral law and that law could be stipulated for everyone without it leading to "contradiction." John Finnis presented Kant's three formulations of the *categorical imperative*:

1. Act only according to that maxim by which you can at the same time will that it should become a universal law.
2. Act so that you treat humanity, whether in your own person or in that of another, always as an end and never as a means only.
3. Act according to a maxim which harmonizes with a possible realm (i.e., a systematic union of different rational beings through common laws). . . . (Quoted in Finnis 1983, 121)

For Kant, the moral law admitted no exception. If we have a duty, there are no exceptions. Further, for Kant, in order for our actions to have moral worth, we must have the right motive, which is to fulfill our duty simply because it is our duty. Although no list of duties has ever been specified as prescriptive, some of the more common duties that Kant and his followers have suggested include the duty to develop one's talents, the duty to avoid dishonest promises, and the duty to respect the freedom of others.

Virtue Ethics

As we have already noted, the three major ethical theories can be distinguished by their answer to the question, "What is the most important aspect of morality?" According to Stephen Cohen, both utilitarians and deontologists look outside of the individual, i.e., outside of the decision maker, to determine the answer to this question. The utilitarian or consequentialist focuses on the consequences of the action to establish the morality of the action, while the deontologist insists that morality is determined by doing one's duty at all times; an examination of the outer world ascertains what that duty is. However, in the virtue theory of ethical behavior, the most important aspect of morality is found within the individual. According to this philosophy of *virtue ethics,* having the right character is the most important aspect of morality. Here, as distinct from utilitarian or deontological theory, the most important issue in morality is having the right "set of dispositions" or virtues. In other words, having a moral character is the basis for choosing the right actions—a person of fundamental integrity can be trusted to do the right thing. Cohen (2004) described this approach as follows:

> A virtue ethics view may see the process more "inside out." Moral behavior should be the result of, and flow from, a person's character. This is not to say that moral behavior is only automatic or spontaneous. It can indeed involve difficult and perplexing thinking and deliberation. . . . Cultivation of an ethical person, then, is very largely a matter of developing the right character. (49, 50)

Aristotle, of course, is the father of virtue ethics. He saw the virtues as those "dispositions" or traits that were in accord with the "golden mean" or the middle course. To him, extremes in behavior or tastes were vices, while moderation—the golden mean—was the primary virtue. For example, in conversation either constant chattering or complete silence would be vices, whereas a reasonable amount of discussion would be a virtue. To Aristotle, the ultimate objective of the golden mean was the "good" or well-being of both the individual and the society, and he offered a non-exhaustive list of virtues or character traits that included *honesty, courage, temperance, friendship*, and the *intellectual virtues*. The intellectual virtue of *practical wisdom* is, according to Aristotle, a prerequisite for all the other virtues.

Other virtue ethicists have suggested some different traits as conditions of being virtuous. Phillipa Foot wrote that "there are four cardinal virtues: courage, temperance, wisdom, and justice" (quoted in Kellenberger 1995, 200). Further, Foot pointed out that what is virtue in one context may not be virtue in another context. For example, courage in carrying out a random act of violence would not be considered a virtue.

Alasdair MacIntyre, in order to identify the nature of virtue, sought a common thread in five different views of the nature of virtue over the ages. First, he noted that during the time of Homer, bodily strength and physical courage were considered major virtues on the grounds that they enabled one to fulfill one's social role. Second, according to Aristotle, "the *telos* [ultimate purpose] of man as a species . . . determines what human qualities are virtues." Traits such as temperance and practical wisdom are considered to be virtues. Third, MacIntyre noted the New Testament virtues of faith, hope, love, and humility that also focus on the good of humanity, but here the "good" includes a spiritual or mystical good. Fourth, MacIntyre identified a "Jane Austen" view of the virtues, which included elements of the three approaches previously discussed, and included a "real affection for people" as a virtue. Finally, MacIntyre described Benjamin Franklin's utilitarian and functional view of virtue, where hard work and early rising are seen as virtues. (Quotes from Kellenberger 1995, 196)

MacIntyre found a common thread in these different and sometimes apparently contradictory views of virtue in the fact that whenever a practice is being performed, like playing chess (or auditing!), we can perform the practice for either external (extrinsic) benefits or internal (intrinsic) benefits. To MacIntyre, performing a practice in such a way as to benefit inherently from that practice is a virtue, because one achieves an intrinsic benefit that can be obtained only from performing the practice properly. To illustrate this, he used the example of playing chess. Assume that you love the game of chess. Now assume further that you wish to play chess, but there are no chess players on hand, and the only person available is a child who does not know the game. If you ask the child to learn chess, he or she will probably refuse. If you offer the youngster candy as an incentive to learn the game, he or she may then agree to be taught. If you then offer the child extra candy to play and some additional candy as a prize for winning, he or she may be more inclined to put extra effort and concentration into the game. Now, if the child were to leave the room during a game, you—who love the game so much— would not be inclined to cheat and move a chess piece. However, if you leave the room, the youngster playing for a candy would almost certainly be tempted to cheat in order to win and obtain the prize. MacIntyre pointed out that the child would be playing for the extrinsic benefit of the prize, but you would be playing for the intrinsic benefit attached to the practice of playing the game as skillfully as possible. To MacIntyre, virtue can be found in performing an action or a practice for its intrinsic benefits. The significance of this in terms of the business world and to the ethics of business— specifically accounting—is self-evident and quite far-reaching.

The Application of Ethical Decision-Making Models in the Business World

Having considered the approach of the three major ethical theories as to the most important aspect of morality, we must now examine how these ethical theories apply to decision making, and ask: "How do we decide what is the right action?" In answering this question, John E. Fleming suggests an eight-step decision-making model developed by Bowie and Velasquez:

1. What are the facts?
2. What are the ethical issues?
3. What are the alternatives?

4. Who are the stakeholders?
5. What is the ethical evaluation of the alternatives?
6. What are the constraints?
   * Ignorance or uncertainty?
   * Ability?
7. What decision should be made?
8. How should the decision be implemented? (Quoted in Pincus 2002, I-2-27, 28)

Under this decision-making model, Fleming describes four approaches to Step 5, i.e., the ethical evaluation of the alternatives:

* The utilitarian/consequentialist model
* The rights approach
* The duties approach
* The justice approach

1. The Consequentialist/Utilitarian Approach to the Decision-Making Model

The consequentialist theory of ethics and morality, as previously discussed, is a particularly practical ethical decision-making approach because it stresses that the most important aspect of morality is to do the right act, and it specifies that the right act is the one that produces the best consequences considering all the parties affected. Therefore, under this approach to the decision-making model, when you are faced with an ethical dilemma, it is vital to identify all of the stakeholders in the decision; that is, you should consider everyone who might possibly be affected by the decision. Further, modern consequentialists agree it is essential to consider the sum or aggregate of all the benefits to all of the stakeholders.

○ The Consequentialist/Utilitarian Approach in the Business World

Let us consider, for example, the case of an auditor contemplating bowing to pressure from a client to give an unqualified audit opinion on a knowingly incorrect set of financial statements. Using this approach, the auditor should first consider all the people who could be affected by the decision:

* Investors could suffer losses if they trade stock at prices based on the incorrect information in fraudulent financial statements.
* All the employees of the company being audited are potential stakeholders. Many internal operating decisions of the firm are made on the basis of accounting data that is used for the financial statements. If that information is wrong, it is very likely that

sub-optimal operating decisions will be made for the company with damaging consequences, such as lower profits and bonuses, or even bankruptcy for the company.

- Employees may choose to contribute to retirement plans that invest in a company's stock; however they may decide on different plans if they were analyzing correct financial statements.
- Potential employees may accept jobs at firms that they would not have joined had they been in possession of correct financial statements.
- Banks and other lenders could make erroneous decisions based on the false information, and this could have serious consequences.
- The auditor could be sued or face other legal action for fraudulently issuing an audit opinion.
- Many employees could lose their jobs due to the fraud.
- The auditor's family could suffer public humiliation if the auditor were criminally prosecuted.
- The auditor's business partners and employees are also stakeholders and their reputations could suffer, as could the entire audit firm as a result of public scrutiny that can follow a failed audit. The firm itself could be sued for monetary damages.
- Our stock markets require valid information in order to operate efficiently. When fraudulent financial statements are allowed to be presented after corrupt audits, this decreases confidence in the capital markets, which, in turn, makes it harder for American firms to raise capital either locally or internationally.

Now let us consider the stakeholders who potentially could suffer negative utility or pain if the auditor *refuses* to issue a fraudulent audit opinion:

- The auditor could be fired and lose compensation and status.
- The family members of the auditor are potential stakeholders because they could suffer due to the auditor losing his or her job; for example, they may have to move to a different house, or change schools.
- The auditor may keep his or her job but lose the client and the fees and possibly lose status or promotion in the firm.
- The auditor may suffer some workplace hostility from colleagues who wanted the auditor to "be more of a team player" and go along with the client and the rest of the team.

According to the consequentialist ethical decision-making model, after identifying all the stakeholders and estimating the potential consequences to them, the decision maker (in this case, the auditor) must choose the action that he or she believes will lead to the *maximum utility or benefit in the aggregate,* taking all the stakeholders into account. Moreover, the mere process of identifying the possible consequences to all the stakeholders would likely increase the decision maker's awareness of the "wrongness" of the unethical act, the risks associated with the "wrong" action, and the importance of doing the "right" or ethical thing. If some of the executives who were found guilty in recent financial frauds had considered their own families as potential stakeholders in their decisions to go along with criminal activity—on the grounds of their families' future suffering or public humiliation—it is possible that some of them may have paused long enough to remember the very good reasons why society made laws against issuing fraudulent financial statements in particular, and against fraud in general. If some of these company officers had paused to imagine their mortification as television cameras filmed their "perp" walks when they were arrested for possible indictments on criminal charges, perhaps they may have had second thoughts before embarking upon unethical paths of action.

2. The Rights and Duties Approach to the Decision-Making Model

Under this approach, when faced with an ethical decision, the decision maker would, again, attempt to identify all the facts and all of the stakeholders affected by a particular decision. However, here, when considering the effects of the decision on others, the most important issue to consider is that of the *rights* of those concerned; thus, following the rights-and-duties approach, the correct decision is the one that would appear to best serve or uphold these rights.

It is important to remember that, frequently, ethical dilemmas involve the possibility of actions that violate or fail to recognize the rights of others. Seen from a slightly different angle, usually the rights of those concerned involve a corresponding duty on the part of others to honor those rights. Therefore, this approach requires the decision maker to fulfill his or her obligation to *recognize and respect the rights of others.* These rights may either be legal rights, or moral rights which are not protected by law. In addition to the focus on natural human rights, issues such as animal rights and potential cruelty to animals could also be a concern.

Philosophers classify rights in many different ways. James Sterba has identified four kinds of rights. First, there are "action" rights or the rights to do things, such as to express your opinion. Second, there are "recipient rights," which are the "rights to receive something;" for example, the right to be paid for services rendered. Third, there are what Sterba has called "in persona" rights, that hold against some "specific, nameable person or persons." An example of an "in persona" right would be the right to have a loan repaid or the right to have a promise kept. Finally, Sterba has identified "*in rem*" rights, which hold against the world. An example of such a right would be the right to liberty. (Quotes from Kellenberger 1995, 212, 213)

○ The Rights-and-Duties Approach in the Business World

Using this approach to the ethical evaluation of alternatives in a decision-making model, a manager under pressure to publish fraudulent financial statements in order to keep his or her job should consider all the people whose rights may be affected by this decision. Note that the list of those affected is virtually identical to the list in the utilitarian model, but the emphasis here is not so much on the negative impact of the decision, but rather on upholding the *rights* of the people involved:

- Users of financial statements, such as potential investors in stock, or people making loans or extending credit to the company have the right to truthful financial statements.
- Society at large relies on the capital markets, which rely on accurate information, and so the society has a right to expect that public companies publish honest financial statements.
- Employees of the company have a right to truthful information about the company.

It is therefore important that the auditor who is under pressure to give an unqualified audit opinion on the fraudulent financial statements must be clearly aware of the rights of all the stakeholders.

On the other hand, what about the rights of the family of the manager or the auditor who may be fired for resisting fraudulent financial statements? What about children's rights to be supported by their parents? How does one balance these rights against the rights of the employees or other users of the financial statements? Conversely, do the relatives of the manager or auditor have the right to expect not to be embarrassed by family members being criminally charged for presenting fraudulent financial statements? For situations when rights clash, ethicist James Kellenberger (2004) made the following two suggestions:

- We should examine the consequences of a decision or course of action—an extension of the utilitarian approach.

- We should also examine the situation of conflicting rights in the context of relationship morality—an extension of the rights and duties model. Relationship morality requires that we treat all human beings with human dignity. It may be helpful for us to consider the special rights and duties that our particular relationships with specific persons demand.

Examining this approach in the auditing context, it is important to remember that the purpose of the auditor's appointment is to give an independent opinion of the financial statements of a company for users of that company's financial statements. Focusing on the resulting *rights* of financial statement users to receive a fair, independent opinion, and on the *relationship* between the auditors and all those who may use the financial statements, should lead auditors to better understand their duties, and why they must not accept limits on the scope of their audits without qualifying their reports. The same goes for the duty of management to produce honest financial statements in the first place.

3. The Justice Decision-Making Model

The third approach presented by Fleming for analyzing ethical dilemmas in the decision-making model in order to identify the *right* or the moral action, is the *justice* approach Once again, as in the other models, all the facts and all the stakeholders impacted by the decision must be identified. Under this model, however, the matter of paramount importance is the "fairness" of treatment of all the individuals involved. Justice, in the ethical sense, is focused more on *distributive* justice than on *retributive* justice—which is more the focus of legal justice. Kellenberger (1995) pointed out, "Distributive justice is concerned with fairness in the comparative treatment of persons" (167). The "good" being distributed in this context is very broad and applies to benefits generally or, conversely, to the general avoidance of burdens or hardships.

Philosophers differ as to the principles of distributive justice. In particular, one school (universalism) argues in favor of universal principles of justice, whereas the communitarianism school recognizes a plurality of communities in which the diversity of the communities must be taken into account. In this case, justice will be determined with reference to community values. At the core, both schools have the concept of equality in common: "Distributive justice, both universalism and communitarianism agree, is treating persons equally" (Kellenberger 1995). According to Joel Feinberg (1993), the principles of distributive justice are equality, need, merit, contribution, and effort.

Certainly, basic human rights must be equally accorded to all people. In some situations, need would be paramount in driving fair distribution, and in other situations one may see merit, contribution, or effort as paramount. For example, when it comes to the distribution of material goods, we can all see the necessity of providing disaster relief to those in need after a natural catastrophe, such as Hurricane Katrina along the Gulf Coast, or to those starving under any other circumstances. In the case of employment compensation, many would also argue in favor of extra distribution of benefits on the basis of merit, contribution, or effort. However, there is little consensus among philosophers on just how far equality in distribution extends and where merit, contribution, or effort overrides equal distribution in the allocation of material goods. Nevertheless, certain aspects of distributive justice are clear enough to be useful.

Of course, both law and morality require that factors such as race, religion, gender, sexual orientation, or national origin should not affect the distribution of benefits or burdens to citizens. Further, the justice approach clearly requires us to ensure that no partiality is used, so as to ensure that all persons falling into the same category are treated equally. For example, all the students taking a particular class must fulfill the same requirements. Some students cannot be required to write more essays than other students, or take more tests, or attend more class sessions. Yet all students taking one course can be required to write five essays in a semester, whereas all students taking a different course could be required to write seven essays in the same semester, and so on.

o The Justice Decision-Making Approach in the Business World

In applying the justice approach to an ethical dilemma in the business arena, the decision maker should:

- Identify all the stakeholders impacted by the decision
- Identify the different categories of stakeholders
- Consider whether all persons in the same category are being treated in the same manner—i.e., that all are being treated equally and fairly

Let us consider the example of year-end bonuses being distributed in a company. In a decision about the size of the bonuses, all employees of the same category (or rank) must be equally eligible for the bonus, and all employees achieving the same target of performance must receive the same size bonus. The overriding concern here is the absence of partiality and prejudice in the treatment of all persons.

Conclusion

All of the previous approaches to the ethical evaluation of alternatives in a decision-making model address the ethical problems quite clearly and offer paradigms to help identify:

- The facts and the alternatives
- The stakeholders
- The dominant ethical issues involved (whether of benefits and consequences, rights and duties, or justice and equality)
- How the decision making may affect the stakeholders

In order to choose the right action, each system requires the consideration of the alternatives and the application of principles in an analytical attempt to make ethical decisions, and therefore to select correct actions.

A number of professional organizations, as well as individuals, have submitted models that either combine two or more of these major philosophical frameworks for the evaluation of ethical issues within a decision-making model, or adapt them to more explicitly operationalize steps in the models.

The American Accounting Association Model (see Appendix A) is a frequently cited model that has strong elements of consequentialism and the rights-and-duties approach, along with specifying some virtues—such as integrity—together with a call to the decision makers' own "primary principles or values" (quoted in Cohen 2004, 134). The Laura Nash Model (see Appendix B) also combines aspects of consequentialism, aspects of a duties approach, and aspects of a virtues approach that encompasses qualities such as sincerity and integrity of intention. It implicitly rejects Kant's categorical imperative when it asks: "Under what conditions would you allow exceptions to your stand?" (Nash 2003, 24).

All ethical dilemmas should be examined against the background of the three major ethical theories of morality: consequentialism, deontology, and virtue ethics. Such analysis and contemplation is highly likely to increase the decision makers' awareness of all the nuances and issues at stake. Like the child who does not appreciate the intricacies of chess and plays the game for an extra piece of candy, the business manager or accountant who does not understand the essence of ethics or morality will be tempted to cheat at the game when no one is looking.

As we proceed from the major ethical theories of morality toward a decision-making model, and test the different approaches for their applicability or usefulness in relation to an ethical evaluation of all the options in a specific business dilemma, the likelihood increases that we will better discern what the right action is, and why it is important to do what is right. Businesses should base their activities on a firm foundation of ethics. Companies should not be in the business of telling fairy tales.

★★★★★

Appendix A: American Accounting Association Ethical Decision-Making Model*

1. Determine the facts—what, who, where, when and how?
   What do we know or need to know, if possible, that will help define the problems?
2. Define the ethical issue.
   (a) List the significant stakeholders
   (b) Define the ethical issues
   Make sure precisely what the ethical issue is—for example, conflicts involving rights, questions over limits of an obligation, etc.
3. Identify major principles, rules, or values.
   For example, integrity, quality, respect for persons, and profit.
4. Specify the alternatives.
   List the major alternative courses of action, including those that represent some form of compromise or point between simply doing or not doing something.
5. Compare values and alternatives. See if a clear decision is evident.
   Determine if there is one principle or value, or combination, which is so compelling that the proper alternative is clear—for example, correcting a defect that is almost certain to cause loss of life.
6. Assess the consequences.
   Identify short and long, and positive and negative consequences for the major alternatives. The common short-run focus on gain or loss needs to be measured against long-run considerations. This step will often reveal an unanticipated result of major importance.
7. Make your decision.
   Balance the consequences against your primary principles or values and select the alternative that best fits.

---

* Quoted in Stephen Cohen. 2004. *The Nature of Moral Reasoning: The Framework and Activities of Ethical Deliberation, Argument, and Decision-Making.* New York: Oxford University Press. pp. 133–134. Model adapted by William W. May for the American Accounting Association from a model suggested by H. Q. Langenderfer and J. W. Rockness. The full article is available online at http://aaahq.org/ic/browse.htm. Published with permission.

Appendix B: Laura Nash Model*

Twelve Questions for Examining the Ethics of a Business Decision

1. Have you defined the problem accurately?
2. How would you define the problem if you stood on the other side of the fence?
3. How did this situation occur in the first place?
4. To whom and to what do you give your loyalties as a person and as a member of the corporation?
5. What is your intention in making this decision?
6. How does this intention compare with the probable results?
7. Whom could your decision or action injure?
8. Can you discuss the problem with the affected parties before you make your decision?
9. Are you confident that your position will be as valid over a long period of time as it seems now?
10. Could you disclose without qualm your decision or action to your boss, your CEO, the board of directors, your family, society as a whole?
11. What is the symbolic potential of your action if it's understood? If misunderstood?
12. Under what conditions would you allow exceptions to your stand?

References

Cohen, Stephen. 2004. *The Nature of Moral Reasoning: The Framework and Activities of Ethical Deliberation, Argument, and Decision-Making.* New York: Oxford University Press.

Feinberg, Joel. 1993. "Distributive Justice." In *Business Ethics: A Philosophical Reader,* edited by Thomas I. White. New York: Macmillan.

Finnis, John. 1983. *Fundamentals of Ethics.* Washington, D.C.: Georgetown University Press.

Kellenberger, James. 1995. *Relationship Morality.* University Park, PA: Pennsylvania State University Press.

Kellenberger, James. December 2004. Personal interview with the author. Northridge, California.

Nash, Laura. 2003. "Ethics without the Sermon." In *Harvard Business Review on Corporate Ethics.* Boston: Harvard Business School Press. Originally published in 1981.

Pincus, Karen. 2002–2003. "Instructor's Notes for Module 2: Management as Users of Accounting Information." In *Core Concepts of Accounting Information.* Boston: McGraw-Hill/Irwin.

"The Surprising No. 1 College Major," *Netscape.com,* December 27, 2004. http://channels.netscape.com/careers/

---

* From: Laura Nash. 2003. "Ethics without the Sermon," In *Harvard Business Review on Corporate Ethics.* Boston: Harvard Business School Press. p. 24. Originally published in 1981. Published with permission.

Accounting Abbreviations

AAER:	accounting and auditing enforcement release
AICPA:	American Institute of Certified Public Accountants
CFFO:	cash flow from operations
CFTF:	Corporate Fraud Task Force
COGS:	cost of goods sold
DSO:	days sales outstanding
EBITDA:	earnings before interest, taxes, depreciation and amortization
EITF:	Emerging Issues Task Force
FASB:	Financial Accounting Standards Board
FIN:	Financial Accounting Standards Board interpretation
FR:	final rule
GAAP:	generally accepted accounting principles
GAAS:	generally accepted auditing standards
IFRS:	international financial reporting standards
IPO:	initial public offering
LR:	litigation release
MD&A:	management discussion and analysis
NASDAQ:	National Association of Securities Dealers Automated Quotations stock market
NI:	net income
NYSE:	New York Stock Exchange
PBGC:	Pension Benefit Guaranty Corporation
PCAOB:	Public Company Accounting Oversight Board
PPE:	property, plant and equipment
PRMA:	price risk management activities
SARS:	stock appreciation rights
SEC:	Securities and Exchange Commission
SOX Act:	Sarbanes-Oxley Act of 2002
SOX Report:	Report Pursuant to Section 704 of the Sarbanes-Oxley Act of 2002
SPE:	special purpose entity
VIE:	variable interest entity

INDEX

About TEXERE

Texere, a progressive and authoritative voice in business publishing, brings
to the global business community the expertise and insights of leading
thinkers. Our books educate, enlighten, and entertain, and provide an
intersection where our authors and our readers share cutting edge ideas,
practices, and innovative solutions. Texere seeks to cultivate, enhance, and
disseminate information that illuminates the global business landscape.

www.thomson.com/learning/texere

About the typeface

This book was set in 10.5 point Bembo. Bembo was cut by Francesco
Griffo for the Venitian printer Aldus Manutius to publish in 1495 *De Aetna*
by Cardinal Pietro Bembo. Stanley Morison supervised the design of
Bembo for the Monotype Corporation in 1929. The Bembo is a readable
and classical typeface because of its well-proportioned letterforms,
functional serifs, and lack of peculiarities.

Library of Congress Cataloging-in-Publication Data

Jackson, Cecil Wilfrid.
   Business fairy tales / by Cecil W. Jackson.
      p. cm.
   Includes bibliographical references and index.
    ISBN 0-324-30539-7 (alk. paper)
     1. Corporations—Accounting—Corrupt practices—United States—
Case studies. 2. Corporations—Accounting—Law and legislation—
United States. I. Title.
HF5686.C7J26   2006
657'.950973—dc22

                                      2006014684